The Discerning Eye

THE
DISCERNING EYE

Studies presented to
Robert Pring-Mill
on his seventieth birthday

EDITED BY
NIGEL GRIFFIN
CLIVE GRIFFIN, ERIC SOUTHWORTH
AND
COLIN THOMPSON

THE DOLPHIN BOOK CO.
1994

This volume has been produced with the aid of grants from the Anglo-Catalan Society; from the Fiedler Memorial Fund made by the Curators of the Taylor Institution in the University of Oxford; from the Interfaculty Committee for Latin-American Studies, Oxford; and from New College, Oxford and St Catherine's College, Oxford.

The publishers and the editors are grateful for this generous support.

ISBN 0 85215 082 2

Printed in Wales by J. D. Lewis and Sons Ltd, Llandysul
for The Dolphin Book Co. (Tredwr) Ltd, Llangrannog.

CONTENTS

III. Twentieth-Century Spain and Spanish-America

PREFACE

TO GIVE AN ADEQUATE ACCOUNT, in the compass of these few introductory pages, of the achievement and influence of Robert Pring-Mill as scholar, teacher, and man is impossible. Fortunately, the volume, range, and quality of his writings are a matter of public record, but the number and variety of the honours that have been bestowed upon him in recognition of his scholarship may well not all be known to many readers of this volume, Robert himself being very much not the kind of person to draw the world's attention to them. Already in his undergraduate years at Oxford, where he specialized in Spanish and French as an undergraduate member of New College, he won two prizes: a Heath Harrison Travelling Scholarship in Spanish (1948) – which he used to cover the expenses of a pilgrimage to Santiago de Compostela – and, in 1949, the year of his graduation as Bachelor of Arts, the Arteaga Essay Prize. Early in 1950, now a research student, he was made a Senior Demy of Magdalen College, and in January 1952 was appointed to a University Lecturership in Spanish. Other honours have followed in accelerating flow: the Premi Pompeu Fabra (Catalonia) in 1956; Magister Maioricensis Scholae Lullisticae in 1957; Leverhulme Research Fellow (1960–61); Fellow of St Catherine's College in 1965 (until 1991, and thereafter Emeritus Fellow of that College); Premi Ciutat de Palma (Mallorca) in 1975; Doctor of Letters of Oxford University (1986); Fellow of the British Academy (1988); Creu de Sant Jordi (Generalitat de Catalunya) in 1990; Comendador de la Orden de Isabel la Católica in that same year; Premi Catalònia (Barcelona) in 1991; and, in 1992, he was awarded the Premi Crítica 'Serra d'Or' de Recerca (Barcelona) and became an Oficial de la Orden de Bernardo O'Higgins (Chile).

The range of these honours itself reflects something of the breadth of Robert's scholarship in that they call to mind three of his principal areas of interest: Catalonia (one thinks in particular of his eminence as critic and elucidator of the poetry and the philosophical works of Ramon Llull); Castile (pre-eminently as a Golden-Age specialist known, in particular, for his work on the prose fiction and drama of the period); and Latin America, where a long-standing interest in the poetry, music, and painting of this region, fomented by a visit in 1949 to the Argentine, Uruguay, and Chile under the aegis of the British diplomat and hispanophile Sir Eugen Millington-Drake, was to give rise, from the early 1970s, to a stream of publications whose central theme was the popular poetry, song, and art rooted mostly in anti-establishment (and therefore often clandestine) movements of the region, movements born of the political and economic confrontations that have shaken Latin America in these last decades. It is typical of Robert that he should be fascinated by the similarities between these apparently disparate areas of research rather than with their more obvious differences: with, that is, the ways in which writers, no matter of what period or which country, work upon their readers in order to persuade them to share the author's vision of the world.

Robert's interest in Catalan culture ancient and modern no doubt owes something to the unusual circumstances of his childhood. Son of a Scottish professional soldier who bore to the end of his life evidence of grievous wounds sustained in Flanders in the Great War and who, obliged to seek a kinder climate after his consequent early retirement from the army, decided in 1931 to take his family to live in Majorca, Robert received his first formal education in the Jesuit school of Montesión in Palma. In 1936, a month or so after the outbreak of the Spanish Civil War and when he would be just about twelve years old, he was taken off the island along with other foreign residents by the British destroyer *Grenville* and spent the next six months in Italy. He then returned to Palma and, in 1939 on the outbreak of the Second World War, to Britain with his family. The early Majorcan years had been spent in Valldemosa, and one of Robert's lesser-known early publications, an English version of Bartomeu Ferrà's book on Chopin and George Sand, derives from his familiarity with the Carthusian monastery there. His critical work on medieval Catalan poetry and philosophy reveals preoccupations that one may recognise as constants in Robert's published work throughout his career: a concern with attitudes towards the relation between the general and the particular; techniques for representing aspects of reality with a view to producing calculated effects on audience or reader; and the effects of these attitudes and techniques on linguistic developments and on the evolution of conventions within a given tradition.

Allied to these concerns is the interest in techniques of communication that also underlies much of Robert's work on the literature of the Golden Age. Hence his interest in the development of conventions: mimesis, verisimilitude, *agudeza*, *conceptismo*, and the exploitation of conceptual and syntactical ambiguities; *ser*, *parecer*, and *desengaño* in prose fiction; the relation between logic, rhetoric and imagery; and dramatic structure as determined by the treatment of particular problems of conscience considered against the background of a highly structured general framework of belief and morality. By pursuing to their logical conclusion a variety of critical insights, he has challenged received ideas and shed new light on the mechanisms of Calderonian thought and its theatrical expression.

Much of Robert's published work associated with the last-mentioned of the three geographical areas whose literature has especially attracted his critical attention, the Latin-American, derives from an aspect of his interest in the work of Pablo Neruda. Neruda is a poet of whom, by virtue of personal acquaintance, indeed friendship, privileged access to autograph draft versions of many of Neruda's works, the critical skills necessary to relate them to the corresponding finished products, and judicious application of a mature and widely-based scholarship, Robert can justly claim a unique position as biographer, disseminator, and interpreter. Their first meeting took place in Oxford in 1965 on the occasion of the poet's visit to receive from the Vice-Chancellor of the University the degree of Doctor of Letters, an award that Robert had played an important part in bringing about. Neruda's arrival in Oxford took place in the very term in which a paper on his work had come, by Robert's initiative, to form part of the University's Final Honour School examination. (Neruda was, in fact, at that time the only living author whose work formed part of the Modern Languages syllabus.)

A particular aspect of the background history of this Latin-American dimension of Robert's scholarship would itself form an absorbing adventure travelogue, had he ever the time to publish it; and, since it bears witness to other important features of his personality, we must make brief reference to it here. Intrigued initially by a change that he had noted in the poetry of Neruda written during the Spanish Civil War, and wishing to know the context of his *Canto general*, wanting also to explore Neruda's connections with the Mexican muralists and to estimate the debt of Latin-American committed poetry to Neruda, and recognising therefore a need to experience more directly the geographical, historical, and political context in which these art forms had

been and were being created, he undertook, in 1967, a carefully-planned, year-
long journey by Land Rover that, starting in Montreal, traversed North
America, Mexico, and the Central-American republics and reached, at its
most southerly point, Puerto Montt in Chile. For large parts of the Latin-
American part of this journey there were no road maps available. Robert,
realising the importance of making the acquaintance of as many local writers
as he could, was carrying with him on the journey letters of introduction from
Pablo Neruda and Miguel Ángel Asturias. Contact with emergent poets,
especially important to him given the nature of his project, was also facilitated
by the many lectures that the British Council and British Embassies arranged
for him to deliver, and by the efficiency of the bush telegraph that passed on
news of his coming.

The Latin-American part of this outward journey alone, even as the crow
flies, must measure some five-and-a-half thousand miles. The return journey
ended, as planned, in New Orleans, and the total distance covered in just the
Latin-American part of this extraordinary enterprise was some twenty-five
thousand miles. For a considerable part of the journey Robert was not alone.
He was able to rely, for some months at least, on the support and technical
experience of a former Flight Mechanic of the women's branch of the Royal
Air Force who could be counted on to see this expedition as one of the things
that a wife naturally does during the children's school holidays provided that
they can come along too. (Thus a separate strand was periodically interwoven
with Robert's quest, as Brigitte, Francis, and Monica set themselves to
investigate aspects of Latin-American geology and handicraft.) Only in the
course of this journey did Robert become aware that song, as well as poetry,
was an important component of the particular culture that was the focus of his
interest. The entire episode says much for the resourcefulness, resolution, and
sheer physical and moral courage not only of Robert but of the whole family.
Robert himself, rejecting as a matter of principle the idea of armed escort, at
one time when travelling alone through a remote part of Ecuador found
himself kicking his heels as a hostage for three days.

A year before the journey just described, Robert had become aware of the
clandestine publications of the other eminent Latin-American poet on whom
he has published seminal critical work, the Nicaraguan Ernesto Cardenal,
though the two were not to meet until 1972 when Robert went to work with
Cardenal on the island of Solentiname in Lake Nicaragua. His one-month
stay with Cardenal on Solentiname, devoted to translation, documentation,

and discussion with the poet, marked for Robert a significant change of rhythm and was a period of particular and intense happiness for him. This scholarly interest in the development of new conventions in committed poetry, in what he himself has termed 'new paradigms', besides adding new courses of University lectures to Robert's repertoire, caused his services as a speaker to be sought after by a much wider public than his Oxford pupils. He has given more than a hundred talks in this country on subjects relevant to his journey, many of them illustrated from his vast collection of coloured slides.

Robert had been, of course, no stranger to foreign travel. Apart from his acquaintance with Majorca, mainland Spain, and Italy, he had, as already mentioned, spent some three months in Latin America almost twenty years before the expedition described above. And a short four years before that he had found himself in Malaya, less than a month after the surrender, on 14 August 1945, of the Japanese forces and just in time to celebrate his twenty-first birthday at the end of a long trail that had led him through India and Burma fighting with the 25th Indian Division. For Robert had enlisted in 1942 in one of the most famed of Scottish regiments, the Black Watch. (Though the minimum age for enlistment was eighteen, he somehow managed to get in at seventeen.) By the end of the war he had risen to the rank of Captain, had become an intelligence officer, and had received a mention in dispatches. Another little-known publication of Robert's dates from this period: a pamphlet entitled *Chinese Triad Societies (An Outline)*.

In addition to his work within the University as lecturer and researcher, Robert has served the many learned societies to which he has belonged as organiser, convenor, president (notably President of the Anglo-Catalan Society, 1973–76), and as presenter of his own papers to these and to many more. He has also served as a member of the editorial boards of such journals as *Estudios Lulianos* and *Romanistisches Jahrbuch* and has, over the years, helped to organize and on one occasion edit the papers of the Anglo-German colloquies on seventeenth-century Spanish drama (*Hacia Calderón*). He has been especially active in fomenting the study of the language and literature of Catalonia and Latin America (and has indeed been prominent in the development of Latin-American studies in this country, especially in the crucial years of the 60s and 70s). He has also been until recently a Trustee of the Oxford–León (Nicaragua) Trust. He has been an indefatigable lecturer in universities of Europe and of the Americas, broadcaster on educational as well as literary topics, propagandist for Hispanic studies in schools – indeed the record of his activities in these areas is much too long to set down in detail here; and he willingly made time to chair the Sub-Faculty of Spanish and Portuguese at Oxford for the year 1977–78.

Academic exchanges with foreign universities being by no means as common forty-five years ago as they are today, it is interesting to note that in the academic year 1949–50 Robert and the late Cyril Jones, of Trinity College, established the Coulthurst Anglo-Spanish Committee to promote academic exchanges with the University of Granada, which brought to Oxford several Spanish students, including a future Spanish Ambassador to the Court of St James.

Everyone has their share of good luck, and part of Robert's share is the intellectual capacity that he was born with. But he would never have achieved what he has achieved on that alone: for this he needed additional qualities and blessings. One of these is a remarkable capacity, legendary among his colleagues, for hard work; long hours of consistent labour, for the sake of which not infrequent periods of indifferent health have habitually been simply brushed aside, as for example during a recent conference in Oxford on Neruda. Part of his colleagues' share of good luck has been that Robert seems never to have been tempted to leave Oxford for any reason. One is of course left to guess at the offers he must have had.

His other notable piece of luck was and is his wife, Brigitte, whom he married in 1950. This resourceful, imperturbable, perspicacious, judicious, good-humoured, unfailingly kind and discreet lady must have been a tower of strength to Robert over the years. To watch them together is very much to receive the impression of a team that operates smoothly on a minimum of spoken communication since each appears to divine at once what is in the other's mind. Running a home, developing her own interests, doing her part in bringing up their two children, and contriving at the same time to be a loyal collaborator and (one guesses) adviser whenever there were problems to be solved: all this, despite having had her own share of ill health, Brigitte has taken in her stride.

A first-rate host but never much inclined to gossip, Robert has been heard to observe in puzzlement on hearing late in the day of a controversial appointment in this or that university or of some spectacular idiocy perpetrated by a common acquaintance: 'Nobody ever tells me these things.' Of course not: the best gossip survives on an element of malice, a quality that Robert is poorly endowed with, much preferring the exercise of Christian charity.

Robert and Brigitte's Catholic faith is indeed a distinctive and central feature of their lives, finding expression in countless acts of kindness to colleagues, pupils, and other friends.

No assessment of Robert could approach completeness without mention of his importance to his Faculty as a teacher, which derives in no small part from his evident enjoyment of the teaching process itself. Ever alert to discover new angles of approach to texts and to devise fresh analytical techniques for research, he would no doubt say that there is, anyway, much to learn from those one teaches. The hundreds of pupils that have passed through his hands – the ultimate arbiters here, of course – will testify to the pains he has always taken on their behalf and his care for their interests. The real wonder about Robert as a college tutor is that he was able to perform that part of his job so well and still produce the extraordinary amount of published work that stands in his name. For he took his teaching no less seriously than his research, ever mindful that a good undergraduate course should be, above all things, a liberal education. One trusts, or rather hopes, that the winds of change now sweeping through our universities will not render his kind obsolete.

To such a man is this volume dedicated, with the respect, affection, and good wishes of colleagues, pupils, and friends. We congratulate him on attaining his seventieth birthday, and we wish him and Brigitte long years of happiness in their well-deserved retirement.

*   *   *   *   *

The editors would like to express their gratitude to all the contributors for meeting the tight time-schedule they imposed upon them and for answering their many queries with patience and forbearance. They are also indebted to Fred Hodcroft, Marcel Ortín, John Wainwright, and Geoffrey Walker, without whose help and expertise *The Discerning Eye* would have been much the poorer; to Joan Gili for once again undertaking the publication of a book of this kind, and for bringing to bear upon it skills he has perfected over half a century as a publisher in Oxford; and to Brigitte Pring-Mill, whose willing co-operation has greatly aided the production of this volume.*

---

*   Nigel Griffin's fellow editors and the other contributors to this volume are keenly aware of their special debt to him. In addition to his share of the editorial work, he has typeset all the copy submitted and compiled the index.

ROBERT PRING-MILL: A BIBLIOGRAPHY OF HIS WRITINGS

IN THE LIST THAT FOLLOWS it has not proved possible to take account of the many hundreds of radio talks given by Robert Pring-Mill, both in this country and abroad; by our calculations, there were well over a hundred broadcasts on the BBC's Spanish and Latin-American services alone before 1972. Nor have we listed unsigned contributions to reference works, such as *The New Caxton Encyclopaedia*. The Taylorian Library in Oxford has the annotated handouts and typescripts of several of the daunting number of illustrated lectures Pring-Mill has given to bodies both august and humble, international and local. Doubtless, more survive, but no unpublished material is recorded here. Work in press and in preparation is only listed where bibliographical details are sufficiently secure for us to be confident of not creating *fausses pistes*.

A   Books and pamphlets

1   *Chinese Triad Societies (An Outline)* (Kuala Kangsar, Malaya: privately published, 1946, iii + 30 pp.).

2   (with Cyril A. Jones) *Advanced Spanish Unseens* (London: George G. Harrap & Co. Ltd, 1958, 122 pp.; rpt 1963 etc.).

3   *El Microcosmos Lul·lià*, Biblioteca Raixa 55 (Palma de Mallorca: Editorial Moll, 1961, 175 pp. + 14 diagrams); rpt, from original plates, as **A4**; corr. rpt in **A13**, 31–112.

4   *El Microcosmos Lul·lià* (Oxford: Dolphin Book Co., 1962, 175 pp. + 14 diagrams). Rpt of **A3**; corr. rpt in **A13**, 31–112.

5   *Ramón Llull y el número primitivo de las dignidades en el «Arte General»* (Oxford: The Dolphin Book Co. Ltd, 1963, vi + 68 pp. + 7 diagrams). Rpt of **D7** & **D9**, plus 'Advertencia preliminar' (i–ii), 'Resumen analítico' (iii–iv), 'Epílogo' (55–59), and indexes (61–68); tr. Albert Soler as 'El nombre primitiu de les Dignitats en l'*art general*' in **A13**, 115–60.

6   *Pregó de Setmana Santa*, Publicacions de la Confraria de sant Agustí
     (Felanitx, Mallorca, 1970, 22 pp. +   frontispiece of a little-known
     miniature of Ramon Llull from Bayerische Staatsbibliothek, Cod. lat.
     10508). Rpt (without the miniature) in **A13**, 333–45.

7   *Both in Sorrow and in Anger: Spanish American Protest Poetry* (Oxford:
     St Catherine's College, 1972, [14] pp.). Reissue of **D29**.

8   *The Scope of Spanish-American Committed Poetry* (Oxford: St Cather-
     ine's College, 1978, [75] pp.). Reissue of **C24**.

9   *The Climate of Current Cuban Poetry*, original unabridged text of **C35**
     (Oxford: [St Catherine's College], n.d. [=1981], typescript, 13 pp.).

10   *Cantas – Canto – Cantemos: las canciones de lucha y esperanza como
     signos de reunión e identidad* (Oxford: St Catherine's College, 1983,
     [38] pp.). Reissue of **D50**.

11   *Dos trabajos sobre los borradores de 'Los versos del capitán'* (Oxford: St
     Catherine's College, 1987, [48] pp.). Reissue of **C47** and **D55**, with
     introductory note.

12   *'Gracias a la vida': The Power and Poetry of Song*, The Kate Elder Lec-
     ture 1 (London: Department of Hispanic Studies, Queen Mary &
     Westfield College, University of London, 1990, 90 pp.). Expanded
     version of the 1st Kate Elder Lecture, delivered 20 February 1990.

13   *Estudis sobre Ramon Llull (1956–1978)*, ed. Lola Badia & Albert Soler,
     Textos i Estudis de Cultura Catalana 22 (Barcelona: Publicacions de
     l'Abadia de Montserrat, Curial Edicions Catalanes, 1991, 360 pp.).
     Collection of studies (see **A3**, **A4**, **A5**, **A6**, **C8**, **C15**, **C21**, **D5**, **D7**, **D9**,
     D17, **D21**, **D26**, **D32**, **D42**), many tr. Albert Soler. Work awarded the
     1992 Premi Crítica «Serra d'Or» de Recerca en Catalanística.

14   *The Uses of Spanish-American So-Called Protest Song*, IPM Occasional
     Paper 4 (Liverpool: Institute of Popular Music, University of Liver-
     pool, 1993, 23 pp.).

B   **Books edited**

1   (tr. & ed.) Bartomeu Ferrà, *Chopin and George Sand in Majorca . . .
     Preceded by an Extract from 'The Memoirs of Aurore Sand'* (Palma de
     Mallorca: Edicions La Cartoixa, 1961, 92 pp.).

2   *Lope de Vega: Five Plays*, tr. Jill Booty, Mermaid Dramabook 20 (New
     York: Hill & Wang Inc., 1961, xli + 278 pp.); extracted in **C37**. See
     also **C5**.

3   Pablo Neruda, *The Heights of Macchu Picchu*, tr. Nathaniel Tarn
     (London: Jonathan Cape, 1966, 47 pp.; rpt New York: Farrar, Straus

& Giroux, 1967, 47 pp.). See also **C7**.

4   Raymundus Lullus, *Quattuor Libri Principiorum (Liber Principiorum Theologiae, Liber Principiorum Philosophiae, Liber Principiorum Juris, et Liber Principiorum Medicinae)*, Mediaeval and Renaissance Classics (Wakefield: S.R. Publishers Ltd. & Paris – The Hague: Mouton, 1969, xxvi + 208 pp.). Facsimile of early edns. See also **C11**.

5   *Pablo Neruda: A Basic Anthology* (Oxford: Dolphin Book Co., 1975, lxxxi + 218 pp.). See also **C18**.

6   (tr. & ed.) Ernesto Cardenal, *Marilyn Monroe and Other Poems: Oración por Marilyn Monroe y otros poemas* (London: Search Press, 1975, 136 pp.). See also **C19**.

7   (with Donald D. Walsh) Ernesto Cardenal, *Apocalypse and Other Poems* (New York: New Directions, n.d. [=1977]). Translations by Mireya Jaimes-Freyre, Thomas Merton, RPM, Kenneth Rexroth, & Donald Walsh. See also **C23** and **D38**.

8   *Antología de canciones de lucha y esperanza*, ed. Gustavo Gac Artigas & Perla Valencia Moncada (Santiago de Chile: Quimantú, 1973). Part re-issue, with selection, assembly and index by RPM (Oxford, 1978, [44] pp.).

9   (with Frederick W. Hodcroft, David G. Pattison & Ronald W. Truman) *Mediaeval and Renaissance Studies on Spain and Portugal in Honour of P. E. Russell* (Oxford: Society for the Study of Mediaeval Languages and Literature, 1981, vii + 226 pp.).

10   (with Hans Flasche) *Hacia Calderón: Quinto Coloquio Anglogermano, Oxford 1978*, Archivum Calderonianum 1 (Wiesbaden: Franz Steiner Verlag, 1983, 100 pp.).

C   Articles in books

1   (tr.) Joan Triadú, 'Introduction' in *Anthology of Catalan Lyric Poetry*, ed. Joan Gili, selected Joan Triadú (Oxford: The Dolphin Book Co., 1953), vii – lxxix. See also **C2**.

2   'Biographical and Bibliographical Index', in *Anthology of Catalan Lyric Poetry* (see **C1**), 371 – 86.

3   'Catalan Literature', in *The Caxton World of Knowledge*, 6 vols (London, etc.: Caxton Publishing Co. Ltd, 1960; rpt 1962), II, 22 – 23. See also **C4**.

4   'Raymond Lully', in *The Caxton World of Knowledge* (see **C3**), II, 232 – 33. Work contains twenty-three further entries on Spanish literature, and five on modern Spanish poets.

5   'Introduction' to *Lope de Vega: Five Plays* (see **B2**), vii–xli; reissued separately (Oxford: TRUEXpress, n.d.);   rpt in Gale publications; extracted in **C37**.

6   'Llull, Ramon', in *Encyclopaedia Britannica* [14th edn], XIV (Chicago, etc.: Encyclopaedia Britannica Inc. (William Benton), 1965), 173–74; rev. rpt 1967; futher rev. rpt in *The New Encyclopaedia Britannica* [15th edn] (1974; rpt 1981 etc.).

7   'Preface' in Pablo Neruda, *The Heights of Macchu Picchu* (see **B3**), vii–xix.

8   'La estructura del *Liber de Natura* del Beato Ramon Llull', in *La Filosofia della Natura nel Medioevo: Atti del Terzo Congresso Internazionale di Filosofia Medioevale, Passo della Mendola (Trento), 31 agosto–5 settembre 1964*, ed. Bruno Nardi & others (Milan: Società Editrice Vita e Pensiero, 1966), 566–75;   tr. Albert Soler as 'L'estructura del *Liber de Natura* del beat Ramon Llull' in **A13**, 203–10.

9   'Escalígero y Herrera: citas y plagios de los *Poetices Libri Septem* en las *Anotaciones*', in *Actas del Segundo Congreso Internacional de Hispanistas, celebrado en Nijmegen del 20 al 25 de agosto de 1965*, ed. Jaime Sánchez Romeralo & Norbert Poulussen (Nijmegen: Instituto Español de la Universidad de Nimega, for La Asociación Internacional de Hispanistas, 1967), 489–98.

10   'Los calderonistas de habla inglesa y *La vida es sueño*: Métodos de análisis temático-estructural', in *Litterae Hispanae et Lusitanae: Zum Fünfzigjährigen Bestehen des Ibero-Amerikanischen Forschungsinstituts der Universität Hamburg*, ed. Hans Flasche (Munich: Max Hueber Verlag, 1968), 369–413.

11   'Ramon Lull's Four *Libri Principiorum*:   An Introductory Note', in Raymundus Lullus, *Quattuor Libri Principiorum* (see **B4**), vi–xxvi.

12   'La «victoria del hado» en *La vida es sueño*', in *Hacia Calderón: Coloquio Anglogermano, Exeter 1969*, ed. Alexander A. Parker & Hans Flasche, Calderoniana 6 (Berlin: Walter de Gruyter & Co., 1970), 53–70.

13   'La elaboración de la cebolla', in *Actas del Tercer Congreso Internacional de Hispanistas, celebrado en México, D.F., del 26 al 31 de agosto de 1968*, ed. Carlos H. Magis (Mexico City: Colegio de México, for La Asociación Internacional de Hispanistas, 1970), 739–51.   A version with many errata, corr. in rpt (see **C20**).

14   'The Themes of Fernando Pessoa's English Sonnets', in *Studies in Modern Portuguese Literature*, Tulane Studies in Romance Languages and Literature 4 (New Orleans: Tulane University, 1971), 9–37.   Re-

vised and expanded version of a paper given at Tulane University under the auspices of the Gulbenkian Foundation.

15   'The Analogical Structure of the Lullian Art', in *Islamic Philosophy and the Classical Tradition: Essays Presented to Richard Walzer by his Friends and Colleagues*, ed. Samuel Miklos Stern, Albert Hourani, and Vivian Brown (Oxford: Cassirer, 1972), 315–26 + 3 figures; tr. Albert Soler as 'L'estructura analògica de l'Art lul·liana' in **A13**, 241–52.

16   'Ramon Lull', in *Dictionary of Scientific Biography*, ed. Charles Coulston Gillispie, 16 vols (plus *Supplement*, vols 17–18, ed. Frederic L. Holmes) (New York: Charles Scribner's Sons, 1970–90), VIII (1973), 547–51.

17   'Estructuras lógico-retóricas y sus resonancias: un discurso de *El príncipe constante*', in *Hacia Calderón: Segundo Coloquio Anglogermano, Hamburgo 1970*, ed. Hans Flasche, Calderoniana 7 (Berlin & New York: Walter de Gruyter, 1973), 109–54. Expanded version of part of a paper read at the Hamburg conference, 21 July 1970. An expanded version of the latter part of that same paper – an study of Calderón's *Summationsschema* – is **C22**.

18   'Introduction' and 'Note on the Texts', in *Pablo Neruda* (see **B5**), xv–lxxxi.

19   'Introduction', in Ernesto Cardenal, *Marilyn Monroe* (see **B6**), 7–32.

20   'La elaboración de la cebolla', in *Aproximaciones a Pablo Neruda*, ed. Ángel Flores, Colección Ocnos: Serie Ensayos 1 (Barcelona: Llibres de Sinera, 1974), 227–41. Corr. rpt of **C13**.

21   'Els *recontaments* de l'*Arbre exemplifical* de Ramon Llull: la transmutació de la ciència en literatura', in *Actes del Tercer Col·loqui Internacional de Llengua i Literatura Catalanes, celebrat a Cambridge del 9 al 14 d'abril de 1973*, ed. R. Brian Tate & Alan Yates (Oxford: The Dolphin Book Co. Ltd, for l'Associació Internacional de Llengua i Literatura Catalanes, 1976), 311–23; excerpted as **C33**; rpt in **A13**, 307–17.

22   'Estructuras lógico-retóricas y sus resonancias: 2ª parte: *Hermosa compostura* y *piedad real*', in *Hacia Calderón: Tercer Coloquio Anglogermano, Londres 1973*, ed. Hans Flasche, Calderoniana 10 (Berlin & New York: Walter de Gruyter, 1976), 47–74. An expanded version of the last part of a paper given at a Calderón conference in Hamburg in 1970 (see **C17**), and subsequently as a separate paper at the Westfield conference in July 1973.

23   'Introduction', in Ernesto Cardenal, *Apocalypse and Other Poems* (see **B7**), ix–xviii.

24   'The Scope of Spanish-American Committed Poetry', in *Homenaje a Rodolfo Grossmann: Festschrift zu seinem 85. Geburtstag*, ed. Sabine Horl, José María Adriaensens Navarro & Hans-Karl Schneider (Frankfurt, Berne & Las Vegas: Verlag Peter Lang, 1977), 259–333; reissued as **A8** and rpt, in abridged version, as **C27**. Some of the arguments expressed also developed in **C26**.

25   'El Neruda de las *Odas elementales*', in *Coloquio Internacional sobre Pablo Neruda (La obra posterior al «Canto general»), organizado en abril de 1975 y abril de 1976*, ed. Alain Sicard (Poitiers: Centre de Recherches Latino-Américaines de l'Université de Poitiers, 1979), 261 –300. Shortened version of a paper read 26 April 1975.

26   'The Nature and the Functions of Spanish-American *Poesía de compromiso*', in *The Search for Identity in Latin-American Literature*, ed. Robert Gurney, Bulletin of the Society for Latin-American Studies 31 (Aberdeen: The Society for Latin-American Studies, 1979), 4–21. Expanded treatment of some of the issues raised in **C24**.

27   'Spanish America: The Social Role of the Committed Poet', in *Social Roles for the Artist*, ed. Ann Thompson & Antony Beck (Liverpool: The Art, Politics, and Society Group, Department of Political Theory and Institutions, University of Liverpool, 1979), 81–88. Abridgement and arrangement of **C24**.

28   'Neruda y el original de *Los libertadores*', in *Actas del Sexto Congreso Internacional de Hispanistas, celebrado en Toronto del 22 al 26 de agosto de 1977*, ed. Alan M. Gordon & Evelyn Rugg (Toronto: Department of Spanish and Portuguese, University of Toronto, for La Asociación Internacional de Hispanistas, 1980), 587–89.

29   'The Redemption of Reality through Documentary Poetry', in Ernesto Cardenal, *Zero Hour and Other Documentary Poems*, ed. Donald D. Walsh (New York: New Directions, 1980), ix–xxi. See also **C30**.

30   (tr.) 'Nicaraguan Canto', in Cardenal, *Zero Hour* (**C29**), 16–36. Tr. of 'Canto nacional'.

31   (tr.) 'Death of Thomas Merton', in *A Merton Concelebration*, ed. Deba Prasad Patnaik (Notre Dame, Indiana: Ave Maria Press, 1981), 83 –98. Tr. of Ernesto Cardenal, 'Coplas a muerte de Merton'.

32   'Un versicle del *Libre d'amich e Amat* de Ramon Llull', in *Anàlisis i comentaris de textos literaris catalans*, 4 vols, ed. Narcís Garolera i Carbonell, Manuals Curial 5–6, 8–9 (Barcelona: Curial, 1982–85), I: *De Llull a Verdaguer*, 11–28. Extracted from **D17**.

33   'Comentaris a un «recontament» lul·lià', in *Anàlisis i comentaris de textos literaris catalans,* I (see **C32**), 29–34. Extracted from **C21**.

34   'Comunicación explícita e implícita en dos poemas de Ernesto Carde-
      nal ('Las ciudades perdidas' y 'Katún 11 Ahau')', in *Actas del Séptimo
      Congreso de la Asociación Internacional de Hispanistas, celebrado en
      Venecia del 25 al 30 de agosto de 1980*, ed. Giuseppe Bellini (Rome:
      Bulzoni, 1982), 825–35.

35   'The Climate of Current Cuban Poetry', in *Caribbean Societies*, ed.
      Christopher Abel & Michael Twaddle, 2 vols, University of London
      Collected Seminar Papers 29, 34 (London: Institute of Commonwealth
      Studies, 1982–85), I, 122–43. See also **A9**.

36   'Calderón de la Barca y la fuerza ejemplar de lo poetizado', in *Hacia
      Calderón: Sexto Coloquio Anglogermano, Würzburg 1981*, ed. Hans
      Flasche & P. Juan i Tous, Archivum Calderonianum 2 (Wiesbaden:
      Franz Steiner Verlag, 1983), 1–15.

37   (with Royston O. Jones & Victor Dixon) *'El perro del hortelano*:
      Burlas, veras y versos', in *Siglos de Oro: Barroco*, ed. Bruce W.
      Wardropper & others [=*Historia y crítica de la literatura española*, ed.
      Francisco Rico, vol. 3] (Barcelona: Editorial Crítica, 1983), 373–80.
      RPM contribution extracted from **B2**.

38   (with Franz-Walter Müller & Ilse Nolting-Hauff) 'Del *Buscón* a *Los
      sueños*', in *Siglos de Oro* (see **C37**), 572–81. Extracted from **D27**.

39   *The Fontana Biographical Companion to Modern Thought*, ed. Alan
      Bullock & R.B. Woodings (London: Collins, 1983). Entries on: Ra-
      fael Alberti (8–9), Miguel Ángel Asturias (25–26), 'Azorín' (31), Jor-
      ge Luis Borges (88–89), Ernesto Cardenal (125–26), Julio Cortázar
      (159–60), Gabriel García Márquez (257), Jorge Guillén (294), Juan
      Ramón Jiménez (366), Federico García Lorca (454–45), Antonio
      Machado (470), Gabriela Mistral (516–17), Pablo Neruda (550–51),
      Octavio Paz (586-87), Miguel de Unamuno (774), César Vallejo
      (779–80), and Mario Vargas Llosa (781).

40   'A Note on the *Canto general*', in *First International Festival of Latin-
      American and Caribbean Culture, 3–8 September 1984, Queen Elizabeth
      Hall & Purcell Room, South Bank, London, England*, ed. Juan Monroy
      (London: Latin-American and Caribbean Cultural Society, 1984), 15.

41   'Both in Sorrow and in Anger: Spanish American Protest Poetry', in
      First International Festival of Latin-American and Caribbean Culture
      (see **C40**), 11–15. Rpt of **D29**.

42   'La estructura de *El gran teatro del mundo*', in *Hacia Calderón: Séptimo
      Coloquio Anglogermano, Cambridge 1984*, ed. Hans Flasche, Archivum
      Calderonianum 3 (Wiesbaden & Stuttgart: Franz Steiner Verlag,
      1985), 110–45.

43   'Ernesto Cardenal and the *Talleres de Poesía*', in *Nicaragua: Pueblo y cultura: Papers Given at Trinity and All Saints College, 9–10 November 1984*, ed. Rob Rix (Leeds: Trinity & All Saints College, 1985), 18–39. Largely a conflation of **D52** and **D53**.

44   '*Cantas/Canto/Cantemos*: Las canciones de lucha y esperanza como signos de reunión e identidad', in *Identidad cultural de Iberoamérica en su literatura*, ed. Saúl Yurkievich, Colección Estudios 30 (Madrid: Editorial Alhambra, 1986), 131–54. Conference paper delivered in 1983 (see **D50**).

45   'Testimonio', in Luis Poirot de la Torre, *Neruda: Retratar la ausencia* (Santiago de Chile: Fundación Neruda, 1986), 162–63. Excerpted in **D54**.

46   'Mayra Jiménez and the Rise of Nicaraguan *Poesía de taller*', in *La mujer en la literatura caribeña: Sexta Conferencia de Hispanistas, 6th–8th abril* [sic] *1983*, ed. Lloyd King (St Augustine, Trinidad: University of the West Indies, 1983 [=1987]), 1–39. See also **D52**.

47   'La composición de *Los versos del capitán*: el testimonio de los borradores', in *Neruda en/a Sassari: Actas/Atti del «Simposio Intercontinental Pablo Neruda» (Sassari, 3–5 mayo/maggio 1984)*, ed. Hernán Loyola, Seminario di Studi Latinoamericani dell'Università di Sassari, Serie Atti 2 (Sassari: Università di Sassari, 1987), 173–204. Published after **D55** but written two years earlier and complementary to it (both reissued in **A11**).

48   Untitled introduction in Marjorie Agosín, *Zones of Pain/Las zonas del dolor*, tr. Cola Franzen (Fredonia, New York: White Pine Press, 1988), i–iii.

49   'The Building of Neruda's "Oda al edificio" ', in *«Sieh den Fluss der Sterne strömen»: Hispanoamerikanische Lyrik der Gegenwart (Interpretationen)*, ed. Gisela Beutler (Darmstadt: Wissenschaftliche Buchgesellschaft, 1990), 198–222.

50   (tr.) 'In the Tower', 'Sonnet VI', 'Sonnet XCIV', and 'Thanks be to Life', in *Tall Poles* (Oxford: North and West Oxford Community Education Committee, 1990), 10–12. Translations of three poems by Neruda ('En la torre', 'En los bosques, perdido, corté una rama oscura', and 'Si muero sobrevíveme con tanta fuerza pura') and one by Violeta Parra ('Gracias a la vida')

51   'La toma de conciencia en la poesía de compromiso hispanoamericana', in *Actas del X Congreso de la Asociación Internacional de Hispanistas, Barcelona, 21–26 de agosto de 1989*, ed. Antonio Vilanova, 4 vols (Barcelona: PPU, 1992–93), I, 33–53.

52 'A Poet for All Seasons', introduction in *A Poet for All Seasons* (see **F13**), 1–8.

53 Introductory note in *Antología popular* (see **F14**), [1].

D Articles in journals

1 'William James Entwistle', *Romanistisches Jahrbuch*, 5 (1952), 43–46.

2 'The Coulthurst Anglo-Spanish Committee, Part I: Spaniards in England', *Anglo-Spanish League of Friendship Quarterly Journal* (London), nr 11 (Apr.–June 1954), 10–13 + plates between 24 and 25. One of the plates is a photograph of the Coulthurst Anglo-Spanish Committee taken in the gardens of New College, Oxford in July 1953, with a youthful RPM on the extreme right.

3 'The Coulthurst Anglo-Spanish Committee, Part II: The Return Visit', *Anglo-Spanish League of Friendship Quarterly Journal*, nr 12 (July–Sept. 1954), 3–7 + plates between 8 and 9.

4 'Two Spanish Mystics and their Methods of Describing Mystical Experience', *The Aryan Path* (Bombay), 26 (1955), 489–92, 536–40.

5 'The Trinitarian World Picture of Ramon Lull', *Romanistisches Jahrbuch*, 7 (1955–56), 229–56; tr. Albert Soler as 'La visió trinitària del món en Ramon Llull' in **A13**, 161–189. A fuller, unpublished study of Trinitarian terminology in Llull, entitled 'Some Lullian Contributions to the Catalan Technical Lexicon, with Special Reference to the Terminological Structure of Ramon Llull's World Picture', on which this was partly based, received the Premi Pompeu Fabra at the Jocs Florals of the Anglo-Catalan Society, Cambridge, 1956.

6 'Actividades lulianas en Inglaterra', *Estudios Lulianos*, 1 (1957), 145–46.

7 'El número primitivo de las dignidades en el *Arte General*, [I]', *Estudios Lulianos*, 1 (1957), 309–34; rpt as **A5** and in **A13**.

8 Untitled summary of paper entitled 'The Roots of the Lullian *ars inveniendi veritatem*' (see **D16**), *Estudios Lulianos*, 1 (1957), 430–31.

9 'El número primitivo de las dignidades en el *Arte General*, [II]', *Estudios Lulianos*, 2 (1958), 129–56; rpt as **A5** and in **A13**.

10 'A Thirteenth-Century Majorcan: Ramon Lull', *Quarterly Journal of the Anglo-Spanish Society*, 28 (April-June 1958), 6–10 + 2 plates.

11 'Spanish Golden-Age Prose and the Depiction of Reality', *Anglo-Spanish Society Quarterly Review*, 32/33 (April-June/July-Sept. 1959), 20–31 + 4 plates.

12   'Las publicaciones medievalistas de Penguin Books', *Estudios Lulianos*, 3 (1959), 96–100.

13   'Interés en Inglaterra por San Vicente Ferrer', *Estudios Lulianos*, 3 (1959), 100–01.

14   'Oxford como preparación para una carrera industrial o comercial', *Asociación para el Progreso de la Dirección*, 1 (1959), 163–68.

15   'Presencia del beato Ramón Lull en en II Congreso Internacional de Filosofía Medieval', *Estudios Lulianos*, 5 (1961), 371–72.

16   'Grundzüge von Lulls *Ars inveniendi veritatem*', *Archiv für Geschichte der Philosophie* (Berlin), 43 (1961), 239–66 + 6 figures + 3 plates. German text by Brigitte Pring-Mill. Expanded and corr. version of a paper entitled 'The Roots of the Lullian *ars inveniendi veritatem*', delivered in the Thomas-Institut of the University of Cologne in October 1957 (see **D8**).

17   'Entorn de la unitat del *Libre d'amich e Amat*', *Estudis Romànics* (Barcelona), 10 (1962) [=*Estudis de literatura catalana oferts a Jordi Rubió i Balaguer en el seu setanta-cinquè aniversari*, ed. R. Aramon i Serra, I], 33–61; extracted as **C32**; rpt in **A13**, 279–306.

18   'Sententiousness in *Fuente Ovejuna*', *Tulane Drama Review* (New Orleans), 7 (1962), 5–37.

19   'La universalitat de la visió lul·liana', *Qüestions de la vida cristiana* (Montserrat), 14 (1962), 46–54.

20   'La lectura del *Libre d'amic e Amat*', *Lluc: Òrgan de la Confraria de la Mare de Déu en Lluc* (Escorca, Mallorca), 42 (1962), 235–37.

21   'Ramón Lull y la *De Divisione Naturae*', *Estudios Lulianos*, 7 (1963), 167–80; tr. Albert Soler as 'Ramon Llull i el *De Divisione Naturae*' in **A13**, 191–202.

22   'Pablo Neruda', *The Oxford Magazine* (Oxford), n.s. 5, nr 21, 27 May 1965, 357. Includes tr. of 'Los libertadores' from *Canto general*. See also **D25**.

23   (tr.) 'Vastness of Pines', *The Oxford Magazine*, n.s. 5, nr 22, 3 June 1965, 375. Tr. of 'Poema 3' of Neruda's *Veinte poemas de amor y una canción desesperada*.

24   (tr.) 'Birth', *The Oxford Magazine*, n.s. 5, nr 23, 10 June 1965, 391. Tr. of 'Nacimiento' from Neruda's *Memorial de Isla Negra*; rpt in **D41**.

25   'Neruda: Doctor Honoris Causa de Oxford', *Ercilla* (Santiago de Chile), 9 June 1965, 4 pp., unpaginated.. Unauthorized rpt of a talk for the BBC Latin-American service to mark Neruda's taking his honorary doctorate, broadcast 30 May 1965. Incorporating **D22**.

26   'Ramón Llull y las tres potencias del alma', *Estudios Lulianos*, 12 (1968), 101–30; tr. Albert Soler as 'Ramon Llull i les tres potències de l'ànima' in **A13**, 211–40. Paper originally delivered 23 April 1960 at Formentor, at the Primer Congrés Internacional de Lul·lisme.

27   'Some Techniques of Representation in the *Sueños* and the *Criticón*', *Bulletin of Hispanic Studies*, 45 (1968), 270–84. Paper first given, with the title 'The Shifting World and the Discerning Eye', at the Strasburg Congress of the Fédération Internationale des Langues et Littératures Modernes, September 1966. Extracted in **C38**.

28   'La *soutenance* del Professor Lluís Sala-Molins en la Sorbona', *Estudios Lulianos*, 14 (1970), 282–85.

29   'Both in Sorrow and in Anger: Spanish American Protest Poetry', *Cambridge Review*, 91, nr 2195 (20 Feb. 1970), 112–22; reissued as **A7** and rpt in **C41**. Includes (117–22) tr. of Pablo Neruda, 'The Liberators' (rpt in **D41** and **F5**) and 'To My Party' (rpt in **D41**); of Eliodoro Aillón Terán, 'Let Me Be Heard'; of Ernesto Cardenal, 'The First Psalm' (rpt in **D43** and **F5**) and 'The Twenty-First Psalm' (rpt in **B6**, **D33**, **D34**); and of Gonzalo Rojas, 'Reading the Omens' (rpt in **D43**).

30   'El mundo nerudiano esencialmente el mundo de la realidad', *La BBC de Londres: información de prensa* (London: BBC, 21–27 November 1971). Excerpt from a broadcast talk on the BBC, subsequently published as **D31**.

31   'Pablo Neruda, premio Nobel: visto desde acá', *El Mercurio* (Santiago de Chile), 5 March 1972, 14–15. Text of a BBC broadcast; excerpted in **D30**. Reissued in **E69**.

32   'Las relaciones entre el *Ars inveniendi veritatem* y los cuatro *Libri Principiorum*', *Estudios Lulianos*, 17 (1973) 18–42; tr. Albert Soler as 'Les relacions entre l'«ars inveniendi veritatem» i els quatre *Libri Principiorum*' in **A13**, 253–75.

33   (tr.) 'The Twenty-First Psalm', *The Catonsville Roadrunner*, 49 (1973). Unauthorized printing of a tr. of Cardenal's 'Salmo 21' (see also **D29** and **D34**), on the back cover of this publication.

34   (tr.) 'The Twenty-First Psalm', *The Tablet* (London), 228, nr 6980/1 (13/20 April 1974), 375; rpt in **B6**. See also **D29** and **D33**.

35   (tr.) 'From *Gethsemani, Ky*', *The Tablet* (London), 228, nr 6990 (22 June 1974), 601; rpt in **B6**. Part of the long sequence of the same name by Cardenal.

36   'A Note on Ernesto Cardenal', *Anthos* (Dublin), 4 (1975), 4–5. Introduction to tr. of Cardenal's 'Coplas a la muerte de Merton' (see **D37**).

37 (tr.) 'Coplas a la muerte de Merton', *Anthos*, 4 (1975), 6–17. See also **D36**.

38 (tr.) 'Apocalypse', *The Tablet*, 229, nr 7050 (16 August 1975), 773–74; rpt in **B7**. Tr. of Cardenal's 'Apocalipsis'.

39 'Pablo Neruda: A Brief Bibliographical Guide', *Bulletin of the Society for Latin-American Studies* (Southampton), 22 (1975), 19–27.

40 'The Anglo-Catalan Society', *Bulletin of Hispanic Studies*, 53 (1976), 99–100.

41 'Pablo Neruda: Three Poems in Context', *Saint Catherine's Year* (Oxford, 1977), 31–35. Contains tr. of 'The Liberators', 'To My Party', and 'Birth', the first two already published in **D29**, the third in **D24**.

42 'La doctrina pueril: conreu i transmissió d'una cultura', *Lluc: Òrgan de la Confraria de la Mare de Déu en Lluc*, 58, nr 682, (1978), 171–76; rpt in **A13**, 319–31. Version of a conference paper given 3 Nov. 1978 at the Estudi Geral Lul·lià, Mallorca, as part of the II Jornades d'Història de l'Educació en els Països Catalans.

43 'Poems at Curfew', *Index on Censorship* (London), 7, nr 1 (1978), 43–51. Introduction and tr. of: Ernesto Cardenal, 'The First Psalm', and Gonzalo Rojas, 'Reading the Omens'. Both tr. already published in **D29**. See also **F5**.

44 'South American *Poesía de compromiso*', *Bulletin of the Society for Latin-American Studies* (Glasgow), 31 (1979), 4–21.

45 'Profile: Ernesto Cardenal', *Index on Censorship* (London), 8, nr 3 (May–June 1979), 49–53.

46 'The Conscience of a "Brave" New World: Orozco', *The Oxford Art Journal*, 4, nr 1 (July 1981, number entitled *Tradition*), 45–50.

47 'La casuística como factor estructurizante en las comedias de Calderón (I)', *Iberoromania* (Tübingen), n.s. 14 (1981), 60–74.

48 'Poesía de la nueva Nicaragua', *Nicaráuac* (Managua), 6 (1981), 150–55.

49 'Acciones paralelas y montaje acelerado en el segundo episodio de Hora O', *Revista Iberoamericana* (Pittsburg, Pa.), 118/119 (1982), 217–40.

50 '*Cantas – Canto – Cantemos*: las canciones de lucha y esperanza como signos de reunión e identidad', *Romanistisches Jahrbuch*, 34 (1983), 318–54; reissued as **A10**; rpt as **D56**. Originally given in Paris as a paper at the XXII Congreso del Instituto Internacional de Literatura Iberoamericana. Not to be confused with the shorter essay of the same title (see **C44**).

51   ' "Porque yo cerca muriese": An Occasional Meditation on a *Concep-tista* Theme', *Bulletin of Hispanic Studies*, 61 (1984), nr 3 (= *Golden-Age Studies in Honour of A. A. Parker*, ed. Melveena McKendrick), 369–78. Based on 'The Linkages of Wit', an unpubl. paper delivered at the Cambridge Conference of the Association of Hispanists of Great Britain and Ireland.

52   'The "Workshop Poetry" of Sandinista Nicaragua (In memoriam K[emlin] M. L[awrence]', *Antilia* (St Augustine, Trinidad), 1, nr 2 (1984), 7–38; corr. rpt in **C43**. Contains many misprints, but comple-ments and also overlaps with **C46**.

53   'New Poetry from Sandinista Nicaragua', *Adelante* (Oxford), 14 (1984), 13–17; rpt in **C43**. Translations of: 'Huelga' by Gioconda Belli, 'En Managua a medianoche' by Cardenal, 'Ayer pasé por este ranchito' by Esperanza Guevara, 'Después del combate' and 'No descansés' by Miriam Guevara, plus an interview with RPM by Kathy Barber & Tom Buchanan.

54   'Neruda visto por sus amigos', *El Mercurio* (Santiago de Chile), 28 May 1986, 1, 4–5. Includes excerpt from **C45**.

55   'La evolución de *Los versos del capitán*: su composición y su reorgani-zación', *Ibero-Amerikanisches Archiv* (Berlin), n.s. 13 (1987), 175–89; reissued in **A11**. See also **C47**.

56   '*Cantas–Canto–Cantemos*: las canciones de lucha y esperanza como signos de reunión e identidad', *Nicaráuac* (Managua), 8, nr 14 (1987), 39–81. A rpt, with many *errata*, of **D50**.

57   'The Roles of Revolutionary Song – A Nicaraguan Assessment', *Pop-ular Music* (Cambridge), 6 (1987), 179–89.

58   'La «dicha sin quebranto» en Matilde Urrutia', *Araucaria de Chile* (Madrid), 40 (1987), 143–44. Text of a speech made on the anniver-sary of the birthday of Matilde Urrutia, 5 January 1986; rpt in **F9**.

59   'El «saber callar a tiempo» en Ernesto Cardenal y en la poesía campesina de *Solentiname*', *Caligrama: Revista Insular de Filología* (Palma de Mallorca), 2, nr 2 (1987), 17–41. A popularising version of **D60**.

60   'El «saber callar a tiempo» en Ernesto Cardenal y en la poesía campesina de *Solentiname*', *Casa de las Américas* (Havana), 28, nr 166, (Jan.–Feb. 1988), 19–34. Text of a paper delivered in Managua in January 1985, during the commemoration of Cardenal's sixtieth birth-day; see also **D59**.

61   'Neruda y Oxford', *Araucaria de Chile* (Madrid), 45 (1989), 137–54.

62   'The Lullian *Art of Finding Truth*:   A Medieval System of Enquiry',
      Catalan Review: International Journal of Catalan Culture (Washington,
      DC, and Barcelona), 4 (1990), 55–74.

63   'Cardenal's Treatment of Amerindian Cultures in *Homenaje a los in-
      dios americanos*', in *Renaissance and Modern Studies* (Nottingham), 35
      (1992), 52–74.

64   'Un comentario sobre el poema «Las garzas» de Alejandro Guevara',
      Nuevo Amanecer Cultural (Managua), 14, nr 673 (3 July 1993), 7.

65   'Neruda en Oxford', *Pluma y Pincel* (Santiago de Chile), nr 168 (1994),
      39–40.

66   'La ejemplaridad del auto y de la comedia: dos modos de argu-
      mentación dramática en Calderón', *Romanistisches Jahrbuch*, 45 (1994
      [= 1995]), in press.

67   'La vigencia sempiterna de Neruda', *Cultura Chilena* (Santiago de
      Chile), in press.

E   **Reviews and review-articles**

1   Review of: M. Sanchis Garner, *Introducción a la historia lingüística*
      (Valencia, 1950) and F. de B. Moll, *Gramática histórica catalana*
      (Madrid, 1952), *Romanistisches Jahrbuch*, 5 (1952), 373–75.

2   'The Literature of Spain', *The Month* (London), n.s. 7, nr 3 (March
      1952), 180–82.   Review of Gerald Brenan, *The Literature of the Span-
      ish People* (Cambridge, 1951).

3   'The Language and Literature of Spain', *Anglo-Spanish League of
      Friendship Quarterly Journal*, nr 9 (Oct.–Dec. 1953), 7–9.   Review of:
      B. J. W. Hill, *A Spanish Course* (London 1952), and Gerald Brenan, *The
      Literature of the Spanish People* (Cambridge, 1951).

4   Review of Francisco de Aldana, *Obras completas*, ed. Manuel Moragón,
      2 vols (Madrid, 1953), *Bulletin of Hispanic Studies*, 31 (1954), 182–83.

5   Review of *The Harrap Anthology of Spanish Poetry*, ed. Janet Perry
      (London, 1953), *Anglo-Spanish League of Friendship Quarterly Journal*,
      nr 10 (Jan.–March 1954), 29–30.

6   Review of: R. Trevor Davies, *Golden Century of Spain* (London, 1937;
      rpt 1954), and Américo Castro, *The Structure of Spanish History*, tr.
      Edmund L. King (Princeton, 1954), *Anglo-Spanish League of Friendship
      Quarterly Journal*, nr 11 (Apr.–June 1954), 9–10.

7   Review of J. A. Pitt-Rivers, *The People of the Sierra* (London, 1954),
      Anglo-Spanish League of Friendship Quarterly Journal, nr 14 (Jan.–

March 1955), 23–24.

8   Review of H. Casteel, *The Running of the Bulls* (London, 1954), *Anglo-Spanish League of Friendship Quarterly Journal*, nr 15 (Apr.–June 1955), 30–31.

9   Review of *The Journal of William Beckford in Portugal and Spain, 1787–1788*, ed. Boyd Alexander (London, 1954), *Bulletin of Hispanic Studies*, 32 (1955), 177–179.

10   Review of John Preston Moore, *The Cabildo in Peru under the Hapsburgs: A Study in the Origins and Powers of the Town Council in the Vice-Royalty of Peru, 1530–1700* (Durham, N.C., 1954), *Anglo-Spanish League of Friendship Quarterly Journal*, nr 17 (Oct.–Dec. 1955), 21–22.

11   Review of Kenneth Tynan, *Bull Fever* (London, 1955), *Anglo-Spanish League of Friendship Quarterly Journal*, nr 19 (Apr.–June 1956), 13.

12   'A Spanish Way of Looking at History', *Anglo-Spanish League of Friendship Quarterly Journal*, nr 19 (Apr.–June 1956), 15–17, nr 20 (June 1956), 12–14. Review of Américo Castro, *The Structure of Spanish History*, tr. Edmund L. King (Princeton, 1954).

13   'Félibrige and Renaixença', *Anglo-Spanish League of Friendship Quarterly Journal*, nr 22 (Oct.–Dec. 1956), 14–15. Review of Richard Aldington, *Introduction to Mistral* (London, 1956).

14   Review of Fernand van Steenberghen, *The Philosophical Movement in the Thirteenth Century* (Edinburgh, 1955), *Estudios Lulianos*, 1 (1957), 282–85.

15   Review of Fernand van Steenberghen, *Aristotle in the West (The Origins of Latin Aristotelianism)*, tr. Leonard Johnston (Louvain, 1955), *Estudios Lulianos*, 1 (1957), 411–12.

16   Review of E. Allison Peers, *Spain: A Companion to Spanish Studies*, 5th edn, revised R. F. Brown (London, 1956), *Anglo-Spanish League of Friendship Quarterly Journal*, nr 23 (Jan.–March 1957), 15–16.

17   Review of Federico García Lorca, *Poet in New York*, tr. Ben Belitt, ed. Ángel del Río (London, 1955), *Anglo-Spanish League of Friendship Quarterly Journal*, nr 24 (Apr.–June 1957), 13.

18   Review of Elias L. Rivers, *Francisco de Aldana, el divino Capitán* (Badajoz, 1955), *Bulletin of Hispanic Studies*, 35 (1958), 49–51.

19   Review of William of Ockham, *Philosophical Writings*, ed. & tr. P. Boehmer (Edinburgh, 1957), *Estudios Lulianos*, 2 (1958), 233–34.

20   'La geometría luliana', *Estudios Lulianos*, 2 (1958), 341–42. Review of José María Millás Vallicrosa, *El libro de la «Nova Geometria» de Ramón Llull* (Barcelona, 1953).

21   Review of: E. L. Dean & M. C. M. Roberts, *Seguimos adelante*
      (London, 1957); and José Picazo, *GCE Examination Papers for Trans-
      lation*, 2nd edn (London, 1958), *Anglo-Spanish Society Quarterly Jour-
      nal*, nr 28 (Apr.–June 1958), 25.

22   Review of Charles Petrie, *The Spanish Royal House* (London, 1958),
      Anglo-Spanish Society Quarterly Journal, nr 29 (July–Sept. 1958),
      28–29.

23   Review of Albert E. Sloman, *The Dramatic Craftsmanship of Calderón:
      His Use of Earlier Plays* (Oxford, 1958), *Romanistisches Jahrbuch*, 10
      (1959), 383–86.

24   Review of Ramon Lull, *Liber predicationis contra judeos*, ed. José
      María Millás Vallicrosa (Madrid, 1957), *Bulletin of Hispanic Studies*, 36
      (1959), 174–76.

25   Review of Francisco de Aldana, *Poesías*, ed. Elias L. Rivers (Madrid,
      1957), *Bulletin of Hispanic Studies*, 36 (1959), 237–38.

26   Review of Ramon Llull, *Obres essencials*, ed. Miquel Batllori & others,
      vol. I (Barcelona, 1957), *Romanistisches Jahrbuch*, 10 (1959), 379–82.

27   Review of Jean Plaidy, *The Rise of the Spanish Inquisition* (London,
      1959), *Anglo-Spanish Society Quarterly Review*, 32/33 (Apr.–June/
      July–Aug. 1959), 32.

28   Review of James O. Crosby, *The Text Tradition of the Memorial
      'Católica, Sacra, Real Magestad'* (Lawrence, Ka., 1958), *The Library*, 5th
      s. 15 (1960), 224–26.

29   Review of D. Hurtado de Mendoza, *A ti, doña Marina*, ed. C.M. Batch-
      elor (Havana, 1959), *Bulletin of Hispanic Studies*, 37 (1960), 200.

30   Review of Eric Allen [Ballard], *The Incredible Adventures of Don
      Quixote: A Retelling*, illustrated David Knight (London 1958), *Anglo-
      Spanish Society Quarterly Review*, 35 (Jan.–March 1960), 36.

31   'El arte de Ramon Llull', *Estudios Lulianos*, 4 (1960), 216–17. Review
      of Erardo (i.e. Erhard-Wolfram) W. Platzeck, OFM, 'Esencia del arte
      luliano', *Orbis Catholicus*, 2, nr 10 (October 1960), 287–95.

32   Review of E. Allison Peers, *Studies of the Spanish Mystics, III* (London,
      1960), *Anglo-Spanish Society Quarterly Review*, 36 (April–June 1960),
      33–35.

33   'Una serie de folletos sobre la filosofía medieval', *Estudios Lulianos*, 5
      (1961), 368-69. Review of vols 19 to 30 of the Aquinas Papers series
      (London: Blackfriars Press, 1952–58).

34   'Cristianos, moros y judíos en la Edad Media', *Estudios Lulianos*, 5
      (1961), 357–60. Review of: N. Daniel, *Islam and the West* (Edinburgh,

1960) and J. Katz, 'Exclusiveness and Tolerance', *Scripta Judaica*, 3 (1961).

35 'Ramón Llull en su mundo', *Estudios Lulianos*, 5 (1961), 349–50. Review of Miquel Batllori, SJ, *Ramon Llull en el món del seu temps* (Barcelona, 1960).

36 Review of H. Peri (Pflaum), *Der Religionsdisput der Barlaam-Legende, ein Motiv abendländischer Dichtung* (Salamanca, 1959), *Bulletin of Hispanic Studies*, 38 (1961), 180.

37 Review of *Semejança del mundo (A Medieval Description of the World)*, ed. William E. Buck & Harry F. Williams (Berkeley & Los Angeles, 1959), *Romanistisches Jahrbuch*, 13 (1962), 353–54.

38 Review of Ramon Llull, *Obres essencials*, ed. Miquel Batllori & others, vol. II (Barcelona, 1960), *Romanistisches Jahrbuch*, 13 (1962), 354–57.

39 Review of A. A. Parker, *The Approach to the Spanish Drama of the Golden Age* (London, 1957; rpt, with corrections, *The Tulane Drama Review*, 4 (1959), 42–59), *Romanistisches Jahrbuch*, 13 (1962), 384–87. The criticisms offered by RPM were largely instrumental in persuading Parker to revise his essay as 'The Spanish Drama of the Golden Age: A Method of Analysis and Interpretation', in Eric Bentley (ed.), *The Great Playwrights: Twenty-Five Plays with Commentaries by Critics and Scholars* (New York, 1970), I, 679–707.

40 Review of Frances A. Yates, *Ramon Lull and John Scotus Erigena* (London, 1960), *Medium Aevum* (Oxford), 31 (1962), 78–80.

41 Review of Richard Walzer, *Greek into Arabic* (Oxford, 1962), *Estudios Lulianos*, 7 (1963), 224–25.

42 'La geografía del medioevo europeo', *Estudios Lulianos*, 7 (1963), 226–27. Review of C. McEvedy, *The Penguin Atlas of Medieval History* (London, 1961).

43 'La filosofía griega y la cristiandad', *Estudios Lulianos*, 7 (1963), 236–37. Review of: Plotinus, *The Enneads*, ed. & tr. S. Mackenna & H. Armstrong (London, 1962), and R.A. Markus, *Christian Faith and Greek Philosophy* (London, 1960).

44 Review of Kenneth R. Scholberg, *La poesía original de Miguel de Barrios* (Ohio, n.d.), *Romanistisches Jahrbuch*, 14 (1963), 370–72.

45 Review of Karl-Ludwig Selig, *The Library of Vincencio Juan de Lastanosa, Patron of Gracián* (Geneva, 1960), *Romanistisches Jahrbuch*, 14 (1963), 366–67.

46 Review of Dámaso Alonso, *Dos españoles del siglo de oro* (Madrid, 1960), *Bulletin of Hispanic Studies*, 40 (1963), 62–63.

47   Review of Julio García Morejón, *Límites de la estilística: el idearium crítico de Dámaso Alonso* (Assis, 1961), *Romanistisches Jahrbuch*, 14 (1963), 352–55.

48   Review of Ángel Antón Andrés, *Geschichte des spanischen Literatur vom 18. Jahrhundert bis zur Gegenwart* (Munich, 1961), *Bulletin of Hispanic Studies*, 40 (1963), 67–68.

49   Review of Francisco de Quevedo, *Obras completas, I: Poesía original*, ed. José Manuel Blecua (Barcelona, 1963), *Romanistisches Jahrbuch*, 15 (1964), 386–88.

50   Review of Eusebio Colomer, SJ, *Nikolaus von Kues und Raimund Llull* (Berlin, 1961), *Archiv für Geschichte der Philosophie* (Berlin), 47 (1965), 105–09.

51   Review of Edward M. Wilson & Jack Sage, *Poesías líricas en las obras de Calderón: citas y glosas* (London, 1964), *Romanistisches Jahrbuch*, 17 (1966), 367–69.

52   Review of *Raimundi Lullii Opera Latina, 118: Liber de Praedicatione*, ed. A. Soria Flores (Palma de Mallorca, 1961–63), *Estudios Lulianos*, 11 (1967), 187–89.

53   Review of Erhard-Wolfram Platzeck, OFM, *Raimund Lull: Sein Leben, seine Werke, die Grundlagen seines Denkens (Prinzipienlehre)*, 2 vols (Düsseldorf, 1962–64), *Estudios Lulianos*, 11 (1967), 192–95. See also **E58**.

54   Review of: Edward C. Riley, *Cervantes's Theory of the Novel* (Oxford, 1962) and Sanford Shepard, *El Pinciano y las teorías literarias del Siglo de Oro* (Madrid, 1962), *Modern Language Review*, 62 (1967), 146–49.

55   'Convocation of Snails', *Times Literary Supplement*, nr 3422, 28 September 1967, 907–908. Review of: José María Castellet, *Un cuarto de siglo de poesía española (1939–64)* (Barcelona, 1960); Castellet, *Poesia, realisme, història* (Barcelona, 1965); and Castellet & Joaquim Molas, *Poesia catalana del segle XX* (Barcelona, 1963). Reissued in **E69**.

56   'Vigour and Gloom', *Times Literary Supplement*, nr 3422, 28 September 1967, 908. Review of: Miguel Arteche, *Resta poética* (Avila, 1966); Enrique Lihn, *Poesía de paso* (Havana, 1966); and Francisco Brines, *Palabras a la oscuridad* (Madrid, 1966). Reissued in **E69**.

57   'States of Suspension', *Times Literary Supplement*, nr 3481, 14 November 1968, 1286. Review of Octavio Paz, *Blanco* (Mexico City, 1967) and *Topoemas* (Mexico City, 1968). Reissued in **E69**.

58   Review of Erhard-Wolfram Platzeck, OFM, *Raimund Lull* (see **E53**)

and *Das Leben des seligen Raimund Lull* (Düsseldorf, 1964), *Bulletin of Hispanic Studies*, 45 (1968), 71–72.

59   Review of *Gesammelte Aufsätze zur Kulturgeschichte Spaniens*, vol. XXI, *Bulletin of Hispanic Studies*, 45 (1968), 80–81.

60   Review of Miriam Thérèse Olabarrieta, *The Influence of Ramon Lull on the Style of Early Spanish Mystics and Santa Teresa* (Washington, DC, 1963), *Bulletin of Hispanic Studies*, 45 (1968), 82–83.

61   Review of Armand Llinarès, *Raymond Lulle, philosophe de l'action* (Grenoble, 1963), *Bulletin of Hispanic Studies*, 45 (1968), 154–55.

62   Review of R. Lull, *Le Livre des bêtes*, ed. Armand Llinarès (Paris, 1964) and *Le Livre du gentil et des trois sages*, ed. Llinarès (Grenoble, 1966), *Bulletin of Hispanic Studies*, 45 (1968), 156–57.

63   'A Poet and his Roots', *Times Literary Supplement*, nr 3555, 16 April 1970, 397–99. Review of: Pablo Neruda, *Obras completas*, 3rd edn, 2 vols (Buenos Aires, 1968);   Neruda, *Aún* (Santiago de Chile, 1969); Hernán Loyola, *Ser y morir en Pablo Neruda, 1918–1945* (Santiago de Chile, 1967);   Jaime Alazraki, *Poética y poesía de Pablo Neruda* (New York, 1965);   E. Rodríguez Monegal, *El viajero inmóvil: Introducción a Pablo Neruda* (Buenos Aires, 1966);   and Margarita Aguirre, *Las vidas de Pablo Neruda* (Santiago de Chile, 1967).   Reissued in **E69**.

64   'Versions of Neruda', *Times Literary Supplement*, nr 3578, 25 September 1970, 1086. Review of: Pablo Neruda, *Twenty Love Poems and a Song of Despair*, tr. W. S. Merwin (London, 1969), and Neruda, *Selected Poems*, ed. Nathaniel Tarn, with translations by Anthony Kerrigan, W. S. Merwin, Alistair Reid, & Nathaniel Tarn (London, 1970). Reissued in **E69**.

65   'Firstborn of the Volcano', *Times Literary Supplement*, nr 3632, 8 October 1971, 1223. Review of: Elisabeth Siefer, *Epische Stilelemente im «Canto General» von Pablo Neruda* (Munich, 1970);   Antonio Melis, *Neruda* (Florence, 1970);   and Pablo Neruda, *Fin de mundo* (Buenos Aires, 1969), *La espada encendida* (Buenos Aires, 1970), and *Las piedras del cielo* (Buenos Aires, 1971). See also **E75**. Reissued in **E69**.

66   'Private and Public Styles', *Times Literary Supplement*, nr 3633, 15 November 1971, 1266–67. Review of: Rafael Alberti, *Roma, peligro para caminantes* (Mexico City, 1968), *El poeta en la calle* (Paris, 1966), and *Libro del mar* (Barcelona, 1968);   and Solita Salinas de Marechal, *El mundo poético de Rafael Alberti* (Madrid, 1968). Reissued in **E69**.

67   'Chilean Whimsies', *Times Literary Supplement*, nr 3673, 21 July 1972, 839.   Review of Pablo Neruda, *Extravagaria* [*sic*], tr. Alistair Reid (London, 1972).

68   'Rotating Signs', *Times Literary Supplement*, nr 3682, 29 September 1972, 1144. Review of Ramón Xirau, *Octavio Paz: El sentido de la palabra* (Mexico City, 1970).

69   'States of Vigour: 20th-Century Poetry in Spanish: Reviews and Review-Articles plus one *Homenaje*' (Oxford: privately printed, n.d. [= ?1972]). Reissue of: **E65, E56, E57, E63, E64, E65, E66**, and **D31**.

70   Review of J. N. Hillgarth, *Ramon Lull and Lullism in Fourteenth-Century France* (Oxford, 1971), *Estudios Lulianos*, 17 (1973), 92–96.

71   Review of Marjorie Reeves, *The Influence of Prophecy in the Later Middle Ages (A Study of Joachimism)* (Oxford, 1969), *Estudios Lulianos*, 17 (1973), 215–18.

72   'Introspection in Autumn', *Times Literary Supplement*, nr 3714, 11 May 1973, 532. Review of: Pablo Neruda, *Antología esencial*, ed. Hernán Loyola (Buenos Aires, 1971), *Geografía infructuosa* (Buenos Aires, 1972), and *Incitación al nixonicidio y alabanza de la revolución chilena* (Montevideo, 1973); Angelina Gatell, *Neruda* (Madrid, 1971); Morris E. Carson, *Pablo Neruda, regresó el caminante: Aspectos sobresalientes de la obra y vida de Pablo Neruda* (New York, 1971); Eliana Suárez Rivero, *El gran amor de Pablo Neruda: Estudio crítico de su poesía* (Madrid, 1971); and Alfredo Lozada, *El monismo agónico de Pablo Neruda: Estructura, significado y filiación de 'Residencia en la Tierra'* (Mexico City, 1971).

73   Review of Francisco Rico, *El pequeño mundo del hombre* (Madrid, 1970), *Bulletin of Hispanic Studies*, 51 (1974), 163–65.

74   'The Christian Revolutionary of Lake Nicaragua', *Times Literary Supplement*, nr 3774, 12 July 1974, 743. Review of: Ernesto Cardenal, *Antología* (Buenos Aires, 1971, etc.), *Homenaje a los indios americanos* (Buenos Aires, 1972), and *En Cuba* (Buenos Aires, 1972); and A. Schwarzer de Ruiz & H. Schulz, *Von der Heiligkeit der Revolution* (Wuppertal, 1972).

75   Review of Elisabeth Siefer, *Epische Stilelemente* (see **E65**), *Bulletin of Hispanic Studies*, 51 (1974), 323–24.

76   'Contrapuntalities', *Times Literary Supplement*, nr 3825, 4 July 1975, 719. Review of Rachel Phillips, *The Poetic Modes of Octavio Paz* (London, 1972).

77   'Testimonials to Neruda', *Times Literary Supplement*, nr 3836, 19 September 1975, 1068. Review of: Jaime Concha, *Neruda 1904–1936* (Santiago de Chile, 1972); Carlos D. Hamilton, *Pablo Neruda: Poeta chileno universal* (Santiago de Chile, 1972); Ángel Flores (ed.), *Aproximaciones a Pablo Neruda* (Barcelona, 1974); and Álvaro Sarmiento & Fina Torres, *Neruda: entierro y testamento* (Las Palmas de Gran Canaria, 1973).

78   'The Winter of Pablo Neruda', *Times Literary Supplement*, nr 3838, 3 October 1975, 1154–56. Review of: Pablo Neruda, *Obras completas*, 4th edn. (Buenos Aires, 1973), *Confieso que he vivido* (Buenos Aires, 1974), *La rosa separada* (Buenos Aires, 1973), *Jardín de invierno* (Buenos Aires, 1974), *2000* (Buenos Aires, 1974), *El corazón amarillo* (Buenos Aires, 1974), *Libro de las preguntas* (Buenos Aires, 1974), *Elegía* (Buenos Aires, 1974), *Defectos escogidos* (Buenos Aires, 1974), *El mar y las campanas* (Buenos Aires, 1974), and *Maremoto* (Santiago de Chile, 1970); Luis F. González-Cruz, *Pablo Neruda y el Memorial de la Isla Negra* (Miami, 1972); and Pablo Neruda, Sara Facio & Alicia d'Amico, *Geografía de Pablo Neruda* (Barcelona, 1973).

79   'The Poetry of Protest', *Times Literary Supplement*, nr 3882, 6 August 1976, 994-95.   Review of: Robert Márquez, *Latin-American Revolutionary Poetry* (New York & London, 1974);   Mario Benedetti, *Letras de emergencia*, 2nd edn (Buenos Aires, 1974) and *Los poetas comunicantes* (Montevideo, 1972);   Jaime Labastida (ed.), *Cuba: jóvenes poetas revolucionarios* and *Obsesiones con un tema obligado* (Mexico City, 1975); Elvio Romero, *Destierro y atardecer* (Buenos Aires, 1975); Jaime Galarza, *El amor en armas* (Quito, 1974); and Ernesto Cardenal, *Canto nacional* (Buenos Aires & Mexico City, 1973) and *Oráculo sobre Managua* (Buenos Aires, 1973).

80   Review of: 'Estudios sobre Pablo Neruda', *Anales de la Universidad de Chile*, 29, nrs 159/160 (1971);   *Atenea* (Concepción, Chile), nr 425 (1972); 'Homenaje a Pablo Neruda', *Taller de Letras* (Santiago de Chile), 2 (1972); *Revista Iberoamericana*, 82/83 (1972); *Cuadernos de Crisis*, 2 (Buenos Aires, 1973); 'Neruda présent', *Europe*, nrs 537/538 (1973); *Mester* (Los Angeles), 4, nr 2 (1974); and *Cuadernos Hispanoamericanos*, nr 287 (1974), all in *Bulletin of Hispanic Studies*, 53 (1976), 91–92.

81   Review of Robert C. Manteiga, *The Poetry of Rafael Alberti: A Visual Approach* (London, 1978), *Romanistisches Jahrbuch*, 32 (1981), 397–99.

82   Review of: René de Costa, *The Poetry of Pablo Neruda* (Cambridge Mass., 1979) and Salvatore Bizzarro, *Pablo Neruda, All Poets the Poet* (Metuchen, 1979), *Review*, 29 (May–August 1981), 75–76.

83   Review article on James Iffland, *Quevedo and the Grotesque*, 2 vols (London, 1978–83), *Romanistisches Jahrbuch*, 38 (1987 [=1988]), 380–85.

F   Other

1   Revisions of Roy Campbell's English tr. of Calderón de la Barca, *La vida es sueño*, for publication in Eric Bentley, *The Classic Theatre*, vol. III: *Spanish Plays* (New York: Doubleday & Co., 1959), 407–80. Also minor revisions to Campbell's English tr. of Lope de Vega, *Fuente Ovejuna*, in same volume, 161–231. The translations rpt in Bentley, *Life is a Dream, and Other Spanish Classics*, tr. Roy Campbell, Eric Bentley's Dramatic Repertoire 2 (New York: Applause Theatre Books, 1985).

2   (tr., with Elizabeth Jennings) Calderón de la Barca, *El gran teatro del mundo*. Staged in Oxford in Exeter College chapel and later broadcast by the BBC, 17 December 1962.

3   'The Interplay of Skills, Techniques, and Information, with Special Reference to the Entrance Examination and to Methods of Instruction in a University', *University of Oxford: Commission of Enquiry: Evidence*, Part XI: *Individuals* (Oxford: University of Oxford, May 1965), 129–53.

4   (ed. & tr.) *Neruda Poems* [also known as the *Neruda Portfolio*], limited edn of a bilingual boxed portfolio of poetry with a set of twelve silkscreen prints by Katya Kohn (London: Central School of Art and Design, 1969).

5   *Poems at Curfew: Poesía del toque de queda: An Evening of Spanish-American Contemporary Poetry at the Poetry Society, London, on 27 October 1977, with the Participation of Robert Pring-Mill and Peter Levi.* Programme, [36 pp.]. Introduction by RPM and translations by him of: Gonzalo Rojas, 'Vaticinio' ('Reading the Omens', see **D29**); Pablo Neruda, 'Los libertadores' ('The Liberators', see **D29** and **D41**); and Ernesto Cardenal, 'Buenaventurado el hombre' ('The First Psalm', see **D29**). See also **D43**.

6   'A Poet for All Seasons', introductory note to theatre programme for evening entitled *A Tribute to Pablo Neruda*, Logan Hall, University of London, 28 September 1979 (London: Chile Committee for Human Rights, 1979, 3 pp.).

7   Untitled set of seven audio cassettes, for use in Optional Subject No.74 of the Final Honour School of Medieval and Modern Languages, University of Oxford: 'Spanish American Committed Poetry' (1982).

8   *Mensaje de solidaridad de Robert Pring-Mill, nerudista británico y profesor de la Universidad de Oxford, Inglaterra, en el 84° cumpleaños de Pablo Neruda* (Oxford, privately printed, 7 July 1988, 2 pp.).

9   *Palabras de Robert Pring-Mill (Universidad de Oxford), el 5 de enero de 1986, en la misa de aniversario de la muerte de doña Matilde Urrutia, viuda de Pablo Neruda* (Oxford, privately printed, 7 July 1988, 2 pp.). Includes a poem 'Te construí cantando', dictated by Neruda to his wife on board the *Giulio Cesare*, 4 August 1952. Rpt of **D58**.

10   (with Jenny Myatt & Rachel Stringfellow). Introductory essay in booklet and audio cassette to accompany *Pablo Martínez 'El Guadalupano'* (Oxford: Oxford–León Association, 1989).

11   'Los sueños del habitante de la casa transparente'. Introduction to a sequence of paintings by Osvaldo Rodríguez-Musso (Valparaíso, 1992), 4 pp. in the exhibition catalogue.

12   *Nerudiana* (London: privately published, 1992, 11 pp.). A catalogue to the exhibition of material from the private collection of RPM held in the Central Library of the University of London, May–June 1992.

13   *A Poet for All Seasons* (Oxford: privately printed, 1993, 50 pp. + 22 unnumbered leaves of illustrations). Catalogue to an exhibition of Neruda material in the Voltaire Room of the Taylor Institution, University of Oxford, Nov. 1993, on the occasion of the International Symposium on Pablo Neruda. Introduction and notes by RPM (see **C52**).

14   *Antología popular de la Resistencia* (Oxford & Warwick: Simposio Internacional sobre Pablo Neruda, 12–16 November 1993, [14] pp.). Conference handout of photocopies from the clandestine 1948 printing of the same title, by Ediciones de la Resistencia, with an introductory note by RPM (see **C53**). For copyright reasons, the texts were only made available in this form.

15   'Neruda un poeta en transición: entrevista a Robert Pring-Mill', *Boletín de la Fundación Pablo Neruda* (Santiago de Chile), 5, nr 16 (1993), 46–50. Interview attributed to a certain 'Martín Ruiz' but loosely based on an interview with RPM recorded by Luis Alberto Mansilla, editor of the *Boletín*, with many of RPM's reported statements fabricated.

16   Oscar Vega, 'Nace Asociación Internacional Nerudista', *La Época* (Santiago de Chile), 24 January 1994, 7. This summary of the proceedings of the Oxford/Warwick Neruda symposium was based on a pseudo-interview with RPM conducted by Florencia Vargas (see **F17**).

17   [credited to] Florencia Vargas, 'Simposio de Neruda en Inglaterra', *El Mercurio* (Santiago de Chile), 248, (24 January 1994), 8. A pseudo-interview, devised in dialogue form by RPM as a way of conveniently summarising the proceedings of the Oxford/Warwick Neruda symposium (see also **F16**).

18 *Brindis declamada en la cena formal en St Catherine's College 'Universidad de Oxford' el 13 de Noviembre de 1993 y décima espinela para Roberto de Inglaterra, por Patricio Manns, declamada en la cena de despedida en Scarman House (Universidad de Watwick) el 15 de Noviembre de 1993* (Oxford: privately printed, 1994, 6 pp.).

N. H. G.   E. A. S.

ONE

—————————

CATALONIA

AUSIÀS MARCH
AS A THEORIST OF LOVE

ONE OF THE FEATURES of the work of Ausiàs March that distinguishes it from the mass of other poetry written in the Crown of Aragon and in Castile in the late fourteenth and fifteenth centuries is the cumulative presence of a system of thought. That is, while one could construct from recurring commonplaces in the work of other poets of the time a general world-view (a topic on which Robert Pring-Mill has carried out some distinguished work), no one who reads March's poetry in its extant entirety can fail to be impressed by his effort to build into his work a structure of apparently interlocking ideas. That he wished to give coherence to these ideas is evident from the fact that he devotes several pieces to expounding them at length, and from the way in which he incorporates theoretical dissertations into other poems which have ostensibly non-theoretical purposes.

This impression of a system of thought behind the poetry has prompted suggestions, since Bishop Torras i Bages's early essay, that March was working from a specific philosophical basis. Theories have been advanced in favour of the *Summa Theologica* of St Thomas Aquinas and the work of Ramon Llull, as well as modified forms of both theses, but it seems fair to say that no convincing case has been made so far in support of either. Pending further research, it seems appropriate to assume that March's ideas are not derived from any particular theologian or specific work but are broadly based on a range of scholastic commonplaces, while in certain poems at least they seem to be closely related to a Romance version of Aristotle's *Ethics*.[1]

---

1. The earliest Thomist interpretation of March is to be found in Josep TORRAS I BAGES, *La tradició catalana: Estudi del valor ètich e racional del regionalisme català* (Barcelona: F. Giró, 1892), rpt in his *Obres completes* (Barcelona: Selecta, 1948). This is taken up by Amédée PAGÈS in his *Auzias March et ses prédécesseurs: Essai sur la poésie amoureuse et philosophique en Catalogne aux XIVe et XVe siècles*, Bibliothèque de l'École des Hautes Études: Sciences Historiques et Philologiques 124 (Paris: Honoré Champion, 1912; rpt Geneva: Slatkine, 1974), now also available in Catalan as *Ausiàs March i els seus predecessors*, tr. Víctor Gómez,

Within this system of thought, love is inevitably a major element, since the bulk of March's poems centres on his relationship with a woman, or with women in general, and he devotes several pieces – XLV, LXXXVII, XCII, CXVII, CXXIIb and CXXIII – to what for all intents and purposes we can call a 'theory of love'. It has usually been assumed since Pagès, and notably in the splendid exposition of March's ideas by Pere Bohigas, that these poems offer an homogeneous basis from which to approach the rest of his work.[2] It is argued here, within the necessarily limited context that these poems offer, that March's ideas on love are in fact a less consistent element in his system of ideas than is generally believed. For reasons of space, I will restrict detailed discussion to XLV, LXXXVII and XCII, without wishing to suggest that CXVII, CXXIIb, and CXXIII are unimportant.

In XLV, probably the first of the poems in the order of chronology, March develops a number of concepts concerning love with the ostensible aim of explaining to those who are 'ignorant of love and its deeds' what love is, and in particular the nature of its effects on himself. He begins with a lengthy *refutatio* (lines 1–20), declaring that those who do not believe what he says must be unworthy examples of mankind. He also includes within these stanzas a description of the physical effects of love in 'fins amadors' like himself, in terms that are purely conventional:[3]

> Foc amagat, nodrit dins en les venes,
> faent gran fum per via dreta i torta;

Col·lecció Politècnica 41 (Valencia: Edicions Alfons el Magnànim & Institució Valenciana d'Estudis i Investigació, 1990). The Lullist position is argued by Pere RAMÍREZ I MOLAS, *La poesia d'Ausiàs March: Analisi textual, cronologia, elements filosòfics* (Basle: privately printed, 1970). Important work on March's system of thought has been carried out by Louis P. A. MAINGON in his 'Melancholy Imagination in Ausiàs March and Florentine Neoplatonists' (unpublished doctoral dissertation, University of St Andrews, 1982).

2. PAGÈS, *Auzias March*, 284–308, 334–41; Ausiàs MARCH, *Poesies*, ed. Pere Bohigas, 5 vols, Els Nostres Clàssics A 71–73, 77, 86 (Barcelona: Editorial Barcino, 1952–59), I, 25–47.

3. Quotations from poems XLV, XCII, CXVII, CXXIIb and CXXIII are from the edition of Pere BOHIGAS (I have regularized the spelling). For LXXXVII I use the text of Robert ARCHER, *Ausiàs March: A Key Anthology*, The Anglo-Catalan Society Occasional Publications 8 (Sheffield: The Anglo-Catalan Society, 1992). Lola BADIA gives a different interpretation of XLV from mine in her stimulating and well-documented study '«E visch de ço que persones no tasten»: De l'«ebrietat» amorosa en els poemes de «Llir entre cards»' in her *Tradició i modernitat als segles XIV i XV: Estudis de cultura literària i lectures d'Ausiàs March*, Biblioteca Sanchis Guarner (Valencia: Institut Universitari de Filologia Valenciana & Barcelona: Publicacions de l'Abadia de Montserrat, 1993), 143–66.

ira dins pau, e turment molt alegre,
llum clar e bell ab si portant tenebres.

(lines 9–12)

The poem starts off, in effect, as an apology for human love: people should
not scoff at the suffering lover, for the power of love is irresistible and terrible
to experience. But in the third stanza it becomes apparent that this description of the workings of love in men like himself in fact represents a norm
against which March intends to gauge the complexity of the particular
experience he claims for himself.

The poet's experience of love has to it a further dimension: not only that
which strikes at the composite nature of man, bringing into play the interpene-
tration of body and soul, but also a form of love in which the flesh has no part
and in which human love transcends sin (lines 21–24). This type of love, to
which at this point March gives the name 'voluntat bona', has only virtue as its
object (line 26) and is the response of one soul to another (line 28); its effects
are, by implication, quite different from those that take their hold on 'fins
amadors', which March has described in lines 9–12 and now summarizes in
line 32 as 'pau e guerra tot ensemble'. This is a grand claim. The poet contends not only that he loves as one who, like others, has elevated human love
to 'fina amor', but also that he is an even finer being who strives for the kind
of love that can only be experienced beyond the flesh:

Aquella amor que·s diu voluntat bona
e solament esguarda part honesta,
aquesta amor ha fet a mi amable
per mon semblant e·l mijançant ministre.

(lines 25–28)[4]

In most of the remainder of the poem, March elaborates the theoretical basis
of his claim.

In the central theoretical section (lines 33–88), he places love in the context of scholastic psychology. Love begins in man as data perceived by the
faculty of the senses. These data (the attributes of the loved person) enter
man firstly through the exterior senses ('nostres senys', line 33), and thence
into the 'comú seny' (line 34), the *sensus communis* or interior sense which

---

4. The 'ministre' here is the soul, not the body, contrary to the interpretation of Amédée
PAGÈS, *Commentaire des poésies d'Auzias March* (Paris: Honoré Champion, 1925), 61, and
MARCH, *Poesies*, II, 156.

distinguishes between the exterior senses and collates them. From here, the perceived forms pass into the understanding ('l'entendre', line 35) at which point the will ('voler', line 36), seeking the good, desires love. March makes it clear that this is not a virtuous form of love, even though the understanding is involved. While it is true that the virtue and intelligence of the loved woman ('totes virtuts e seny', line 39) are part of the lover's desire, these are not loved for their own sake but rather because they serve to augment the overall pleasure which the lover takes in his beloved.

March now defines the two extreme forms of love between which lies 'fina amor'. In purely carnal love, the kind of pleasure he has just described is not possible since the understanding, by definition, has no part in it. Rather, it is a short-lived form of love since its cause – purely physical appetite – is itself only brief (lines 41–49). At the other extreme is the type of love in which the senses have no part, that is, purely spiritual love. Few have actually attained it, but those blessed few have experienced the only form of enduring love. It is evident here that March does not include himself among the number of these spiritual lovers. What he has actually claimed, in lines 25–28 quoted above, is that he feels the pull of the spiritual form of love and aspires to practise it, while he continues to be subject to 'fina amor'. This form of love lies between the two extremes, and is in practice a refined form of the properly human 'amor homenívol', which partakes of man's composite nature. The refinement lies in its tendency to incline more towards the spirit than towards the flesh (lines 49–56).

In the next few stanzas March explains why 'amor homenívol' (including 'fina amor') is so much more beset with strong desires ('volers . . . punyents', lines 63–64) than the simple forms (carnal, spiritual). This is because, in the struggle for domination between body and soul, the flesh always manages in the end to impose its will upon the spirit (although, as March has asserted in line 54, in 'fina amor' the spirit has a more pronounced role). This is due to the fact that in human love man loves unaided by virtue (lines 65–72).

In this properly human type of love, desire, pleasure, and the passions all play their part. Desire comes first, the primary movement identified by March elsewhere as the 'primer moviment' or 'prim moviment'.[5] The passions (that

---

5. IV, 34; LXI, 40; LXXI, 95 (*prim motiu*); CVI, 426. See also RAMÍREZ I MOLAS, *La poesia d'Ausiàs March*, 328–32; Xavier RENEDO I PUIG, 'Edició i estudi del *Tractat de luxúria* del *Terç del Crestià* de Francesc Eiximenis' (unpublished doctoral dissertation, Universitat Autònoma de Barcelona, 1992), I, 320 ff.

is, the emotions) follow the onset of love, which will last only as long as pleasure endures (lines 73–76). At this point March includes some very elliptical clarification of his terms of reference: he reminds us that the form of 'amor homenívol' he is discussing is that of 'fina amor', and that he uses the word pleasure (*delit*) without wishing to imply the carnal act. Rather, the pleasure to which he refers is one in which the lover aspires to another form of love, more spiritual than carnal, which is sustained solely by the hope of achieving reciprocation. Because 'fina amor' is subject to the passions (or so we may infer), once hope is lost (hope is in scholastic terms a passion), only the opposite passion, fear, can follow (lines 77–80).

This idea is developed in the following stanza in the form of a eulogy of true 'fins amants': those who give themselves up to the passions of 'fina amor' live in the hope of requited love, and once this is lost only a martyr's death can follow (lines 81–88). At this point an underlying irony starts to make its presence felt in the poem: March proclaims that those who would be worthy adherents of such love need first to renounce the use of their reason:

> Cell qui d'amor del tot no·s lleixa vençre,
> sí que raó de son consell no llunya,
> no mereix pas la corona de martre.

(lines 81–83)

Not only, then, is the lover in 'fina amor' unaided by virtue, but he has also to be blind to reason. In the final full stanza the irony of these words of praise is brought out still further by their contrast with March's encomium of *bona amor*, the spiritual love that earlier in the poem he had called 'voluntat bona' (line 25). This type of love is infinite, transcending death itself, and thus can hold no fears for the lover since it lies beyond the passions. Dante's love for Beatrice is cited as an example. This form of love has its origins in virtue itself – virtuous friendship – and it is for this reason that the senses (the fallible basis of 'fina amor') cannot bring about its undoing (lines 91–92).

At this stage it becomes apparent that March has shifted ground from the exaltation of 'fina amor' in the first stanzas to the recognition of its underlying moral defects. By the end of the poem, he is willing to tolerate only spiritual love as the object of his praise.

If we read XLV in this way, its *tornada* turns out to be less surprising than it might at first appear, since the final perspective of March's somewhat tangled disquisition on love is an exclusively moral one that is perfectly consonant

with the *sententia* of the last four lines. The terms of reference here continue
to be broadly scholastic, but it is useful to relate March's ideas to their Aristotelian roots, at least in the form accessible to him in a Catalan translation of
Brunetto Latini, used by him on at least two other occasions.[6]

March's final words are as follows:

> Llir entre cards, tres són les grans carreres
> on veritat per negun temps passeja:
> ira i amor ab si no la consenten,
> e l'altra és general ignorança.

(lines 97–100)

In the compendium of the *Ethics* in Brunetto, Guillem de Copons translates:

> Pobrea de seny e de discreció és occasió de mal e de tots hòmens mal-
> vats ... Mas pensen les gents que·ls ... hòmens fellons, quant fan mal,
> que·u fan per ignorància, e ço és per no saber. E jassia que ells sien
> no-sabents o ignorants en lurs afers, però la occasió del mal no és fora de
> l'home ... E la occasió d'açò és concupiscència e ira, que són occasió de
> totes males obres que hom fa per voluntat.[7]

I am not suggesting that Brunetto is the source of March's ideas here.[8]
However, the parallel is worth drawing as it allows us to see that the poet is
not saying anything unusual, but rather is drawing on commonplaces of
medieval Aristotelianism. It is plain from Brunetto that *ignorància* becomes a
culpable condition when sinful acts are committed; such sinful acts are always
prompted by *ira* and *concupiscència*. In March, the three terms appear as *ignorança*, *ira*, and *amor*. The 'general ignorança' to which March alludes in the
very last words of his poem is set up in deliberate contrast with the ignorance
of those whom March decries in his opening line: 'Los ignorants amor e sos
exemples'. This manifestation of ignorance fades into insignificance by the

---

6. See Robert ARCHER, 'Una font aristotèlica d'Ausiàs March,' in *Miscel·lània Joan Fuster:
Estudis de llengua i literatura*, ed. Antoni Ferrando & Albert G. Hauf, 7 vols (to date), Publicacions de l'Abadia de Montserrat (Barcelona: Departament de Filologia Catalana, Universitat
de València & Associació Internacional de Llengua i Literatura Catalanes, 1989–   ), IV,
59–74, a revised version of which is contained in ARCHER, *Aproximació a Ausiàs March:
Tradició, estructura, metàfora* (Barcelona: Empúries, in press).

7. BRUNETTO LATINI, *Llibre del Tresor*, tr. Guillem de Copons, ed. Curt J. Wittlin, 4 vols, Els
Nostres Clàssics, Col·lecció A 102, 111, 122, 125 (Barcelona: Barcino, 1971–89), II, 127–28.

8. The idea is taken up by Aquinas (*In quatuor sententiarum P. Lombardi libros*, II, d.22, q.II,
a.2), where distinctions between types of ignorance are elaborated further and there is specific
reference to universal (general) ignorance.

end of the poem since March makes a full retreat from his initial position: no form of human love that involves the senses, even 'fina amor' with all the attendant wonders described in lines 1–16, can lead man towards truth. It is universal culpable ignorance, in close alliance with the concupiscent and irascible wills, that March finally denounces.

This, I suggest, is the moral position that underlies a great deal of March's love poetry.[9] If he rarely allows it to occupy the centre of his discourse, this seems to be precisely because he was concerned with exploring other ways than those of didacticism by which to show the falsity of the ideal of 'fina amor', especially by acting out the process of perception. In this sense, XLV is an important point of reference for numerous other poems, including all the *Plena de seny* and *Llir entre cards* pieces. In it we see clearly how March decries 'fina amor' even as he celebrates it.

By the time March came to write his longest piece of theorizing on love, poem LXXXVII, the legitimacy of 'fina amor' as a transcendent form of love is no longer the matter in dispute. There is no reference to 'fina amor' or 'fins amants'. Rather, March returns to the claim made in XLV, lines 17–24, namely that he loves in both the spiritual/physical and purely spiritual forms, or at least that he feels strongly pulled towards the latter type. But what makes this poem so interesting is the way in which March strives to get beyond the moral perspective that comes to the fore in XLV and which provides the underlying context for much of what is assumed to be his early and mature work. Allowing himself 340 lines to move at will amidst the complexities of the relationship between spiritual/physical and spiritual love, he is able to posit some unconventional ideas about love of which XLV contained not a hint.

In this poem, as in XLV, March at once identifies his audience. Here he is not speaking to the ignorant and incredulous in matters of love. Quite the contrary: he addresses the 'entenent amador', the hypothetical reader who is deemed to have developed, through the practice of the higher forms of human love, a subtle understanding of its nature.

March next delimits the area of his discussion of love and of his relationship to it. Following the Aristotelian division of the objects of human desire

9. For an elaboration of this viewpoint see Robert ARCHER, *The Pervasive Image: The Role of Analogy in the Poetry of Ausiàs March*, Purdue University Monographs in Romance Languages 17 (Amsterdam: John Benjamins, 1985), a book based on a doctoral dissertation supervised by Robert Pring-Mill.

(they are called *profitable*, *delitable*, and *bona* in Brunetto) he distinguishes three kinds of love, and states from the first that he refuses even to discuss the lowest of the three, 'lo profit amable', a form in which the lover does not seek the reciprocation and furtherance of love but rather is motivated by the desire for personal advantage.[10]

Most of LXXXVII, both in its purely theoretical part (lines 1–194) and in its more personalized remainder (lines 195–340), is an attempt to define the workings of the appetites of body and soul in relation to the passions of spiritual/physical love. March's view of this has an underlying basis in the then generally (but not universally) accepted concept of hylomorphism. That is, man is a composite being of which the soul is the substantial form and the body the primal matter; he is not two substantial beings (as body and as soul) as Augustine and Plato had maintained. It is important to bear this in mind if we are to avoid making assumptions of duality behind March's references to the two natures of man (as in line 22, for instance).

Spiritual/physical love, which inevitably fails to give man the contentment he seeks from it, derives from the sensitive will of the soul, not from the rational will (lines 44–45). However, since the two wills do not operate discretely in this form of love, it is in practice impossible to distinguish one from the other; they form a 'mesclat voler' (line 19). The two wills – sensitive, and intellectual/rational – are in a state of constant flux, with dominance continually shifting from one to the other (lines 51–70). For its part, the soul can only participate in this mixed form of love ('amor... mixte', CXVII, 151) through the body, and although it derives pleasure from it, this comes only at the cost of its abasement, and the temporary forgetting of its own nature (lines 71–90). The state of flux that characterizes the 'mesclat voler' points to the absence of virtue; if virtue were present, such love would be stable and not subject to the shifting movements of body and soul (lines 91–100). Given this condition, neither body nor soul is able to achieve contentment and each is goaded constantly by its own desire until such time as the object of love ceases to be desired, a development which is usually felt in the body first (lines 101–30).

Since this form of love involves passions which debilitate body and soul, it is destined to extinction. But spiritual love, even though it too begins in the senses like the 'mixed' form, does not have as its end the fulfilment of sensual

---

10. *Llibre del Tresor*, II, 120.

desires, but rather virtue and wisdom (lines 131–50). Such love, however, is rarely practised. While most men want the woman they love to be virtuous, the end of this desire for virtue is not virtue itself but the pleasure that is to be derived from virtue (lines 151–60), a point also made in XLV, lines 38–40. Few men love virtue in women for its own sake; most lovers, even those who are virtuous themselves, are given up, at best, to the mixed form, which obstructs man's passage to the truth (lines 161–80).

It is at this point that March praises the power of spiritual love for its capacity to impose itself in certain circumstances over the claims of the flesh, even where the mixed type is active (lines 181–90). The pleasure felt by the soul is not subject to the flux of the passions, so that when the body's urges subside, the soul is left free, for a time, to reach towards what it glimpses beyond its corporal prison (lines 191–200). March makes it clear at once that he is not claiming that he loves with the spirit only, but rather that he experiences some form of the love of the spirit during those spells when the desire of the flesh abates. It is this aspect of 'mixed' love – its moments of virtuous love during lulls in the movements of the body – that, he affirms, gives meaning to his life (lines 201–30).

He knows, then, what it is to love spiritually, even if only during brief remissions of the carnal urges. The question inevitably follows: why, knowing that this spiritual love is the only true good for those who would devote themselves to love, does he not channel all his love into this form? In his attempt at an answer in the next four stanzas (lines 231–70) he can only partially explain his failure, attributing it to the power of his own fickle sensuality (lines 245–47) and to the inherent fallibility of the proposed object of this spiritual love:

> Assats a mi és causa descoberta
> que pura amor no pot en dona caure.

(lines 267–68)

Such a form of love is beyond both the immediate capacities of the poet and the innate capabilities of the beloved.

This is the first point in the poem where March takes a step down from the higher abstractions of his theory to clarify that the object of the spiritual love he has briefly described is the same as that of spiritual/physical love. His is a *vita contemplativa* whose spiritual journey is not into God, but rather towards a female beloved. And yet it would be easy to assume up to this point that the virtuous love he speaks of is directed at the Creator, its only true end from any theological standpoint: there are no references to Dante to invite us to think otherwise (as there are in XLV). It is an assumption that leads us to the real cause of the poet's failure in his striving for virtuous love: the only end that could ever give fulfilment to the lover is God, and the only true love is charity.

These ideas provide the moral backdrop to the rest of the poem. Two stanzas follow (lines 271–90) in which March describes his amorous *vita activa*. The effects of the 'mesclat voler' which he lists are the classical symptoms of *amor hereos*; the connection between the lover's malady and 'amor homenívol' is much clearer here than in XLV. This leads to some conjecture about the problems he had described in lines 241–50: if he cannot turn those moments of spirituality into an enduring habit, it is because he is simply one of those men who are, as the severity of the symptoms attest, predisposed to love with body and soul (lines 291–300).

He finds no solutions to the problem. He can only reaffirm the superiority of spiritual love (lines 301–10) and define – by means of the last of the seven comparisons that he uses in the second half of his poem – his own perception of the mixed form of love (lines 311–16). Like the armour made from an alloy of steel and iron so that it will stand up to the blows of combat, the enduring love of the spirit tempers the carnal appetite and gives it strength. More importantly still, as he goes on to say a few lines later, it can happen at times that the sensitive appetite temporarily dies, dissolving for a while the ties of the soul to the body, so that the soul, while still operating within the 'mesclat voler', loves purely as soul for as long as the carnal appetite is dormant:

> En cert cas mor nostra amor sensitiva
> e l'esperit junt ab ell se destempra.
> Amen ensemps, e l'esperit sols ame,
> perque tot l'hom no·s trop que en res desame.

(lines 317–20)

March contends, in effect, that human love, as practised by him and by the 'tot entenent amador', contains moments of transcendence that overlap with, or are identical with, spiritual love. It is significant that immediately after these lines March apologizes for any unconventional ideas that the reader may find in his theory:

Doncs, si d'amor algun parlar m'escapa
que la raó no·l lloe ne l'aprove,
no sia algú que los dits meus reprove.

(lines 325–27)

This is not simply a modesty topos: the apology is entirely ironic, coming within a *peroratio* that is full of hyperbolic claims to privileged knowledge:

Dels grans secrets que amor cobre ab sa capa,
de tots aquells puc fer apocalipsi.
Io defallint, amor farà eclipsi.

(lines 328–30)

In the final stanza, March describes this apocalypse, and discards from his scheme of things every chance of there being any other 'entenent amador' but himself: he deletes from his poem the very audience that he had inscribed into its first line.[11] Only the poet, by constantly seeking to transcend the confines of the *compositum*, takes human love as far as it will go. Striving is all, and no one else in the world is even trying:

pus hom no s'afina
en ben amar, ans cascú veig que·s llasse.

(lines 337–38)

The transcendence described in LXXXVII becomes more than fleetingly possible once the object of love ceases to have a carnal form. The death of the loved woman that prompts the *Cants de mort* (poems XCII–XCVII) forces March to look afresh at the question of spiritual love within the context of grief, which itself raises for him important theoretical issues.[12] This is dealt with in the longest, and what is probably the first, of the six poems (XCII).

March affirms that the love he feels for the dead 'muller aimia' is one of 'amistança pura' (lines 29–30) – the virtuous friendship he had described in XLV, 93–94 – while trying to define the roles of the other two forms of love (physical and spiritual/physical) in these new circumstances. He recognizes initially that purely physical desire has not entirely disappeared, but he expects this to happen soon (lines 41–42). The mixed love formed of the wills

---

11. The end of the world described by March has its roots both in the tradition of the signs of Judgement Day, such as those he uses in his poem XLVI, and in the Bible (Isaiah 13. 10, 34. 4, and Mark 13. 24).

12. The way in which March addresses problems associated with grief and its moral and literary context is studied in chapter 2 of ARCHER, *Aproximació a Ausiàs March*.

of body and soul, and with no element of virtue to control it, is identified as the principal cause of his continuing grief; the third, spiritual, form of love is not a cause since it is united with reason, which will not admit grief (lines 43 – 70).

In lines 71 – 100 March elaborates his ideas on the mechanism of grief. Since it is impossible to distinguish between the workings of body and soul when the mixed form of love is operative, it would be inaccurate to describe this grief as belonging to either body or soul. Such grief may begin in the body, for instance, but it then extends through the *compositum* to affect the soul. Pain, such as grief, is felt by man within this mixed love in much the same way as he experiences his pleasures, a process described in XLV and LXXXVII.

After several stanzas of a much more personal kind in which he describes the emotional experience of his grief, and affirms the predominant spirituality of his love for the deceased woman (lines 101 – 88), March turns his attention to an important problem that underlies the theory he has developed so far (lines 191 – 220). While his grief has its causes in a persisting mixed love, a new, spiritual, love has arisen from the beloved's death. How is it possible for the two forms to coexist?

March's solution is that his grief is caused by the memory of pleasure experienced in spiritual/physical love ('lo record del plaure', line 212), while his spiritual love arises from a new condition in which the flesh, since it has lost its object in the lady's body, can feel no desire (by this stage in the poem, the previous suggestion of a lingering physical desire has been discarded). This explanation of the coexistence of the two forms of love enables March to affirm that, beyond his persisting grief, he now feels a spiritual love that is enduring, rather than the fleeting form he had described in LXXXVII:

> si voler tinc, pec és lo qui no creia
> que l'esperit de pura amor s'enflame.

(lines 227 – 28)

Compared to these three poems, CXXIIb, which we can assign with confidence to March's later years, contains no more than the empty rehearsal of worn propositions on the nature of love, enlisted for the purposes of a plea to an enamoured King Alfonso (significantly, the other known version of the poem has no theoretical content). In this jocular request for a favour, March distinguishes between forms of love according to his basic taxonomy and asserts (as he did in XLV, 50–51) that whoever loves spiritually is closer to the angels than to man. But by this stage of his poetic career, March seems to have abandoned the notion that *amour mixte* could contain its own level of spirituality. In poems CXVII and CXXIII March does not mention spiritual love except as a theoretical possibility inextricably linked to the other forms of love:

> Lo qui amor per tres parts ha sentit,
> toca de tot: d'angel e d'hom e brut.

(CXXIII, 29–30)

By now the striving has gone, and so has the vitality of the theory: love is discussed according to a tripartite schema which leaves no room for unconventional transcendence. The virtue of the poems we have studied is precisely that in them March is seen to push out beyond the limits of the threefold classification of love, and to affirm the real possibility of transcending the human *compositum*, both within properly human love and within the condition of grief.

ROBERT ARCHER

La Trobe University, Melbourne

AUSIÀS MARCH
AND THE MEDIEVAL IMAGINATION

IN A PREVIOUS ARTICLE, I tried to examine the nature of introspection in Ausiàs March – roughly speaking, what it meant for a fifteenth-century poet to write in the first-person singular, and what kind of adjustments a modern reader needed to make in order to gauge the original effect.[1] This, clearly, has to do with the nature of the self which is expressed in the poems: except in a small number of didactic poems, March never speaks from a fixed point of view; the 'I' of the poems, in other words, is never taken for granted, but has to be constructed each time in terms of the poetic discourse itself. Moreover, however one interprets his presentation of the self, it seems clear that for March, as for other late medieval writers, the essence of analysis is to make the invisible visible. Allegory, of course, is the principal means by which the inner may be described in terms of the outer; what is more difficult to grasp is the sense in which medieval conceptions of inner and outer differ from modern ones. And this in turn has to do with the rules by which one distinguishes between subjective and objective. As Stephen Medcalf puts it:

> Among the medieval philosophers, *subjective* does not have our connotation of 'imaginary', nor *objective* of 'existing as it would do if we were not conscious of it'; rather, *subjective* means 'existing in itself' and *objective* 'presentational', with no sense of consciousness as a film between the two, or as something projected on reality.[2]

This difference of emphasis is very obvious in medieval theories of the imagination, which affect the nature of introspection at every turn. To begin with, imagination, for the Middle Ages, is never 'free' in a post-Romantic

---

1. Arthur TERRY, 'Introspection in Ausiàs March', in *Medieval and Renaissance Studies in Honour of Robert Brian Tate*, ed. Ian Michael & Richard A. Cardwell (Oxford: The Dolphin Book Co., 1986), 165–77.

2. Stephen MEDCALF, 'Inner and Outer', in *The Context of Literature: The Later Middle Ages*, ed. Medcalf (London: Methuen, 1981), 108–71 (134).

sense; still less is it to be equated with idle fantasy. Instead, as Douglas Kelly observes: 'Imagination is a mental faculty. It governs the invention, retention, and expression of Images in the mind.'[3] The important thing is that all this takes place in the mind, where imagination, as I shall explain in a moment, is associated with memory and reason. Imagination, then, invents, not by starting from scratch, but by working on the material which is provided by the senses. This means that the image does not so much mirror external reality as provide the reason with raw material for ideas which are then conveyed to the reader through other images. So, when March writes that 'Sobresdolor m'ha tolt l'imaginar' (XXVII, line 1), what he has lost is the power of creating images in this sense. And the reason for this is given a few lines later: '... ma dolor és tanta | que mon voler en parts ne tinc partit' (lines 5–6).[4] In other words, if the imagination represents visually the idea which gives unity to what is materially diverse, then it is unable to function if one of the faculties – in this case, the will – is divided.[5] And the same notion appears, in a different form, in Poem LX. Here, the speaker's powers – his 'voluntats' – have been reconciled by the woman he loves, so that the imagination is no longer needed to bring harmony to his previously confused thoughts: 'A imaginar no em cal d'huimés assiure | per aplegar ma pensa molt confusa'. In both instances, the notion is the same: the image expresses visually the whole – the single idea – which the mind forms from the disparate evidence of the senses. Or, as Kelly puts it: 'Imagination is visual representation of a unified whole in material diversity, a diversity that is formed by *interpretatio* to reveal the idea, and not just the literal parts of the representation'.[6]

This notion of a controlling idea is central to an understanding of the medieval imagination, as I shall try to show in a moment. But first we must deal

---

3. Douglas KELLY, *Medieval Imagination: Rhetoric and the Poetry of Courtly Love* (Madison: University of Wisconsin Press, 1978), xi–xii.

4. My texts are taken from *Les poesies d'Ausiàs March*, ed. Joan FERRATÉ (Barcelona: Quaderns Crema, 1979).

5. This does not prevent March from using his imagination in the rest of the poem. Compare Lola BADIA, *Tradició i modernitat als segles XIV i XV: Estudis de cultura literària i lectures d'Ausiàs March*, Biblioteca Sanchis Guarner (Valencia: Institut Universitari de Filologia Valenciana & Barcelona: Publicacions de l'Abadia de Montserrat, 1993), 213: 'La meva opinió és que al primer vers March fa una irada declaració de principis de caràcter retòric, expressada en termes hiperbòlics, que no s'ha de prendre òbviament al peu de la lletra ... l'«art» i la «imaginació» no manquen, doncs, als textos marquians; el que passa és que el poeta deliberadament els maltracta, els castiga.'

6. KELLY, *Medieval Imagination*, 84.

with the second of Kelly's terms: retention. What is meant by this emerges very clearly from a statement by the medieval French theorist Jehan le Bel:

> Imagination is a cognitive power in which the images of things perceived by the senses are retained. This force extracts the appearance of things from sensible objects more than do the senses. For the sense impression receives the appearance of things only from those things which are present, while the former retains the appearances and images even when the things are withdrawn.[7]

The imagination, then, is more powerful than the senses since it can retain the appearances of things even when they are absent – hence the connection with memory. But notice also how he talks about 'extracting the appearances of things from sensible objects', as if 'appearances' and 'sensible objects' were two separate things. And, of course, to the medieval imagination, they are: in the majority of medieval courtly love poems (and many of March's own poems come under that heading) the woman of flesh and blood becomes an archetype – an idea – whose abstract perfection is literally inexpressible. As another medieval theorist, Alain de Lille, puts it:

> When, through a certain recall of sensual perceptions, to which the senses have gone out, the soul inscribes in itself, as it were, an *exemplum* in memory, the entire attention of the soul, removed from the presence of the sensible objects upon which it reflects, seems to be suspended figuratively in the imagination of them.[8]

That last phrase – 'suspended figuratively in the imagination of them' – takes us to Kelly's last term: expression. Imagination, on this view, is essentially a two-way process. The senses provide the imagination with raw material, which is then processed – selected, and at the same time transformed – until it forms an archetype, or idea, in the memory. This archetype is strictly

---

7. JEHAN LE BEL, *Li ars d'amour, de vertu et de boneurté*, ed. Jules Petit, 2 vols (Brussels: Victor Devaux et Cie, 1867–69), I, 199–200: 'Ymaginations est une poissance comprendans, en laquele les ymagenes des choses senties sunt gardées. Ceste vertus si soustrait plus le sanlance des choses de matères sensibles que ne font li sens. Car li sens ne rechoit le sanlant des choses, fors les choses présentes, et ceste si garde ces sanlants et ces ymagenes, encore soit la chose absens.'

8. ALAIN DE LILLE, *Textes inédits, avec une introduction sur sa vie et ses oeuvres*, ed. Marie-Thérèse d'Alverny, Études de Philosophie Médiévale 52 (Paris: Librairie Philosophique J. Vrin, 1965), 315: 'Cum in quadam sensibilium ad que sensus exierat rememoratione, anima penes se quasi quodam memoriale exemplum inscribit, ut tota animalis intentio preter sensibilium de quibus cogitat presentiam, in eorundem ymaginationem comparabiliter videatur esse suspensa.'

ineffable: it lies beyond the reach of the senses and in itself is not amenable to reason.[9] At the same time – and this is where the process goes into reverse – this invisible image has the power to generate other, more visible, images, and these are the images which eventually get into the poem. There is a paradox here, in that what is essentially a rational process – the conscious invention of appropriate images – is a means of access to ideas and feelings which ultimately defy rational analysis. Another way of putting this would be to say that it is abstract conceptual relationships which determine the choice of material for the image, however 'concrete' this may appear. And this affects the way we see the image itself; it can no longer be thought of as a single, monolithic unity, but rather as a complex, or configuration, in which abstract and concrete are brought together in a peculiarly resonant way. Medieval rhetoric has a term for such a 'bringing together': *frequentatio*, which the *Ad Herennium* describes as 'when the points scattered through the whole cause are collected in one place'.[10] This is why, earlier on, I described the imagination as 'representing visually the idea which gives unity to what is materially diverse'; in other words, however individualized the image may appear, its peculiar configuration is held in place by the underlying idea which the author sets out to convey to the reader. And, returning to Ausiàs March, this seems to give a further justification to Robert Archer's claim that the similes which appear so often in March's poems are not merely decorative, but have an organic function within the poem as a whole.[11] If, as Aristotle asserts, 'the soul never thinks without a mental picture', these particular mental pictures are March's way of suggesting what cannot be conveyed in simple, expository verse and his way of creating overtones which cannot be entirely explained by rational analysis.[12]

---

9. This applies not only to poetry, but to other genres. Compare Frances YATES, *The Art of Memory* (London: Pimlico, 1992), 96: 'Yet the similitude spoken in the sermon is not strictly speaking the similitude used in artificial memory. For the memory image is invisible, and remains hidden within the memory of its user, where, however, it can become the hidden generator of externalized imagery.'

10. *Ad Herennium*, IV. xl. 52: 'Frequentatio est cum res tota causa dispersae coguntur in unum locum.'

11. See Robert ARCHER, *The Pervasive Image: The Role of Analogy in the Poetry of Ausiàs March*, Purdue University Monographs in Romance Languages 17 (Amsterdam: John Benjamins, 1985).

12. ARISTOTLE, *De anima*, 432 a.17.

Though this account of the workings of the medieval imagination is true as far as it goes, it hardly accounts for the tensions which occur at many points in March's verse. For one thing, an image not only conveys a likeness; it may also embody an intention, and this intention, in its turn, will have the power to move the soul to rational ends. Thus, in Frances Yates's example:

> An image to remind one of a wolf's form will also contain the *intentio* that the wolf is a dangerous animal from which it would be wise to flee; on the animal level of memory, a lamb's mental image of a wolf contains this *intentio*. And on the higher level of the memory of a rational being, it will mean that an image chosen, say, to remind us of the virtue of Justice will contain the *intentio* of seeking to acquire this virtue.[13]

In March's later poems, on the other hand, there is often a split between contemplation and action; more specifically, the distance between the imagination and the senses – the difference between the idealizing tendencies of the imagination and the senses as instruments of desire – frequently takes the form of an opposition between the contemplation and the practice of love. There is a simple example of this in Poem CXVII, which is introduced by one of March's typical similes:

> Així me'n pren com a aquell qui contempla
> l'ésser de l'hom e com és de Déu obra
> e, puix ell ve a contemplar sos actes,
> tant avorreix trobar-se en lo món home:
> com, de amor, son ésser imagine
> e els gentils fets que en l'entendre em romanen,
> jo m'adelit, e com al voler passe,
> per llur excés e qualitat m'agreuge.

(lines 57–64)

Here, the division is clear-cut: love is a source of pleasure as long as it remains in the understanding; once it is put into practice, however – once the will begins to act – it turns to disgust. Elsewhere, though, the situation is more complex, and in one of the late poems, CXIX, the emphasis falls, not so much on the ideal, as on the work which the imagination performs in going beyond sensual content to find pleasure in more spiritual qualities.

The general sense of this poem is based on a paradox: how is it that the speaker can love a woman whom, on the face of it, he detests? However,

---

13.   YATES, *The Art of Memory*, 76.

early on in the poem, March attempts to resolve this paradox by means of a
contrast between the senses – sight and touch – and what he calls 'gest':

> Tant és l'escalf que pel gest m'enamora
> que no sent res del fred que el toc me porta,
> ans tot és foc quant la pensa em reporta:
> l'imaginar l'amarg dolç assabora.

(lines 15 – 18)

Later on, this contrast is qualified:

> L'ull de per si e el toc llur bé no hi senten:
> per los senys dins llurs delits se assenten.

(lines 49 – 50)

And, later still, we are told:

> Si el pens en parts, la pensa d'ella aparte
> e, quan la veig o toc sens alt, no em farte.

(lines 89 – 90)

What does all this mean? The key, I think, is in that reference to the 'inward
sense' – 'los senys dins' – which are clearly connected with the imagination.
To the outer senses – the senses in their normal meaning – the woman's body
is ugly and incapable of inspiring love; 'gest', on the other hand, suggests
more inward qualities, or rather, inward qualities making themselves visible.
Also, of course, there is a wholeness, an integrity, about 'gest' which the individual parts of the body do not possess, and this wholeness corresponds to the
imagination's attempt to bring the disparate materials provided by the senses
under control.

   This particular poem, in fact, keeps coming back to the question of imagination. Sometimes the verb 'imaginar' is used in its modern sense: 'Quan
imagín d'aquesta amor la causa' (line 31), or 'que no imagín que en amor jo
retorne' (line 94), though even an apparently obvious example like this last
one takes on a special edge when seen in terms of the medieval imagination,
as if the speaker were saying: 'No images occur to me which suggest that I
might return to love', or, more simply, 'No images of such a situation occur to
me'. There is one central passage, however, in which imagination is given its
full medieval sense:

> Lo toc per si molt no s'hi adelita:
> quan pren delit, l'imaginar lo hi porta

pel gest, que tal pensament me reporta
que, tot mi ensems, per ella tota em cita.

(lines 51–54)

This brings together a lot of what I have been trying to explain. To begin with, it more or less repeats what has already been said about 'touch', or rather 'lo toc per si'. But then it goes on to refer directly to the imagination: touch in itself brings no pleasure; when it does, it is through the functioning of the imagination, in other words, as the result of an inward process. And the agency of this process is the woman's 'gest', something which is remade in the imagination and which issues in thought. It is this 'thought' which then operates within the speaker to attract him to the woman, seen now as a whole – an integral form – and not merely as her separate parts. Yet the important thing, as always with the notion of 'gest', is that the superior qualities should be made visible, and this, as I have already claimed, is one of the main functions of the medieval image.

I have been speaking up to now as if all images had their roots in the senses. There is, however, a special aspect of the imagination, often known as *phantasia*, which includes both the power to recall the form of sense experience as images, and the power to recombine those forms into forms of things never experienced. (The *locus classicus* here is St Augustine's famous example, according to which he can picture in his mind Carthage, which he knew, but also, in some approximate way, Alexandria, which he had never seen.)[14] There is one poem of March's (LXXXVII) which exploits this possibility in a very striking way by imagining an ideal woman – one who would correspond to the kind of spiritual love described earlier in the poem:

Mon esperit contemplant se contenta
e dintre si una persona forja.
D'ella no pens braços, peus, mans ne gorja,
car tot semblant altre semblant presenta.
Solament vull d'ella tan clara pensa
que res de mi no el fos cosa secreta,
apta i sabent, e d'amor fos estreta,
lo contrafer prengués en gran ofensa,
de son voler volgués ésser celosa
e que per mi vers mort fos animosa.

(lines 231–39)

---

14. AUGUSTINE, *De Genesi ad litteram*, XII. vi. 15.

The point about this is that the woman March describes exists only in the imagination; as the rest of the poem makes clear, no woman on earth can attain to such perfection, so that the speaker is left loving an abstraction. To put it another way, the senses have no part in the creation of such an image, except by contrast; the imagination has gone beyond the senses to create its own image, and this can only be done in a state of contemplation, that is to say, in a state from which no possible action could issue. Thus the image is an abstraction in a special sense: it discards what might be thought of as the distinguishing features of a particular woman − 'D'ella no pens braços, peus, mans ne gorja' − since these, seen from this Olympian viewpoint, are always the same. The only qualities which survive, then − which are abstracted from the idea of any particular woman − are spiritual ones: clear thought, strictness in love, honesty, and chastity. Here, clearly, perfect correspondence transcends the physical level, and so removes the obstacles − such as the inability to see into another's mind − which are overwhelmingly present in other poems.[15] However, this is all in the mind, or rather in the imagination which is a part of the mind, and in the rest of the poem, this imagined figure is recognized as the pure product of contemplation, in sharp contrast to the realities of practice.

This state of contemplation which cannot lead to action is seen most clearly in the series of poems − from XCII to XCVII − on the death of a woman. Here, as I pointed out in my previous article, the general sense is that the death of the loved one has brought about the one kind of circumstance in which love can exist in a pure state.[16] The result is a kind of clarification: hence the number of images which have to do with 'bringing to light':

> Lo voler cec del tot ella il·lumena,
> mas no en tant que lleve el cataracte,
> e, si posqués fer sense empatx son acte,
> no fóra al món ull ab gota serena.

(XCII, lines 35−38)

The effect of death, in other words, is to clarify − to the extent that is possible in a fallen world − the inner life of the lover by externalizing it; as March puts it: 'Tots los volers que en mi confusos eren | se mostren clar per llur obra

---

15. Compare Poem LXXVIII, lines 33−34: 'No imagín de mi us puscau altar, | car dintre meu jo creu que no veeu.'

16. TERRY, 'Introspection in Ausiàs March', 176.

forana' (lines 21–22). And elsewhere, in Poem XCIV, the same situation is described in terms which indicate even more forcibly the movement from the invisible to the visible:

> De tots aquests passions m'atengueren
> mescladament, sí com mesclats jaien,
> mas bé distints són aprés de son opte
> e separats los sent, quasi visibles.

(lines 53–56)

This is perhaps the clearest expression of a process which, in one way or another, determines the whole thrust of March's self-analysis. If his passions are now 'quasi visibles', this is not only because the situation has simplified itself, but also because the language itself has brought them to the surface. The language here is discreetly allegorical: the passions are described almost as if they were concrete things – they 'reach' the speaker and 'lie mixed' within him – until their separate identity emerges in their 'almost visibility'. As I said earlier, allegory, in particular the use of personified abstractions, is the chief means by which the inner may be described in terms of the outer. Yet, as John Burrow has observed: 'personifications are not themselves suitable subjects for analysis, but represent precisely the point at which, in any given text, a writer has chosen to *stop* in the almost endless process of breaking human behaviour into its constituents'.[17] This sets a limit to March's powers of introspection and at the same time returns us to the role of the imagination. Whether this feeds directly on the senses or creates independently of matter, it refers ultimately to something – an idea – which is strictly speaking ineffable and in the last instance irrational. This, for the medieval imagination, is the vanishing-point, the limit beyond which allegory and the whole process of image-making cannot go. Yet, paradoxically, this vanishing-point is also the centre from which images are generated by the rational part of the mind – images which gather together the confused impressions of the senses and project them in a public, accessible form.

*   *   *   *   *

---

17. John A. BURROW, *Medieval Writers and Their Work: Middle English Literature and its Background, 1150–1500* (Oxford: Oxford University Press, 1982), 91.

Marie-Claire Zimmermann writes:

> La imatge va caminant, subreptícia, subterrània, en el text, es metamor-
> fosa després de portar tota una sèrie de signes contradictoris, entre altres
> imatges molt nombroses que fan d'Ausiàs March el poeta més metafòric
> del segle XV.[18]

This is well said, and emphasizes once again the complexity of the imaginative
process which is at work in these poems. Above all, it underlines the fact that
very few of March's images exist in isolation – that, more often than not, a
particular image will intersect with the rest of the text to alter it and to disturb
its stability. Or as Robert Archer puts it: 'In March, the simile is never a
rhetorical embellishment or elegant variation on metaphor, but a vital poetic
process'.[19] And as Archer himself has shown, this process entails a high degree of self-criticism, a constant questioning of the attitudes on which the
poems seldom come firmly to rest. If, as I hope to have shown, the nature of
March's introspection depends crucially on the kind of imagination which is at
work in the poems, an understanding of the medieval imagination in general
and the ways it determines March's image-making in the actual process of
writing can only increase one's admiration for a poet who, while working
strictly within the conventions of his age, pursued these to their limits in a
poetry of astonishing range and power.

ARTHUR TERRY

University of Essex

---

18.   Marie-Claire ZIMMERMANN, 'Metàfora i destrucció del món en Ausiàs March', in *Actes
del cinquè col·loqui internacional de llengua i literatura catalanes: Andorra, 1–6 d'octubre de
1979*, ed. J. Bruguera & J. Massot i Muntaner, Biblioteca «Abat Oliva» 19 (Barcelona: Publicacions de l'Abadia de Montserrat, 1980), 123–50 (147).

19.   ARCHER, *The Pervasive Image*, 180.

POSTIL·LES NATURALS
A LLULL I JORDI DE SANT JORDI

I. Premissa

ALS SEGLES QUE VAN del XII al XV hom creia que el cervell era el centre del coneixement sensible. La noció, que arrenca de Galè i té orígens anatòmics i fisiològics, va ser perfeccionada per la tradició mèdica àrab (Râzî, Hali Abbâs, Avicenna), que va haver de resoldre, a més, l'exigència musulmana (compartida pel cristianisme) d'una ànima espiritual individual, capacitada per al coneixement dels universals i destinada a la vida eterna de pena o de glòria després de la mort del cos. Les solucions dels metges-filòsofs àrabs havien circulat eficaçment per l'Occident cristià d'ençà dels temps de Constantí l'Africà, a través del qual s'havien instal·lat al cor de la filosofia natural dels mestres chartrians del XII i de la cultura mitjana general d'aquell segle (i això inclou la lírica dels trobadors). L'esclat de les traduccions del grec i de l'àrab al pas del XII al XIII no va fer més que potenciar la recepció dels materials mèdico-filosòfics esmentats, la qual cosa va permetre que sant Albert Magne i sant Tomàs des d'un aristotelisme recuperat, tinguessin ocasió de recompondre el quadre *natural* amb les seves conseqüències *morals*, per a ús de la tradició escolàstica posterior i de la divulgació, homilètica o no, d'aquesta tradició entre els laics.[1]

Tot i que mai no va deixar de ser sentit com un dels nusos de la unió entre el sensible i l'espiritual, el cor, que Aristòtil havia consagrat com a centre de l'esperit vital (i també del coneixement i de les emocions), va romandre en un segon pla en la psicologia escolàstica, que es construeix a partir de la descripció natural del cervell. En la formulació reductiva per a ús de laics, que

---

1. Per a la història de la psicologia mèdica antiga, E. Ruth HARVEY, *The Inward Wits: Psychological Theory in the Middle Ages and Renaissance*, Warburg Institute Surveys (Londres: The Warburg Institute, 1975). Per a la circulació europea de la medicina àrab, Danielle JACQUART & Françoise MICHEAU, *La Médecine arabe et l'occident médiéval*, Islam – Occident 7 (París: Maisonneuve & Larose, 1990).

retrobo des del *Drogmaticon philosophiae* de Guillem de Conches al *Lilium medicinae* de Bernat de Gordon, el cervell posseeix materialment tres cambres, cèl·lules o ventricles. El primer ventricle, situat al darrera del front, estatja la funció sensitiva de copsar i reunir les dades dels cinc sentits externs (vista, oïda, olfacte, gust, tacte). El ventricle frontal també coordina les dades de fora, que ara esdevenen imatges sensibles, i les passa al segon ventricle, situat al darrera d'aquest, al damunt del paladar, on resideix la funció fonamental del coneixement sensitiu, que és la de relacionar aquestes imatges les unes amb les altres, inicialment per a valorar-les com a favorables o desfavorables en la subsistència immediata. El tercer ventricle, situat a la nuca, és la memòria sensitiva, entesa com un arxiu permanent d'imatges. Aquest esquema descriu el coneixement sensible tant dels animals com dels homes; explicar amb precisió la inserció de les potències superiors de l'ànima racional en aquest quadre unànimement acceptat com a natural pertany a un nivell elaborat d'especulació científica, que no deixa de transcendir al vulgar, fins i tot en contextos purament literaris.[2]

Si descomptem Llull, que sempre és un cas a part, la via d'entrada dels laics, usuaris del vulgar, en la discussió sobre el coneixement sensible i intel·lectual sol ser la legitimació científica del discurs sobre l'amor. L'enorme prestigi de la tradició trobadoresca havia transformat la passió amorosa en centre d'interès primordial per als homes de lletres, en principi per a exaltar-la, però després també per a debel·lar-la. L'òptica naturalista al·ludida més amunt, vehiculada per la literatura mèdica, situava el tema central de la lírica entre les disfuncions del coneixement sensitiu, concretament les vinculades a les operacions del segon ventricle. La passió d'amor deriva d'una hipertròfia en la valoració de la imatge sensible de l'ésser estimat; la funció del segon ventricle que es desregla sol anomenar-se cogitativa o estimativa (Llull, però, en diu fantasia). L'estudi de la passió d'amor com a disfunció ens porta a la patologia mèdica: és la famosa malaltia d'amor o *amor*

---

2. He pretès de fixar conceptes bàsics (defugint la variació terminològica) amb lectures d'Aristòtil, Avicenna, Guillem de Conches i sant Tomàs d'Aquino, entre d'altres. Per al *Drogmaticon philosophiae*, veg. la nota 15 i per al *Lilium Medicinae*, del qual n'existí una versió catalana del XV, Bernardo GORDONIO, *Lilio de medicina, edición crítica de la versión española, Sevilla 1495*, ed. John Cull & Brian Dutton (Madison: The Hispanic Seminary of Medieval Studies, 1991). Per a la Castella del XV, Pedro M. CÁTEDRA, *Amor y pedagogía en la Edad Media (Estudios de doctrina amorosa y práctica literaria)* (Salamanca: Universidad de Salamanca, Secretariado de Publicaciones, 1989).

hereos.[3] Debatre la responsabilitat moral del subjecte davant de l'amor comporta afaiçonar una determinada teoria sobre la inserció de l'ànima espiritual en el cos; sembla feina de moralistes, però també ho va ser de poetes: Cavalcanti va incidir-hi amb una colpidora càrrega tràgica. Com Ausiàs March, *mutatis mutandis*, cent-cinquanta anys més tard.[4]

Les postil·les que segueixen volen mostrar, un cop recuperat el marc general que acabo d'esbossar, que cada llengua romànica esdevé un horitzó de referència per a situar els coneixements naturals dels escriptors que en són usuaris. Per al cas del català cal tenir presents, en principi, les traduccions d'obres de divulgació dels segles XII i XIII, com el *Llibre de Sidrac*, textos més ambiciosos d'educació del laicat produïts al segle XIV directament en vulgar, com els sermons de sant Vicent Ferrer, els tractats d'Eiximenis o les escasses contribucions en aquest terreny d'Arnau de Vilanova, i les versions de monografies tècniques del XIV.[5] A més, comptem amb l'obra de Ramon Llull (1232–1316, actiu a partir de 1274), un home que es va avançar a la primera Universitat de la Corona d'Aragó (Lleida 1300) com a promotor d'una síntesi local del saber, creativa i innovadora, i que va usar en diverses ocasions el vulgar com a vehicle de difusió del discurs savi.[6]

---

3. El *Lilium medicinae*, citat a la nota anterior, defineix l'amor hereos com una espècie de la melancolia. Mary Frances WACK, *Lovesickness in the Middle Ages: The 'Viaticum' and Its Commentaries* (Philadelphia: University of Pennsylvania Press, 1990); Arnaldi de VILLANOVA, *Opera Medica Omnia*, III: *Tractatus de amore heroico. Epistola de dosi tyriacalium medicinarum*, ed. Michael R. McVaugh (Barcelona: Universitat de Barcelona, 1985), 11–54; Lola BADIA, *Tradició i modernitat als segles XIV i XV: Estudis de cultura literària i lectures d'Ausiàs March*, Biblioteca Sanchis Guarner (València: Institut Universitari de Filologia Valenciana & Barcelona: Publicacions de l'Abadia de Montserrat, 1993), 143–50.

4. El problema de les relacions precises entre el cos i l'ànima varia molt des dels platònics de Chartres als escolàstics del XIV i del XV; els usuaris de la llengua vulgar, però, podia ser que llegissin en ple segle XV traduccions d'obres del XII, com ara el *Drogmaticon philosophiae*, on el problema se soluciona a través de sant Agustí, veg. el MS esmentat a la nota 15, 147r. Per a les especulacions des del vulgar, Guido CAVALCANTI, *Rime, con le rime de Iacopo Cavalcanti*, ed. Domenico de Robertis (Torí: Giulio Einaudi Editore, 1986), 93–107; Maria CORTI, *La felicità mentale* (Torí: Giulio Einaudi Editore, 1983). Remeto a la nota 31.

5. Estic treballant en l'edició de la versió catalana del *Drogmaticon philosophiae* per a l'editorial Brepols de Turnhout, amb Josep Pujol, de la Universitat Autònoma de Barcelona. Per a les concomitàncies de la filosfia natural chartriana i Llull, Lola BADIA, 'La filosofia natural de Guillem de Conches en català', *Boletín de la Real Academia de Buenas Letras de Barcelona*, 40 (1985–86), 137–69. Com que aquest paràgraf apunta un programa de recerca, m'abstinc de donar més referències, llevat de la tesi doctoral de Xavier RENEDO, 'El tractat de luxúria de Francesc Eiximenis: Edició i estudi' (Universitat de Girona, 1993), de pròxima publicació. Per al *Sidrac*, vegeu la nota 21.

6. Tomás CARRERAS ARTAU & Joaquin CARRERAS ARTAU, *Historia de la filosofía española:*

Robert Pring-Mill ens ha explicat que Ramon Llull creia que els principis
fonamentals de la filosofia natural (els elements i les seves qualitats, els cels i
la seva jerarquia) responien a una estructuració lògica interna que els feia
anàlegs dels principis espirituals, rectors essencials de la realitat en sentit
ontològic.[7] Aquesta atenció al món natural, tan evident a les Arts de la
primera època, a partir de 1290 s'esborra del pla de la mecànica artística go-
vernada per les accions *ad extra* de la figura A i pels principis correlatius.
Pràcticament només sobreviu la noció que el coneixement de la filosofia
natural forneix uns esquemes racionals aptes per a actualitzar la memòria dels
principis ètics (*Arbre exemplifical* de l'*Arbre de Ciència*, 1295). Aquesta doble
valoració dels continguts de la filosofia natural (que inclou la medicina) enco-
ratja Llull a fer de divulgador científic (a més de teològic) des dels temps de
la *Doctrina pueril* (1275) als del *Llibre de virtuts e de pecats* (1312–1313).[8] És
des d'aquesta perspectiva que reuneixo aquí unes postil·les naturals a Llull i a
Jordi de Sant Jordi i no perquè hagi detectat cap influència concreta del beat
sobre aquest o cap altre poeta català de la baixa Edat Mitjana, inclòs Ausiàs
March.

II.   Funcions cerebrals, follia i pecat en Llull

Exposar tècnicament la natura, les causes i les conseqüències de la passió
d'amor no era un objectiu prioritari de Ramon Llull, però en la mesura en
què la seva Art assumeix la totalitat dels continguts del saber, no ha de
sorprendre trobar als seus escrits, de forma dispersa, informacions precises

---

Filosofía cristiana de los siglos XIII al XV (Madrid: Real Academia de Ciencias Exactas, Físicas
y Naturales, 1939), I, 233 ff. qualifiquen la filosofia de Llull d'«escolasticismo popular»; Anthony BONNER, *Selected Works of Ramon Llull*, 2 vols (Princeton: Princeton University Press,
1985), edició catalana: *Obres selectes de Ramon Llull (1232–1316)*, 2 vols (Mallorca: Editorial
Moll, 1989).

7. Em refereixo inicialment a 'El microcosmos lul·lià', a Robert PRING-MILL, *Estudis sobre
Ramon Llull (1956–1978)*, ed. Lola Badia & Albert Soler, Textos i Estudis de Cultura Catalana
22 (Barcelona: Publicacions de l'Abadia de Montserrat, Curial Edicions Catalanes, 1991),
33–114, però també als altres assaigs del recull. Els treballs pioners de Frances A. YATES sobre la filosofia natural i el beat, al seu *Lull and Bruno: Collected Essays*, I (Londres: Routledge
& Kegan Paul, 1982); edició catalana (Barcelona: Editorial Empúries, 1985).

8. Per a l'evolució del sistema lul·lià i per a la bibliografia sobre la seva medicina, remeto a
BONNER, *Obres Selectes*. Per als canvis que experimenten les Arts lul·lianes abans i després de
1290, Josep M. RUIZ SIMÓN, 'De la naturalesa com a mescla a l'art de mesclar (sobre la fona-
mentació cosmològica de les arts lul·lianes)', *Randa* (Palma de Mallorca), 19 (1986), 69–99. El
nivell superdivulgatiu de les qüestions que debato aquí es troba per dessota d'aquests canvis.

relacionades amb aquesta qüestió. Heus ací alguns exemples. El darrer paràgraf del cap. 68 de la *Doctrina pueril*, que tracta 'De ley de natura', esmenta la
percepció dels cinc sentits com a fenomen natural, per a poder explicar que el
coneixement sensible que en deriva és transcendit per l'intel·lectual:

TEXT 1

... e natural cosa és que la ànima ab la ymaginativa prenga tot so que
prenen los seyns corporals e que·u dó a l'humà enteniment en la fantasia,
qui es entre lo front e·l tos, e que l'enteniment se leu a ensús sobre la fantasia, entendre ço qui li és offert de la noblea e de la granea de Déu, e
que la volentat am e obeescha a Déu.[9]

Aquesta formulació tan senzilla de la gnoseologia lul·liana ens torna a ser
presentada al cap. 85 de la mateixa obra, que tracta 'De ànima':[10]

TEXT 2

... Sàpies, fill, que la ànima ab la ymaginació pren e ajusta en comú tot
ço que li offeren los v senys corporals, veent, oent, odorant, gustant, sin-
tent; e offer-ho en la fantasia a l'enteniment, e puxes lo enteniment puya
més a ensús entendre Déu e àngels e les coses intellectuals les quals la
ymaginativa no pot ymaginar. La phantasia és cambre qui és en lo paladar sobre lo front; e en lo front la ymaginativa ajusta ço que pren de les
coses corporals, e entra-sse'n en la phantasia açò que pren, e il·lumina
aquella cambra per ço que l'enteniment pusque pendre ço que la ymaginativa ly offer. On, com per algú accident açò se desordona, adonchs esdevé lo home fantàstich, o à gros enteniment, o és orat ... Com lo cors
de l'home se mor, no·t cuyts, fill, que muyra la ànima racional, ans va en
paradís o en purgatori o en infern, segons que ha perservit. Mas la ànima
vegetal e sensitiva e ymaginativa moren en la mort del cors ...[11]

---

9. Ramon LLULL, *Doctrina pueril*, ed. Gret Schib, Els Nostres Clàssics, col·lecció A 104
(Barcelona: Editorial Barcino, 1972), 158–59.

10. Llull separa netament el coneixement sensible de l'intel·lectual, en la línia agustiniana
esmentada a la nota 4; veg. Eusebi COLOMER, *De la Edad Media al Renacimiento: Ramon
Llull, Nicolás de Cusa, Juan Pico della Mirandola* (Barcelona: Editorial Herder, 1975), 57–77.
La qüestió no es fàcil d'esquematitzar. Heus ací aquest fragment del *Libre de home* (1300),
recollit per Miquel COLOM I MATEU, *Glossari General Lul·lià*, 5 vols (Mallorca: Editorial Moll,
1985), V, 122–23, *s.v.* TOÇ: 'Ha ànima en lo cos òrguens e struments en los quals mou les sues
potències: axí con lo cor qui és orguen de la volentat, e·l cervell del front del enteniment, e·l
cervell del tozc de la memòria, e en lo mig d'amdós la ànima mou la ymaginativa a ymaginar los
obgects ymaginables'. Veg. la nota 13.

11. LLULL, *Doctrina pueril, ed cit.*, 204.

El diccionari del pare Colom documenta el mot *toç* o *tos* en el sentit d'occípit o nuca (V. 122) i assenyala la confusió paleogràfica amb *cos* (I. 452), que és una *lectio facilior* de molts copistes antics i editors moderns.[12] En restituir el mot *tos* al Text 1, al lloc de *cos*, com diuen els manuscrits, precisem l'indret on Llull situa la fantasia: al mig de l'interior del crani, entre el front i el clatell. Deixo per a una altra ocasió dilucidar la filiació concreta de les doctrines lul·lianes sobre el suport anatòmic i psicològic del coneixement sensible, per cridar l'atenció sobre dos detalls.[13]

Al Text 2 la imaginació és la funció de prendre i reunir en comú les dades dels sentits, mentre que la imaginativa és la facultat cognoscitiva sensible que *en lo front . . . ajusta ço que pren de les coses corporals* i, fent-ho entrar a la cambra de la fantasia, *il·lumina aquella cambra* per fer possible l'enteniment racional. La part del crani situada sobre els ulls, el front, està associada, doncs, en Llull a una forma de coneixement, en uns termes semblants a l'accepció del terme 'memòria' que associa aquest mot amb l'occípit.[14] La localització de la fantasia al Text 2, una funció del coneixement sensible que, com he dit, en altres autors sol dur altres noms, com cogitativa, imaginativa o estimativa, és qualificada de 'passatge obscur' a l'aparat de notes de l'edició citada a la nota 9. No m'ho sembla: la indicació *qui és en lo paladar* designa la zona intermitja del cervell entre el front i el clatell, com es diu al Text 1 i a la literatura divulgativa d'aquestes matèries.[15] El *sobre lo front* que segueix,

---

12. COLOM I MATEU, *Glossari*. La versió catalana del *Drogmaticon philosophiae* de Guillem de Conches anomena *tos* l'occípit en una descripció de les parts del cervell (veg. la nota 15).

13. A Lola BADIA, *Teoria i pràctica de la literatura en Ramon Llull*, Assaig 10 (Barcelona: Quaderns Crema, 1991), 45–46, hi ha una nota sobre el terme fantasia en Llull, que apunta les dimensions del problema. La proximitat del discurs lul·lià al del *Drogmaticon* fa estrany que a la *Doctrina pueril* s'anomeni fantasia el conjunt de les funcions del segon ventricle, quan aquest mot, que en el grec del *De anima* aristotèlic volia dir tan sols imaginació, sol ser usat a les fonts del XII per a designar el poder de rebre les impressions dels sentits, situat al primer ventricle; en fonts del segle XIII (sant Tomàs) la fantasia apareix al segon ventricle i no és la funció estimativa/cogitativa, sinó la capacitat de combinar imatges, amb el control de la raó o sense. Llull maneja, doncs, també materials escolàstics de mitjan segle XIII; però, quins? Veg. la nota 10.

14. Antoni M. ALCOVER & Francesc de B. MOLL, *Diccionari català-valencià-balear* (Palma de Mallorca: Editorial Moll, 1962–69), VII, 337, *s.v.* MEMÒRIA: 'part posterior del cap'. Veg. el text citat a la nota 10, on es documenta aquesta associació.

15. 'En lo cap a tres cellules, 1 en lo front, altra en lo tos et la tercera en lo mig. La primera çellula apela hom fantastiqua, que vol dir visual, cor en ela veu la anima e entén . . . La miyana çelula és dita canbra logistica, que vol dir raonable, cor aquí conex la anima ço que a vist . . . La derrera cambra del tos es dita memorial . . . Et si lo cerveill de la cambra miyana es de tot en tot destemprat es hom orat e sens raó', traducció catalana del *Drogmaticon philosophiae* de GUILLEM DE CONCHES (Bibl. Nacional de París, MS espanyol 225, 133r–v).

per estrany que ens sembli el *sobre*, només pot designar, com veurem al Text 4, el segon ventricle del cervell.

La darrera frase que he copiat del Text 2 explica, en els termes elementals propis d'una *Doctrina pueril*, en què consisteix la perversió del coneixement o condició d'*home fantàstic* o *foll* : cal que un accident interfereixi en el procés pel qual l'enteniment copsa les espècies sensibles de la imaginativa que la fantasia li presenta des de la seva cambra. Aquesta explicació pertany a la tradició galènica, que descrivia formes de follia diferenciades segons la cambra cerebral que resultés afectada, la de la percepció, la de la valoració d'aquesta percepció o la de la memòria.[16] Una explicació tan escarida com aquesta, tanmateix, resulta útil per entendre, per exemple, en quins termes Llull podia considerar que ell no era un fantàstic en el seu fingit diàleg amb el clergue Pere de l'any 1311: la cèl·lula central del seu cervell no estava perturbada per cap accident quan presentava al seu intel·lecte unes dades que li permetien d'elevar-se a un coneixement que l'impulsava a percaçar empreses espirituals i no mundanes, com era el cas del seu interlocutor.[17] Vist així el procés, no costa gaire de connectar amb la filosofia moral, que estableix un judici ètic negatiu a propòsit de determinades perturbacions de la imaginació i de la fantasia, que l'intel·lecte podria corregir i no corregeix.

Saltant a l'extrem oposat de la bibliografia lul·liana, heus ací dos passatges d'un sermó sobre els vicis de gola i luxúria, on emergeixen alguns punts essencial del discurs natural i moral sobre la follia i el pecat, aplicat, per més claredat, al que els trobadors anomenaven amor i Llull, 'puteria'.[18]

TEXT 3

Qui continua e menuga molts ays e beu vi forts, corromp la sedula que está sobre lo front en los locs hon participen los çervels denant e detrás,

---

16. 'Lo duc dix: Aquestes coses con las poyràs provar? Lo filosof dix: Per les nafres que hom pren en aqueles partz; cor, con hom fos de bon engin e de bona memoria e de bona raó provaren los fisicians que con alscuns eren nafratz en la primera cambra del cerveill, ço es en les partz del front, no avien puxes tan bon seyn . . . E asó reconta Galienus qui axí o avia provat . . . ', *Drogmaticon philosophiae* (nota 15), 133v.

17. Per a la *Disputatio Petri et Raimundi* (1311), veg. el vol. XVI de les *Raimundi Lulli Opera Latina*, del *Corpus Christianorum* (Turnhout: Brepols, 1988), 1–30, i Lola BADIA, 'Estudi del *Phantasticus* de Ramon Llull', a BADIA, *Teoria i pràctica*, 31–54. Veg. les notes 10 i 13 per a problemes semàntics i lèxics.

18. 'Los joglars veem, Sènyer, que de nits van sonant los estruments per les places e per les carreres, per tal que moven lo coratge de les fembres a puteria, e que facen traïció a lurs marits', Ramon LLULL, *Libre de Contemplació en Déu*, cap. 118, a *Obres Essencials*, Col·lecció Perenne (Barcelona: Editorial Selecta, 1960), II, 356. El terme joglar engloba el de trobador.

en la qual sedula se fan les ymprecions intelligibles; e açó matex en la çedula detràs en lo tos hon se fan les ymprecions recolibles. E per ço, per trob calor e secor es torbat lo cerveyl qui es fret e humit, per lo qual torbament hom es foyl e fa folies per trob menjar e per trob beure. Açó matex pot hom dir de luxuria, car home qui longuament membre, entén e ama los plaers de luxúria es torbat son çerveyl per trob entendre [e] remembrar luxuria; e açó matex del seu cor per trob amar luxuria. E alscunes vegades, quant se volen partir, no se'n poden partir, car longa perseverança no pot esser destruyda per son poc contrari, si doncs Deus no l'ajuda.[19]

La cel·lula 'que està sobre lo front' és el segon ventricle, perquè hi participen la part anterior del cervell i la posterior: en el termes dels Textos 1 i 2, és la cambra de la fantasia. La luxúria (amor) pertorba la delicada operació valorativa de les impressions sensibles i provoca un comportament estult, des del punt de vista natural, i culpable des del moral. Vegem-ho en un altre fragment del mateix sermó:

TEXT 4

Com home glot e luxuriós veu taverna e sardina salada o carn salada, per ço que molt pusca beure consira menjar la sardina e la carn salada. E si veu gras capó o bel pex, desija menjar forts salses e, si veu bela fembra, desija luxuriar. E abdosos los desirers s'ajusten en la ymaginació que emflama la carn, la qual flama nax e diriva del grex qui participa ab los renyons, dels quals diriva en los genitius qui són corsos e·spirits en qui buyl la esperma, dels quals ixen vepors e calors caldes, seques e humides qui escalfen, crexen e humplen la verga. E si lo racional consent per membrar, entendre e amar les condicions de luxúria, es fet lo pecat mortal . . . Aytals obres en partida son naturals e en partida son morals. No dich que tu qui preyques enaxí les digues al poble con les trobes escrites, mas que digues lurs semblançes en tal guisa que u pusquen entendre, car paraules serien vergonyosas.[20]

La part moral de l''obra' de gola i luxúria, és a dir el consentiment de les tres facultats superiors de l'ànima, memòria, enteniment i voluntat, en un acte contrari a l'impuls de recordar, entendre i estimar Déu, s'insereix en la divulgació de la teoria que hem resumit a l'apartat 1: el apetits entren a través del

---

19. Ramon LLULL, *Llibre de virtuts e de pecats*, ed. Fernando Domínguez Reboiras, Nova Edició de les Obres de Ramon Llull 1 (Palma de Mallorca: Patronat Ramon Llull, 1990), 128–29, sermó 52, 'De glotonia e de luxuria'.

20. LLULL, *Llibre de virtuts*, 127.

sentit de la vista (*com home . . . veu*) i provoquen que la imaginació, que com s'ha dit al Text 2, *pren e ajusta en comú tot ço que li oferen los V senys*, actuï directament sobre els organs del cos (ronyons, genitius).[21] Heus ací que, si la diferència entre l'home i l'animal resideix en la capacitat del primer de controlar racionalment els apetits, l'abandonament a l'animalitat, que era estultícia o follia en termes naturals, esdevé pecat en termes morals. Al Text 3, a més, s'adverteix de la dificultat afegida que comporta una 'longa perseverança'.

Així, doncs, malgrat el sever desinterès de Llull pel tema, les nocions de fisiologia i psicologia presents als Textos 1, 2, 3 i 4 presenten els elements científics sobre les perturbacions de l'amor, que permeten discutir la qüestió en els escrits lírics o narratius de la tradició vulgar que s'interessen pel fenomen. Vegeu el llenguatge del Boccaccio català de 1429: 'sobiran foch que en mon enteniment avia consebut, ab fort desaretglat appetit'. I és que poden canviar les 'opinions', però no la 'ciència de natures'.[22]

III.   Just lo front port vostra bella semblança

«Dins del crani hi ha el centre del coneixement sensible, sobre el qual opera l'abstracció que condueix al coneixement intel·lectual: allí és on tinc instal·lada la impressió sensible procedent de la meva estimada i és tan extraordinàriament bella i ocupa un tal lloc de privilegi en el meu cervell que la mort no podrá esborrar-la'n.» El text que genera aquesta paràfrasi natural és la primera estrofa del poema 9 de Jordi de Sant Sant Jordi :

---

21. El *Drogmaticon philosophiae*, quan tracta de la generació (fol. 115v), no explica d'on procedeix la calor que encén l'home i congria l'esperma. No se n'oblida el *Llibre de Sidrac* català: 'La primera coza sí és la volentat de l'home, què ell desyia fer, e per aquell desig totz los membres flamegen e la natura qui és en ell o demana. La segona coza sí és l'escalffament, què ell s'escalffa en aquella volentat': Vincenzo MINERVINI, *Il «Libro di Sidrac» : Versione catalana* (Bari: Lerici, 1982), 149. Es retroba la mateixa explicació al text francès del *Placides et Timéo ou li secrés as philosophes*, ed. Claude A. THOMASSET, Textes Littéraires Français 289 (Ginebra: Droz, 1980), 102. En canvi el paper dels ronyons en la producció de l'esperma no és gaire popular: no s'esmenten en aquesta funció a Danielle JACQUART & Claude THOMASSET, *Sexualité et savoir médical au Moyen Âge*, Les Chemins de l'Histoire (París: Presses Universitaires de France, 1985), 74–98; BERNAT DE GORDON en fa un esment de passada al *Lilium Medicinae*, VII, 1.

22. Joan BOCCACCIO, *Decameron: Traducció catalana, publicada segons l'únic manuscrit conegut (any 1429)* (Barcelona: Editorial AHR, 1964), 3.

TEXT 5

Jus lo front port vostra bella semblança
de què mon cors nit e jorn fa gran festa,
que remirant la molt bella figura?
de vostra faç m'és romasa l'empremta;
que ja per mort no se'n partrà la forma,
ans quan serai del tot fores d'est segle,
cells qui lo cors portaran al sepulcre
sobre ma faç veuran lo vostre signe.[23]

El primer hemistiqui d'aquesta cobla fa referència al segon ventricle del cervell, en el qual es produeixen les alteracions accidentals de la percepció, causa de la passió d'amor. La preposició 'jus' segurament és una mala lectura del manuscrit únic (veg. la nota 23); els Textos 2 i 3 porten 'sobre lo front' per indicar el segon ventricle, senyal que es feia difícil d'explicar en un llenguatge no estrictament tècnic l'indret exacte de la seva localització.[24]

L'adjectiu que acompanya 'semblança', un terme usat en contextos científics, revela que la percepció de la impressió sensible de la dama està magnificada d'entrada, tal com explica el segon vers; on cal entendre 'mon cors' com la forma enfàtica habitual de designar la primera persona.[25] El mot 'festa' té unes vagues ressonàncies litúrgiques que dignifiquen la dimensió contemplativa de l'enamorat.[26] El vers 2 evoca el procés natural de la percep-

23. Martí de RIQUER & Lola BADIA, *Poesies de Jordi de Sant Jordi, cavaller valencià del segle XV*, Biblioteca d'Estudis i d'Investigacions (València: Tres i Quatre, 1984), 168. Text procedent del MS 184 de la Biblioteca Universitària de Saragossa, 98v; és obra d'un copista descurat. Una autocita de l'autor al seu poema XVIII, vers 65 (274) diu: 'En lo front port vostra bella semblança | de què mon cor nuit e jorn fa gran festa'.

24. Que 'just lo front' vol dir 'en el pensament' i no 'en els ulls', sense recórrer a la filosofia natural, ja ho va assenyalar Josep ROMEU I FIGUERAS, 'Comentaris al cançoner de Jordi de Sant Jordi', *Serra d'Or* (març de 1977), 156.

25. No s'ha de llegir 'cor', per bé que també fa sentit. Com ja he insinuat, malgrat la filosofia natural, el cor no va perdre mai el valor simbòlic de centre dels sentiments; veg. RIQUER & BADIA, *Poesies de Jordi de Sant Jordi*, 169–71, s'esmenten alguns passatges trobadorescos, on el cor o el ulls porten la marca indeleble de l'estimada, i aquest lloc del *Canzoniere* de Petrarca: 'Amor, che nel penser mio vive et regna | e'l suo seggio maggior nel mio cor tene, | talor armato nella fronte mi vène, | ivi si loca et ivi pon sua insegna': Francesco PETRARCA, *Canzoniere*, ed. Gianfranco Contini & Daniele Ponchiroli (Torí: Giulio Einaudi Editore, 1962), 195 (sonet CX).

26. És el sentit del v. 1 del poema XIII d'Ausiàs March, 'Colguen les gents ab alegria *festes*' o de LIII, v. 43, 'lo sant haïr, aquell del qual tinch *festa*': Ausiàs MARCH, *Poesies*, ed. Pere Bohigas, 5 vols, Els Nostres Clàssics, col·lecció A 71–73, 77, 86 (Barcelona: Editorial Barcino, 1952–59), II, 46, III, 30.

ció: l'acció de mirar (noteu l'increment re- del verb 'mirar' que suggereix
una acció repetida, relacionable amb el context obsessiu de l'amor) produeix
la imatge sensible, la qual dóna lloc a una 'empremta'. Aquest mot, a més de
ser una rima difícil que satisfà les exigències de la sonoritat del estramps,
recorda un lloc comú de la filosofia natural: les dades dels sentits im-
pressionen l'intel·lecte sensible com el segell la cera.[27]

El vers cinquè descriu un impossible natural; llegiu les dues darreres línies
del Text 2. La 'forma' també és un terme present als textos tècnics sobre la
percepció. Si aquest vers introdueix un *adynaton* just a la meitat de la cobla,
els tres versos finals creixen retòricament perquè cal llegir-los com una hipèrbola molt ultrada. Que el signe de l'estimada quedi reflectit al rostre de
l'enamorat és una metàfora nascuda per analogia del que ha succeït al segon
ventricle del cervell, en uns termes que transcendeixen l'experiència natural
(ja que la semblança encara hi és després de la mort de l'ànima sensitiva).
Com imaginar físicament que el posat, el capteniment, o l'actitud d'un
cadàver revelen la innatural empremta indeleble de l'amor? [28] Joan Roís de
Corella que, trenta anys després de la mort de Jordi de Sant Jordi, va esde-
venir mestre en l'art de dir l'inefable, proposa el següent a la seva poètica fic-
ció sobre Hero i Leandre. Quan el desventurat nadador està a punt de morir
ofegat a l'Hel·lespont, acomiada el seu propi cos i li recomana que navegui
fins a la torre de l'estimada: 'ffes-te present a la plorosa Hero'. I comenta
Corella: 'La darrera sillaba del nom de Hero en aquest mon fon terme del
seu parlar, amar e viure . . . hi en la boca morta aquell gest guardava, ab lo
qual lo nom de Hero se pronuncia'.[29] Que Corella no estava gaire lluny de
Jordi de Sant Jordi ho mostren aquests versos seus: 'Puix que, dins mi, vos

---

27.   És una noció aristotèlica (veg. n. 1). Al v. 37 del poema que ens ocupa s'esmenta
Aristòtil com el savi burlat per l'amiga del seu deixeble Alexandre del *Lai d'Aristôte*: RIQUER
& BADIA, *Poesies de Jordi de sant Jordi*, 174–75. Al v. 38 amor desferma els cinc sentits i a
l'estrofa IV del poema III, 'El setge d'amor', s'explica que els cinc sentits traïcionen el poeta
perquè d'amagat de la seva voluntat pacten amb l'enemic: RIQUER & BADIA, *Poesies de Jordi
de sant Jordi*, 110–11.

28.   El motiu de la perdurabilitat de l'amor respon a la tradició folklòrica de 'l'amor és més
poderós que la mort': no cal imaginar res, basta anunciar l'hipèrbola (tan grata a la poesia
barroca!), com fa Gilabert de Próixita: 'car tant n'hay duyt que'n fau la sapultura; | mas,
enquer mort, celhs qui volran mirar | dins en mon cor, veyran vostre figura': *Poesies de
Gilabert de Próixita*, ed Martí de RIQUER, Els Nostres Clàssics, col·lecció A 76 (Barcelona:
Editorial Barcino, 1954), 66.

29.   *Obres de J[oan] Roiç de Corella*, ed. Ramon MIQUEL I PLANAS (Barcelona: Biblioteca
Catalana, 1913), 109–10.

tinch en bella forma, | treta del viu en perfeta figura, | ab les colors sobre·l fresch, hi l'apremta, | que ni la mort, ni'l temps, ni l'altre segle, | raure no us pot, ni del riu Letes l'aigua'.[30]

Proposo de retenir que Jordi de Sant Jordi, en l'eufòria de la recuperació trobadoresca de la primera cort del Magnànim, presenta alguns símptomes de la intel·lectualització científica (moral i natural) del llenguatge líric que consagrarà Ausiàs March i que també apunta en el seus predecessors immediats Pere i Jaume.[31]

LOLA BADIA

Universitat de Barcelona

---

30. *Obres de J[oan] Roiç de Corella*, 419.

31. RIQUER & BADIA, *Poesies de Jordi de sant Jordi*, 55–80; Pere MARCH, *Obra completa*, ed. Lluís Cabré, Els Nostres Clàssics, col·lecció A 132 (Barcelona: Editorial Barcino, 1993); Josep PUJOL, '*Dos son los alts*: La teoria amorosa i els seus problemes a la poesia lírica de Jacme March', *Boletín de la Real Academia de Buenas Letras de Barcelona*, 42 (1989–90), 185–207.

THE ELEVENTH ELEGY OF CARLES RIBA

THE *Elegies de Bierville* of Carles Riba (1893-1959) are generally considered a landmark in twentieth-century Catalan poetry. The work consists of eleven elegies, plus an envoi. They were written during the poet's exile in France, where, together with his wife, he had taken refuge after the collapse of the Catalan Government, joining the exodus of January 1939 towards the frontier ahead of Franco's invading forces.

The eleventh elegy was written in agonizing circumstances. Riba and his wife had left on one of the last trains to leave Paris as the Nazis advanced; they went to Bordeaux in the hope of finding an escape route through Pétain's France, eventually reaching Montpellier, where they lived for two years before returning to Barcelona in April 1943. It is not difficult to imagine how critical must have been the plight of people, already refugees from their own country, and now fleeing from the Nazis. The elegy poignantly reflects both the state of the poet's mind and his tormented heart; his profound soul-searching makes this one of the most obscure of his elegies. We are fortunate, however, to have some insight into its meaning through the poet's own words at a public reading in Barcelona in February 1956: 'This elegy marks the passing of an idea of undefined gods, if you wish − I'll not deny that they could be pagan − towards a personal God, the loving redeemer, towards the Christian God, who had never abandoned me, even when He was silent. Jansenists speak of these sudden illuminations peculiar to the soul, of a kind of Divine revelation, with God's grace penetrating one's being. This brings with it moments, hours, of ineffable joy, and what follows, even if it be another silence from the revealed God, ceases to *be* solitude; one has to exert oneself in order to sustain such grace, but one is not alone in doing so. Therefore in this elegy will be found the idea that our life and our salvation lie in realizing the idea that God had of ourselves when He sent us to this Earth. And, in this state of mind, one sees oneself already fulfilled, divided in two, as it were, into what remains of one's temporal life, and what will be when integrated in the end.'

E L E G I A   X I

Era en la llibertat i en el cel de la meva paraula,
  transfigurat pel déu que en els meus anys ha sofert;
sota els meus ulls, la terra vivia per mi – com un rostre
  dins la diversitat de l'amorós pensament;
entre la serra, que porta, mirada enllà, a la distància
  pura, camins ocults, serpentejants com desigs,
i la ciutat dels Feliços que no conec ni em coneixen,
    alta en llur èter natal, més que les albes del risc,
incomparable reia, fill gran de la meva puixança,
    el meu efímer vol. Ah! no temptat per l'engany
esplendorós del foc que ens barra la vostra ventura,
    ni per l'atzur, oh divins indiferents! que no pot
sostenir de nosaltres sinó el que en va se us assembla:
    no: ans perquè Algú, dintre de mi, on la nit
brusca de vagues pors em combatia, s'havia
    tot de sobte estimat; amb el meu cor estremit
violentament i virginal va estimar-se,
    com si em necessités per a conèixer-se en mi,
per a plaure's en mi i en la meva joia expandir-se
    i vessar-se en el vent, amb abundància de flor
que dilapida el seu maig. Oh gran cor satisfet, oh més plena
    possessió de mi des de la idea d'un déu!
Pur en el meu enigma, he cantat, segur que la flama
    que parlava per mi no tocaria el meu cos;
i que l'ull absolut que a través del meu somni mirava
    no deixaria el cristall humiliat sobre el món.
Sols l'inefable abús i acreixement l'un per l'altre
    dels perfectes amants fóra una imatge adient;
com en cad'un es compensen i mútuament s'ultrapassen
    l'ànima i el subtil dolç instrument corporal.
Jo amb el fast he *pogut* que el meu déu de mi desplegava;
    del que de mi mateix ell em donava, he donat.
Foren uns instants que jo comptaria per vida
    i per avenç d'això: ésse' integrat en el fi;
ja en mi mateix no pertànye' a l'obscur destí de les coses
    ni al precari pols de la memòria en la sang.

ELEGY XI

In the freedom and zenith of my word, I was
      transfigured by the god who throughout my years has suffered;
under my eyes, the earth was alive for me – as a face
      within the diversity of the loving thought;
between the mountain-range that leads, a glance away, to the pure
      distance, hidden paths, turning and twisting like desires,
and the city of the Blissful, whom I neither know nor am known to,
      lofty in their natural ether, higher than daybreaks of risk,
my ephemeral flight, the first-born of my power,
      was uniquely laughing. Ah! not tempted by the splendorous
deception of the fire that bars us from your happiness,
      nor the azure, O unconcerned deities!, unable to
support itself from us except in what vaguely resembles it:
      no: but because Someone, inside me where a harsh
night of veiled fears struggled against me, had
      suddenly loved himself; with my heart trembling
violently and pure, he fell in love with himself,
      as though he needed me to know himself in me,
to delight in me and in my joy to expand and scatter
      himself in the wind, with an abundance of blossom
that his May squanders. O great satisfied heart, O most perfect
      self-possession emanating from the idea of a god!
Pure in my enigma, I sang, confident that the flame
      that spoke on my behalf would not touch my body;
and that the absolute eye, vigilant as I dreamed,
      would not abandon the humbled crystal upon the world.
Only the ineffable indulgence and growing attraction one towards the other
      of perfect lovers would be a suitable image;
how they compensate each other and mutually transcend
      their soul and the sweet subtle instrument of the body.
With the magnificence that my god from me unfolded, I *could*;
      from what of my own self he gave me, I've given.
They were instants that I would value as a life
      and as an advance on this: to be integrated in the end;
myself no longer belonging to the obscure destiny of things
      nor to the uncertain throb of memory in the blood.

Dolça, ells esvaïts, la transparència me'n dura;
    que no en sabria dir *seguretat* ni *record*:
tant m'és present la meva secreta figura salvada!
    com si des d'ara em veiés dintre la llum d'un mirall.
Com l'apassionat, que entre dues tanques fa via
    per la vall vesprejant, deixa endarrera el seu pas
i omple els seus ulls asservits en el pensament de l'encontre
    i s'acompanya ja de l'abraçada i la veu,
ara, jo, tornat a l'exili on callen les coses,
    on es mesura el temps pel que s'espera tan sols,
pujo per retrobar el qui és jo mateix i madura,
    únic, de mi mateix i del meu déu salvador,
i en l'impuls consentit cap a l'harmonia fixada,
    dins la posta que em venç creo l'aurora brillant.
Res no pot ser com abans. Comprenc, més enllà del silenci
    i ah! més enllà del meu cor, que l'invisible Vivent
que es coronà de mi i del meu crit gloriós, no em va prendre
    com un alberg de pas per al seu goig foraster;
ans havia en mi renascut del seu cel, amb el germen
    més preservat del meu cast fantasieig pueril,
i en els meus anys de fruit, profund, completava el meu compte
    de sofriment terrenal amb el seu propi diví;
fins que *tot* fos amor. I de sobte em mostrà què seria.
    El que, però, ja és, basta al meu cant i al meu do.
És la certesa. Aquesta: saber, sense pes, en la vetlla
    dura del pensament i en la llangor de l'oblit,
què ha de ser pels orígens. Saber-nos, jo i Qui no em deixa,
    fills tots dos de la pau, en la discòrdia engendrats
contra la Indiferència, absent atzur, oh immutables!
    home entre els homes jo, déu contra els déus el meu Déu!

NOTE : The Catalan text conforms to that in *Obres completes*, ed. Joan-Lluís
Marfany, 2 vols, Clàssics catalans del segle XX (Barcelona: Edicions 62,
1965–67), I, 236–37. I am grateful to Eulàlia Riba who, on behalf of the heirs,
gave me permission to translate the whole of the *Elegies*.

Once they've vanished, their sweet clearness stays with me;
        which I would not call *surety* nor *remembrance*;
thus much my redeemed secret figure is present in me!
        as though from this moment I were to see myself within the light of
Like the passionate one, who between two hedges hurries   [a mirror.
        along the darkening valley, outstripping his step,
and fills his enslaved eyes with thought of the encounter
        and accompanies himself already with the embrace and the voice,
now I, returned to exile where all is silence,
        where time is measured solely by hours of hope.
I climb to rediscover who I really am and what matures,
        unique, from my own self and from my redeeming god,
and in the concerted impulse towards a fixed harmony,
        within the sunset that conquers me I create the bright dawn.
Nothing can be as before. I understand, beyond silence
        and ah! beyond my heart, that the invisible Living One
that crowned himself with me and my joyous cry, did not take me
        as a transient shelter for his alien pleasure;
rather that from his sky he is reborn in me, with the germ
        of my innocent childish fantasies kept intact,
and in my fruitful years, profound, I completed the reckoning
        of my earthly suffering with that of his divine own;
until *all* was love. And suddenly he revealed to me what it would be.
        But what already is, satisfies my song and my gift.
It is certainty. It is this: to know, simply, in the hard
        vigil of thought and in the languor of oblivion,
what it has to be by its origins. To know ourselves, I and He who never
        both of us offsprings of peace, born in discord   [leaves me,
against Indifference, absent azure, O immutables!
        I a man among men, my God a god against gods!

JOAN GILI

Oxford

TWO

———————

GOLDEN-AGE

SPAIN

ANALOGY AND ARGUMENT IN
JERÓNIMO MEROLA'S *REPÚBLICA ORIGINAL*

IN HIS MANY STUDIES covering a dauntingly wide area of investigation, Robert Pring-Mill has repeatedly addressed himself to the processes by which writers of very varied kinds and backgrounds have expressed structures of meaning in the terms and conceptual framework provided by a given 'world-picture'. The following brief essay is concerned with a notable example of this from late sixteenth-century Barcelona; and although the work in question is non-fictional in character, it is not, I think, without interest as regards the larger literary context of the time.

In the intellectual history of Early Modern Europe the transition from 'medieval' to 'modern' is not infrequently expressed in terms of the breakdown of the analogical habit of mind as applied to the order of nature. That analogical perception of things has been characterized by W. R. Elton thus:

> Levels of existence, including human and cosmic, were habitually correlated, and correspondences and resemblances were perceived everywhere. Man as microcosmic model was thus a mediator between himself and the universe; and knowledge of one element in the microcosm-macrocosm analogy was knowledge of the other. Blending faith with knowledge, actuality with metaphysics, analogy also joined symbol with concept, the internal with the external world. Analogy, indeed, provided the perceiver with the impression of aesthetically and philosophically comprehending experience.[1]

The universe, thus seen, was a continuous and teleologically directed whole, containing within itself the existence of all possible kinds, linked in unilinear gradation to form 'the great chain of being'. This mental model, made more problematic in the sixteenth century by the epistemological

---

1. W. R. ELTON, 'Shakespeare and the Thought of his Age', in *A New Companion to Shakespeare Studies*, ed. Kenneth Muir & S. Schoenbaum (Cambridge: Cambridge University Press, 1971), 181.

questioning now associated especially with Montaigne, was finally undermined
in the seventeenth century by Descartes. As Elton again writes:

> Putting aside, like Bacon, as unknowable or uncertain, final causes – the
> 'why' or purposefulness of things – Descartes considered objects as
> intelligible only as we bring our judgements to bear on them. If only such
> knowledge alone were possible, it would follow that the analogical
> method of knowing the universe was thenceforth outmoded.[2]

The seventeenth-century 'scientific revolution', centred on the principle of ex-
perimental verification, was greatly advanced thereby.

Spain was not, of course, prominent in furthering this change or rapid in re-
sponding to it. The work to be considered here stands mainly as a vivid
illustration – so vivid as to be almost baffling at times – of the hold which the
older, analogical view of things continued to maintain in at least some sectors
of educated society in Spain towards the end of the sixteenth century. This is
made the more intriguing by the fact that this work contains passages that
could easily be taken to be indicative of a striking intellectual modernity. In
its small way, it serves to remind us of the complex factors involved in the
transition of mental outlooks which Elton and others have traced.

*   *   *   *   *

The work in question is Jerónimo Merola's *República original sacada del
cuerpo humano*, published at Barcelona in 1587.[3] We learn that its author was
aged fifty or so when he wrote it, that he was from Balaguer, near Lérida, that
he had studied medicine at Montpellier and was now 'doctor of philosophy
and medicine' and professor of medicine at the university of Barcelona.

He acknowledges (sig. B$_7$r) Plato's *Republic*, V, 462–64, as the source of
the central idea of his work: 'Civitas bene instituta similis est fabricae
corporis humani'. (He does not mention that other obvious source for the
idea, John of Salisbury's *Policraticus*.)

His declared aim is to show why certain 'estates' in society are, or ought to
be, paid more honour than others. Book I of his treatise is centred on his ex-

---

2. ELTON, 'Shakespeare and the Thought of his Age', 186.

3. *Republica original sacada del cuerpo humano. Compuesta por Hieronimo Merola, doctor en
Philosophia y Medicina, Catalan, y natural de la ciudad de Balaguer*. En Barcelona. Impresso
en casa de Pedro Malo en el año M.D.LXXXVII. The work was reprinted by the same house
in 1595 and again in 1611.

position of the analogy stated in the title. Book II is concerned with a particular aspect of his main theme: the long-debated question (pursued with much energy in Italy especially) whether the medical or the legal profession is superior to the other.[4]

He begins, however, by considering at length the universal order of things. The human body is a copy and summary of the world at large; human nature joins earth and heaven, combining material elements inferior to man with a rationality that finds its full realization only in the angelic orders of creation above him (fols 2v–5v).[5] Man finds his place within an all-inclusive scheme of related ends: the larger world (or macrocosm) is by its nature directed towards 'the little world that is man', while God is the aim or goal of both (fol. 20v).[6] The body was created to serve the soul, and the material things bestowed by fortune were created for the sake of the body. Thus was formed 'a three-stranded cord' – *funiculus triplex* – or 'golden chain' (fols 22v–23r). In this context, the specific role and aim of man is to complete a circular process ('hazer una circulación'), returning to the God from whom he derives his origin and thus completing a larger process of derivation and return, descent and ascent, within the scheme of things at large.[7] This line of argument has an

---

4. This debate related to the distinctive character of the Italian universities. In Kristeller's words, 'at Bologna and the other Italian centers, there were only two faculties, that of law and that of the arts . . . Within the faculty of arts, medicine was the most important subject of instruction [while] logic and natural philosophy were considered as preparatory for medicine': Paul Oskar KRISTELLER, *Renaissance Thought: The Classic, Scholastic, and Humanist Strains*, Harper Torchbook (New York: Harper & Row, 1961), 36. Kristeller remarks further (45) that 'in the period preceding Galileo . . . the various sciences differed in their traditions and mutual relations . . . Medicine was [a] science distinct from philosophy, but more closely linked to it since medicine and philosophy were considered as parts of the same study and career, and since such medical authorities as Galen and Avicenna were Aristotelians'. William A. WALLACE, OP, commenting on 'the close alliance that was promoted between the practical science of medicine and its speculative underpinnings as found in the study of nature', points out that 'physicians in the late Middle Ages and the Renaissance saw themselves as both *philosophi* and *medici*, with their university degrees qualifying them in this way': *Cambridge History of Renaissance Philosophy*, ed. Charles B. SCHMITT & Quentin SKINNER (Cambridge: Cambridge University Press, 1988), Part VI (8): 'Traditional Natural Philosophy', 201–35 (205).

5. See also Book I, chapter xxiv: 'Que el hombre es un mundo pequeño y abreviado'. Textual references are to the edition of Barcelona 1611, the foliation of which is identical to that of 1587. Punctuation has been modernized in quotations and accents have been added.

6. Merola returns to the point in his Conclusion: 'Y todo esto para que se guarde la vida deste pequeño mundo: al qual, como a su fin, está dirigido el grande, y todo lo que en su ámbito está contenido, hasta los mismos cielos, su mouimiento, y luzeros' (fol. 315v).

7. 'Porque lo que pretende el hombre es hazer vna circulación y boluerse a Dios de quien tiene su origen, y esto mediante la virtud, con la qual viene a hazerse tan virtuoso, tan perfecto,

obvious Neoplatonic aspect;[8] and the latter is emphasized by Merola's several (and at times lengthy) borrowings from the Hermetic works: the *Asclepius* and (especially) the *Pimander*, which he quotes in Ficino's Latin version, showing the wonderful order of the created scheme of things, where the invisible Deity is to be discerned in the harmonious movement of the planets and stars and in the structure and constitution of the human body.

When he moves on to the central topic of Book I of his treatise, Merola first applies his analogy as a whole and then elaborates a series of more particular applications.[9]

The body has three 'principal parts', which, in ascending order of dignity and excellence, are the kidneys, the heart and the brain. To these three there correspond three professions in society, which are, respectively, those of civil law, medicine, and 'theology'.[10] These are the three 'artes architectónicas' – a term deriving ultimately from the opening of the *Nicomachean Ethics*, where Aristotle distinguishes between 'master arts' and subordinate skills. As the three physical organs work cooperatively together, so too should these three professions (fols 102v–103v). Merola notes with regret, however, that medical men and lawyers are in fact very ready to speak ill of each other, and indeed shows something of this himself in Book II, where he argues at length and with vigorous *parti pris* for the superiority of the medical profession against the claims of the lawyers.

Recalling the 'great and divine' St Paul in Romans 12. 4 ('. . . even as we have many members in one body and all the members have not the same office . . .', fols 111v–112r), Merola next speaks of the three more inclusive sectors of society between which he again looks for cooperation and mutual

y semejante a Dios, que por la similitud es atrahído por el summo bien (porque Dios enamórasse del ánima, viendo en ella muchas cosas suyas, que puede dezirse que se enamora de sí mesmo en el ánima) para que allí le goze de manera que se haga otro como Dios por participación y fruyción' (fols 20v–21r).

8. There is a strong resemblance between Merola on this point and Nicholas of Cusa and Ficino. See Charles H. LOHR, SJ, in *Cambridge History of Renaissance Philosophy*, Part X (16): 'Metaphysics', 537–638 (552–53, 571–72). Lohr points out the respects in which Renaissance Neoplatonists drew on Ramon Llull.

9. 'La Analogía de más calidad, y en la qual más que en otra ninguna [se] funda todo este libro, es la que ay entre los bienes que en la República y en el cuerpo se pretenden, y las artes que essos bienes tratan en la exterior polycía de los hombres, y las partes que disponen los [=bienes] de la interior de la naturaleza' (fols 100v–101r).

10. Throughout this work the term 'teólogos' signifies not those who pursue the intellectual discipline of theology but those whose concern is with spiritual things. 'Teología' here means the principles and pursuit of that concern.

concern: those who govern but are not themselves governed (that is, 'consejeros o consules');   those who are governed but do not themselves govern (that is, the plebs);   and those in between, who command some people while obeying others (those, that is, who assist in council those who have the government of society in their hands). To express the harmony that results when these all work together as they should, Merola turns (fol. 114r–v) to St Augustine's frequently remembered image of musical concord applied to the proper relationship of the highest, middle and lowest orders of society (*De civitate Dei*, II, 21; from Cicero, *De republica*, II, xlii).

After this introduction Merola now elaborates over the space of ten chapters (25–34) a series of particular analogies between the human body and aspects or elements of human society. In the body one finds a representation of royal government, for as a king rules his kingdom, so nature 'rules' the human body. But the latter is also a 'vivid portrait' of rule by aristocracy, seen in the combined control of the bodily functions by brain, heart, and kidneys together. The body also provides a model of the well-ordered life of a perfect family. On the other hand, it gives us a picture of warfare and military discipline, for as the king's army attacks an enemy, so the body 'attacks' a disease. Not only that but, as the title of Chapter 30 promises us, 'las centinelas en la guerra, las enseñas y pendones se hallan cifrados en nuestro cuerpo' (fol. 148r). So far as disease is concerned, the body is also like a legal tribunal, in so far as nature 'judges between an illness and its sufferer'. At this point it should be stressed that these and the like are not passing figures of speech; each analogy is worked out in detail in a chapter to itself.

Sometimes Merola admits to having difficulties, as when he finds that society has three 'arms' – the ecclesiastical, the military, and 'el braço real' (which signifies all that is included in public administration and services) – all three being 'arms' of society because they offer it strength and protection in the way that arms protect the body, and yet of the latter, alas, there are only two.[11]

It is unnecessary to add to this account of Merola's analogies to show that, for the modern reader, the problem is to understand in what sense Merola thought that he was making meaningful statements in employing this kind of discourse. Early in Book I he acknowledges that 'si en alguna cosa auía de cobrar temor el hombre de echar mano de la pluma, hauía de ser en las cosas

---

11. Book I, chapters 32 ('Qve nvestro cverpo es la cifra de los tres braços: Ecclesiástico, Militar, y Real') and 33 ('Por qvé no teniendo más que dos braços nuestro cuerpo admitimos tres en nuestra República').

de analogías y semejanças' (fols 12v – 13r). What, nevertheless, gave him intellectual confidence was his belief, emphasized in his chapter on the three 'arms' of society, that 'art imitates nature' (fol. 159v). Artificial, man-made things imitate natural things. But, continues Merola syllogistically, no natural thing so perfectly contains within itself the *cifra* or sum of artificial things as the human body. Therefore it follows that 'in imitation of the human body have all other artificial things been made'. Merola adds that he has desired to establish this point lest anyone should think that these things of which he is speaking are 'imaginary' and merely ingenious comparisons.[12]

To look, here, for anything that might to modern eyes commend itself as rational argument may, in view of the foregoing, seem a vain endeavour. However, in the very chapter immediately preceding the one on which I have just been drawing, one finds a passage that at once attracts attention to itself by reason of its rationality and, indeed, apparent modernity. The title of the chapter ('Que nuestro cuerpo es la cifra de un tribunal') does not immediately seem to promise that. However, Merola makes this the occasion to argue against quack cures and superstitious remedies in contrast to the rational application of natural means for restoring health. He attacks as 'abogados con especie de santimonia' those who instruct a patient

> que se ponga vna medida, o reliquia, o vn cordón, o nómina, o que beua de la agua de sancta Catalina, o de sant Magín, y que se encomiende a Dios, que es el verdadero médico y los demás matasanos (como si se nos entregassen tales) y que se dexen de hazer remedios naturales . . .

This, he continues, is offensive to God:

> pues a los médicos, y a los remedios naturales, Dios por su bondad les a dado para las dolencias, que son necessidades naturales. Y siempre que para semejantes necessidades ay remedios naturales, es temeridad querer obligar a Dios a milagro . . .

Natural and supernatural means should be employed together:

> que vayan juntos los remedios naturales y sobrenaturales, porque guíe Dios a los remedios, y a su instrumento y ministro el Médico en la elección de los medios conuenientes, no digo que es bueno solamente, pero necessario.

---

12. 'Esto e querido prouar para que no pensasse alguno que estas cosas son imaginarias y que son como apodos bien assentados, y no porque se an de auer regulado por el modelo de nuestro cuerpo. Agora entremos en nuestros braços . . .' (fol. 160r – v).

Merola returns to his initial attack:

> Pero que los [remedios] sobrenaturales vayan solos, es querer parecer a la generación praua y adúltera quae signum quaerit.[13] Y sería como quien a poder de oraciones quiziesse matar la hambre, o remediar el frío, sin comer ni cobijarse ... También son abogados de la dolencia las supersticiosas y supersticiosos, con sus bocesos [*sic*] cruzes y palabras que baxo de sí no tienen ningún supuesto.[14]

What led Merola to write with the emphasis that he did at this point was his view of the order of nature.

That order, with its 'concurso de causas' derives from God; it is his 'mayordomo'; therefore whatever is said about nature cannot but be in praise of God. Since God created nature and works through it, it is proper to investigate the way in which it operates, that is, its 'causes'. To talk only in terms of the First Cause 'sería cerrar la puerta a todo buen discurso y Philosóphico' (fol. 290r). Therefore the things of nature must be resolutely investigated and their proper scope of operation recognized: 'las cosas naturales a porfía an de buscarse'. It sounds like an exhortation to scientific method, and in a sense it is; but the religious perspective is maintained: 'Que las cosas naturales a porfía an de buscarse, y por ellas como por la escalera de Iacob yr subiendo a la diuinidad de aquel que todo lo haze y manda' (fol. 290v). Merola here cites Romans 1. 20: 'For the invisible things of [God] since the creation of the world are clearly seen ... through the things that are made ... '.

Merola's thought moves in the same upward direction when he takes up the topic, in another chapter, that Natural Philosophy is 'more excellent' than Moral Philosophy. The 'end' of Natural Philosophy is 'más común y más general' than that of Moral Philosophy, and

> ... de más preeminencia es el discurso de los efectos a las causas, y de las conclusiones a sus principios, que no al contrario, porque el entendimiento es más amigo de lo más vniuersal: y el sentimiento de lo más particular ... (fol. 223v).

---

13. The reference is to Matthew 16. 4.

14. fols 155r – 156v. Merola refers here to Pedro CIRUELO, *Reprobación de las supersticiones y hechicerías*, Book III, chapter vii ('En que disputa contra los comunes saludadores'). The latter are attacked here 'porque todo lo que hacen los saludadores son palabras y cerimonias vanas para querer sanar algunas enfermedades fuera del curso natural de las medicinas': ed. Justo García Morales, Joyas Bibliográficas 7 (Madrid: Joyas Bibliográficas, 1952), 94. However, the point is not expanded in conceptual terms there as it is in Merola.

Natural Philosophy stands behind medicine; Moral Philosophy stands behind the law (fol. 223r); and Merola gives much of Book II of his treatise to
arguing that the status or 'dignity' of the medical profession is superior to that
of the legal profession.[15]

Merola was aware that he was thus entering a long-continuing polemic. As
he explains, he had been prompted to do so by two prominent French jurists
who, in two massive works often mentioned by Spanish writers, argued the
case for their own profession: Barthélémy de Chasseneux (Cassaneus) in his
Catalogus gloriae mundi (Lyons, 1529) and André Tiraqueau (Tiraquellus) in
his *De nobilitate* (Paris, 1549). However, behind these Frenchmen was a
debate which, in Italy, had run on at least from the time of Petrarch, who in
the 1350s had roundly attacked medical men who had pretensions to invading
the field of letters. Through the fifteenth century, humanists such as Salutati,
Bruni, and Poggio Bracciolini made common cause with the lawyers against
the practitioners and professors of medicine, and the debate continued
through the sixteenth century into the seventeenth.

While professional *parti pris* and the character (noted earlier) of Italian
universities provided much of the driving force for this debate, larger and
more significant issues were involved. Claims for the superior 'dignity' or
'nobility' of the legal as distinct from the medical profession centred on the
role of law within the moral function of civil society; that is, on its part in
promoting the moral life of the individual within society and thus society's
good at large. On the other hand, assertions of the superior standing of
medicine rested on the alleged superiority of systematic knowledge over action, the superiority of the speculative or 'contemplative' life over the 'active'
life, and, finally, on the superiority of the object of its concern (the human
body) over that of the lawyers (mere things). On the one side much was made
of Cicero and his argument (as in *De officiis*, I, xliii–xliv) that the claims of
human society take precedence over speculative knowledge. On the other,
appeal was made to Aristotle and his argument (in *Nicomachean Ethics*, X,
vii–viii) that the activity of the reason in contemplation is superior to the
activity of the practical virtues in political or military affairs, and that it is in
such contemplative activity that man is most like God.

---

15. Merola in fact readily concedes, and argues at some length, that the role of 'teólogos'
gives them superiority over both medicine and the law. The consideration of all three
'facultades' in relation to each other itself belongs to a larger context of discussion in Italy, but
this is not of immediate relevance here.

Medicine is 'contemplative' in that it studies the order of the 'grande mundo' as found in 'el mundo pequeño que es el hombre' (fol. 234v). As Merola says, 'aquí veréys el mundo grande abreuiado'; the body is a 'mappamundi' of that larger world (fol. 313v); and so, 'si queréys saber el poder de Dios de la manera que se puede, mira y escudriña las obras de naturaleza en nuestro cuerpo . . . ' (fol. 313r).

From this it follows that medicine enjoys a superiority over law as an intellectual activity and method, in that medical knowledge has a coherent, systematic, and unvarying character which jurisprudence lacks. Merola takes it as axiomatic that, among the 'sciencias', 'aquella será de más excelencia que tuviere mejor méthodo y procediere con mejor orden' (fol. 236v). He soon moves on to echoing the opening observations of Aristotle's *Physics*: 'Que en toda sciencia que tenga principios, causas, o elementos, se a de començar la doctrina por éstos, como más simples, y como piedras fundamentales del edificio' (fol. 239r–v). The study of medicine exemplifies this principle, whereas law (specifically here, the Civil Law) lacks such method: it proceeds 'a su aluedrío y sin orden alguna' (fol. 239r). Laws, he has earlier noted, vary from place to place and from time to time (fols 212v–213v); and jurisprudence, since it gives so much weight to the principle of authority, is very much open to frequently conflicting legal opinions; whereas medical men set less store by 'authorities' than by reason (fols 271v–272v); and that to which they apply their reason is the perfect ordering of nature by God (fol. 214r–v).

It follows that Merola is much more eager to base his claims for the 'dignity' of medicine on its theoretical basis than on its empirical practice. He accepts that 'todas las sciencias an tenido origen de la espiriencia, la qual tiene por subjecto las cosas sensibles . . . ' (fol. 314r). However, granted the complex character of the human body and the difficulty involved in medical study,

> [¿] cómo es posible que pueda ni ose exercitar esta arte vn empírico, con vna sola espiriencia, vana y de ningún valor, aunque pudiesse tenerla de mil años [?] Porque como dize Galeno, Exercitatio quantumuis longa sine arte & ratione nihil horum inuenire potest. La exercitación y espiriencia por más que larga y de muchos años sea, sin razón y arte no puede inuentar algún remedio (fol. 316r–v).

The scheme of things portrayed by E. M. W. Tillyard in his *The Elizabethan World Picture* and by others since, with its hierarchies and correspondences and analogies ordering the world's diversity, held an evident appeal for other writers, markedly different in background or career, who were Merola's contemporaries in the Crown of Aragon. A notable example of a work where, within that larger conceptual context, society as a whole is presented in terms of the analogy of the human body is the *Microcosmia y govierno universal del hombre christiano, para todos los estados y qualquiera de ellos* of Marco Antonio de Camós y Requeséns, published at Barcelona in 1592. The question that arises here (and in other such works) is how far the thematic analogy in fact serves as a coherent and effective integrative principle for the argument of the work at large. Merola, as we have seen, acknowledged that analogical exposition (even when it was in essence of a highly traditional kind) posed problems. The very strong attachment which he nevertheless displayed to this mode of discourse is to be explained by underlying convictions as to the way things ultimately are and the kind of argument that is appropriate to them. We have seen how Aristotle's authority is invoked on behalf of deductive reasoning as applied to a cosmology to which Merola gives a strongly Neoplatonic aspect. The work thus comes to express an intellectual position possessing particular importance for one of Merola's profession – as he conceived that to be.

Merola introduces us to a professional debate, vigorously conducted in fifteenth- and sixteenth-century Italy especially, whose intellectual significance ran well beyond its immediate terms and application. His own treatise (and Book II of it in particular) thereby becomes a document of importance as regards the fortunes of the ideology of civic humanism in the Spain of this period and its relations (conflictive or otherwise) with Aristotelian and Neoplatonic traditions. Within its own span, the work illustrates how a given mental model will sustain and foster a particular mode of reasoning, and in so doing illuminates the relativities of rationality.

RONALD TRUMAN

Christ Church, Oxford

A NOTE ON SCENIC FORM
IN *EL CASTIGO SIN VENGANZA*

THE INTRODUCTION to Cyril Jones's admirable 1966 edition of *El castigo sin venganza* consists of several pages on the MS and printed witnesses of the text, on the play's sources, on the reasons for its single performance in Madrid, and on its versification. The main discussion, however, centres on the play's title and designation as *tragedia*, its treatment of the honour code, and its 'intention' (by which is meant its exemplary moral teaching).[1] By contrast, the treatment of style is perfunctory (17–19), while the half page devoted to 'staging' (5–6) refers the reader to Hugo Rennert's general book of 1909 on *The Spanish Stage in the Time of Lope de Vega*, remarks briefly on the geographical setting of the three acts, and ends with Rennert's astounding declaration that Golden-Age theatre-goers 'went to *hear* the play', not see it.

This introduction was typical of 1960s scholarship on Golden-Age drama, except that it gave a good deal more attention to staging than was usual. The ruling methodology of that generation, which sought to detect messages in plays through close discussion of moral or political themes, has been overtaken by two developments in the approach to the Spanish drama of the Golden Age. The first of these has been the formulation of a proper theory of dramatic poetics – of a criticism, that is, which treats plays as special kinds of texts whose meaning is inseparable from performance, and where stagecraft is a primary concern of the critic.[2] The second is one pioneered by Robert Pring-Mill. As early as 1961 he began to question the anagogical or inductive search for general moral themes in the action of plays, which made characters into embodiments of Good and Evil; instead he suggested a more delicate

---

1. Lope de VEGA, *El castigo sin venganza*, ed. C. A. Jones (Oxford: Pergamon, 1966), 1–21 (quotations are from this edn). Several of Jones's concerns were, of course, provoked by Lope's important 'Prólogo' to the 1634 *suelta* edn (121): 'Señor lector, esta Tragedia se hizo en la Corte solo vn dia, por causas que a v. m. le importan poco . . . Su Historia estuuo escrita en lengua Latina, Francesa, Alemana, Toscana, y Castellana . . . està escrita al estilo Español, no por la antiguedad Griega y seueridad Latina, huyendo de las sombras, Nuncios, y coros'.

2. See, for example, the recent volume of collected essays (1964–87) by John E. VAREY, *Cosmovisión y escenografía: El teatro español en el Siglo de Oro*, Nueva Biblioteca de Erudición y Crítica 2 (Madrid: Castalia, 1987).

analogical or deductive model, seeing actions as concrete individual *casos* or illustrative examples whose relation to moral problems might be indirect, autonomous, and open-ended:

> The structuralized vision of Creation forms the background against which every play is enacted: the framework within which it is constructed and in terms of which it is articulated. The individual drama is related outward to the framework by subtle use of interlocking images which bring out the analogical correspondences, by mythological references endowed with an allegorical force, and by the constant use of generalized statements (*sentencias*, the Latin *sententiae*).[3]

Tempting as it is to assume that these remarks refer to Calderón, it is worth underlining that Pring-Mill's earliest formulations were concerned with Lope.[4]

The two approaches I have just described, through stagecraft and through analogy, do not seem to have much in common. Nevertheless, the present study seeks to suggest how both may come together in a reading of Lope's most mature and challenging play. It seeks, first, to show how we might begin to read the play as a play, and then to discuss the light which the peculiar features of its stagecraft may throw on its 'relation outward to the framework'. Pring-Mill himself observed (*Five Plays*, xv) that

> while Lope is obviously fascinated by the ultimate moral values at issue, he seems . . . no less interested in the illustration of the title proposition [*Justice without Revenge*] by means of a highly melodramatic action, which is developed with at least as great a concern for its theatrical as for its moral potentialities.

The following attempt to meld the theatrical and analogical approaches tries to meet the challenge posed by the last phrase of this quotation.

What, then, is meant by reading the play as a play? Two factors are involved: first, that we should avoid treating a drama as if it were a narrative poem or novel, and second that we should avoid interpreting its text in the same way as we interpret real life. To take the second and easier point first, a

---

3. Lope de VEGA, *Five Plays*, ed. R. D. F. Pring-Mill, tr. Jill Booty, Mermaid Dramabook 20 (New York: Hill and Wang Inc., 1961), 'Introduction', vii–xli (viii).

4. In addition to the essay mentioned in the preceding footnote, see his 'Sententiousness in *Fuente Ovejuna*', *Tulane Drama Review*, 7 (1962), 5–37. In a letter of 3 August 1984 commenting on an early version of this paper, Robert Pring-Mill revealed that his fascination with analogical models (in science as much as literature) arose not from his studies of Calderón, but from his early work on medieval analogical thinking in connection with Ramon Llull.

play is a calculated rational artefact, and hence as different from life as it is possible to be. The dangers of mistaking such an artefact for a 'literal transcript of . . . what, at that given time and place, an interlinked set of people said and did' – the documentary fallacy, as it has become known – may be exemplified by a detail from E. M. Wilson's reading of the character of Aurora in *El castigo sin venganza*.[5] Upset by Federico's crush on another woman – his stepmother, as it happens – Aurora decides to bring him to heel by the well-tried trick of flirting with another man. Wilson astutely argues that this implies a contrast with Casandra, who tries to bring her husband to heel by flirting with another man – as it happens, her stepson. But Aurora 'can do this legitimately as a single woman', whereas Casandra is married and hence acts 'criminally'; furthermore, Aurora 'refuses to act as a cloak for this crime [the incest of Federico and Casandra]'. Armed with this favourable estimate of Aurora, Wilson is emboldened to opine that at the end of the play she 'probably' goes off to Mantua with the Marquis – 'she has our sympathy . . . and we feel she is really fortunate' in her choice, for 'on the whole she behaves well. Her love for Federico has been destroyed, and she decides to make a new start'.[6] This inference concerns the following lines from *El castigo sin venganza* (lines 3000–08):

DUQUE.	Tú, Aurora, con este ejemplo,
	parte con Carlos a Mantua,
	que él te merece, y yo gusto.
AURORA.	Estoy, señor, tan turbada,
	que no sé lo que responda.
BATÍN.	Di que sí, que no es sin causa
	todo lo que ves, Aurora.
AURORA.	Señor, desde aquí a mañana
	te daré respuesta.

Salga el Marqués.

---

5. The term 'documentary fallacy', and the quotation, come from chapter 2 of A. J. A. WALDOCK, *Sophocles the Dramatist* (Cambridge: Cambridge University Press, 1951, rpt 1966), 11–24 (15); the idea goes back to L. C. KNIGHTS, 'How Many Children had Lady Macbeth?' (1933), rpt in his *Explorations* (London: Chatto & Windus, 1946), 1–39.

6. E. M. WILSON, 'Quando Lope quiere, quiere', in his *Spanish and English Literature of the 16th and 17th Centuries: Studies in Discretion, Illusion, and Mutability* (Cambridge: Cambridge University Press, 1980), 155–83, 261–63 (176), first published in Spanish in *Cuadernos Hispanoamericanos*, nr 161/162 (May–June 1963), 265–98.

But to speculate from 'desde aquí a mañana te daré respuesta' that Aurora will shortly marry Mantua is to suppose that the lines are what a duke, a lady, and a servant are saying, when in fact they are nothing of the kind; they are what the playwright has chosen to make his Duke, his lady, and his *gracioso* say. To put it another way, if Aurora were a real person, her announcing 'I shall answer tomorrow' might mean that she was going to answer yes, or no, or that she did not know what she was going to answer, and we should be free (at least until tomorrow) to speculate about what the answer was going to be; but when Lope makes his character announce 'I shall answer tomorrow', it means only that there will be no answer. Speculation about Aurora's future is thus rendered academic; paradoxically – and this is the heart of the mysterious difference between the pragmatics of stage language and the pragmatics of ordinary discourse – Aurora's promise that she will give an answer actually guarantees the opposite, and invites us to contemplate not the answer, but the absence of the answer. Since the marked absence of an answer is a very different thing from not having mentioned an answer at all, it is permissible to surmise, if we are being invited to conclude anything about Aurora's fate at this point, that her indecision, which by seventeenth-century standards is rather rude (and which pointedly ignores Batín's prompting to say yes), indicates that she is assailed by doubts about the desirability of marriage to the Marquis, and perhaps uncomfortable about the fate of Federico and Casandra.[7]

There is, besides, a more potent fact about this dialogue to be taken into account. The stage direction which directly follows Aurora's last words shows that the Marquis himself has made an exit behind the discovery-space curtain with sword in hand before the Duke begins speaking (line 2996), and is off-stage in the very act of murdering Aurora's erstwhile lover even as the conver-

---

7. It is hard to know what to make of Lope's first draft of lines 3000–02, struck out by his own hand in the MS: 'Aurora, qual quieres mas | ser Duquesa de Ferrara | o yr a Mantua con Carlos?'; but the fact that the playwright even entertained the idea of Aurora's marrying the Duke seems to indicate that Wilson was reading too much into the match with Mantua. See the editor's note *ad loc.* in Lope de VEGA, *El perro del hortelano. El castigo sin venganza*, ed. A. David Kossoff, Clásicos Castalia 25 (Madrid: Castalia, 1970), 366; and, for Lope's autograph corrections (and all other textual matters), Hugo Albert RENNERT, 'Ueber Lope de Vega's *El castigo sin venganza*', *Zeitschrift für Romanische Philologie*, 25 (1901), 411–23, and the indispensable critical edition by C. F. Adolfo VAN DAM, *El castigo sin venganza: Tragedia de Frey Lope Félix de Vega Carpio, edición conforme al manuscrito autógrafo de la Ticknor Library de Boston* (Groningen: P. Noordhoff; Madrid: Ediciones de «La Lectura»; & Paris: Honoré Champion, 1928), 278–81.

sation takes place ('FEDERICO. ¡O padre! ¿Por qué me matan?', from behind the curtain, line 2997; 'MARQUÉS. Ya | queda muerto el Conde', lines 3008–09).[8] I submit, therefore, that the last thing the dialogue does is to invite the spectator to forget what is going on behind the curtain and to consider Aurora's marriage prospects; its function is rather to mark the moment, the heart of darkness in the play, not with Aurora's future complacence, but with her present horror, perplexity, and incomprehension ('tan turbada | que no sé lo que responda'). That is why Batín has to intervene with his piece of cold comfort ('que no es sin causa | todo lo que ves, Aurora', lines 3005–06).

It is hard to make a discussion of this small example seem other than sophistic, but the basic point – that we must grasp the distinction between what the language of a play, as opposed to the language of real life, can and cannot tell us when properly considered as two hours' traffic on a stage – has a direct bearing on Pring-Mill's notion of analogical reading. For if we consider Wilson's argument about Aurora, it seems clear that his conviction that she is to be rewarded in the incomprehensible *mañana* of time outside the play with the conventional happy ending of an advantageous marriage springs not from the dialogue and certainly not from the action of this scene, but from his earlier inductive judgment of her moral merit. And though I can find no cogent reason to challenge Wilson's analysis of Aurora's character, dispassionate consideration forces one to admit that there is no reason to agree with it either. The real explanation of the riddle of Aurora's *respuesta* appears to be that her morality was a problem which it never occurred to Lope to solve. Wilson's critique is hence about a Platonic moral idea of Aurora, and Platonic ideas, though theoretically inconceivable to merely human minds, are rational; the Aurora of Lope's play, on the other hand, is enigmatic and passionate, human and practically impossible to judge. What shall we make, for example, of the dialogue at the beginning of Act III where she reveals to the Marquis her discovery of the lovers' dreadful incest (lines 2031–2110)? She begins by claiming coolly that she is revealing the secret 'para pedirte consejo' (line 2035), though a moment later she says she does not trust men (line 2047); nevertheless, when she repeats her plea it is not for advice to do with the incestuous pair but for reassurance that Gonzaga really means to marry her

---

8. The *Parte XXI* edition of the play, prepared with the poet's approbation just before his death (27 August 1635) and issued by his daughter Feliciana shortly after it, adds a stage direction at line 2997 to make the point clear, «*Vanse todos riñendo con èl*» (VAN DAM, *ed. cit.*, 278n.).

(lines 2103–10). The Marquis is quite sure that he does (lines 2111 ff.), but perhaps he has not been listening with attention, for Aurora has simultaneously confessed that she is madly jealous of Federico, and that her favours to the Marquis have been mere ploys to make Federico jealous in return (lines 2040–57). It is jealousy that has reduced her to spying in mirrors ('como celos son linces | que las paredes penetran', lines 2064–65), but the reward of this lynx-like optical acuity has been a 'terrible disaster' – to see her man measuring another woman's rosebuds with his lips (lines 2074–77). The wistful Petrarchan lyricism of this vision contrasts poignantly (or is it piquantly?) with the pain it has inflicted, but nothing can rob Aurora of her ability to frame her passion in elegant zeugma and further measured ophthalmological conceits: 'Con esto, y sin alma, fuime, | donde lloré mi desdicha, | y la de los dos que viven, | . . . tan ciegos (lines 2078–81).

Is this agony genuine? And, if it is, do we believe also in her tears for the faithless couple who have inflicted it? As so often in this play, one is left almost swooning with the power and emotion of the poetry – but not necessarily with a fixed idea of what the emotion is. We need not believe that it is the mirrors, rather than Aurora's own preternaturally sharp eyes, that cloud over at the filthiness of the spied embraces (lines 2089–92); but is this from moral outrage or jealous fever? Is it lovesick curiosity or vengeful prurience that makes her keep looking until 'the ultimate insult' has been witnessed (lines 2093–96)? What strange gust of inconsistency makes her compare Federico and Casandra's incest to the grossest perversions of 'naked kaffirs in their sealskin clothes' (lines 2086–87)? In short, is this whole speech the outpouring of a wounded soul, or is it a cynical ploy to work upon the Marquis?

It is natural that spectators should ask these questions, but critics must resist the temptation to answer them from the throne of some inductive interpretation. It is easy to imagine two actresses performing the speech I have just discussed in diametrically opposed ways; Aurora could be portrayed as a hard woman, or as a hurt one, or as a number of permutations of the two, without violating the structure of the text. The aim of the sort of dramatic criticism I have in mind is not to instruct actors on how to interpret their individual parts on stage, but rather to reveal the inner workings of the play's theatrical architecture. One of the great merits of Wilson's excellent essay is to have revealed the profound importance of Aurora; of that one is more persuaded on every reading. But there is no need for a cut-and-dried decision about her morality, for that, as my discussion of her final speech has tried to show, is a concern which the text actively seeks not to determine.

One of the factors involved in reading the play as a play, then, is not forcing its text to yield more answers than it is capable of providing; not trying to turn the picture-frame over to see if there is anything on the back of the canvas to elucidate the work of art on the front. But here is the drawback of an anagogical-inductive reading; once the comparison with Casandra has been set up, it must determine the point of Aurora's morality because it demands that the allegorical theme be projected through every detail of the structure. Pring-Mill's more generous analogical approach, on the other hand, allows us to accept that Aurora is merely a part – a complex and autonomous part – of a suggestive and open-ended dramatic whole, her character linking into and fleshing out the main action with suggestive resonances of its own rather than dovetailing into a rigid and aprioristic scheme of poetic justice.

I return now to the first of those two factors which I mentioned as being involved in a properly dramatic criticism: that is, not treating a drama as if it were a narrative poem or a novel. It is evident that Golden-Age plays tell stories, and to this degree share certain elements of plotting, structure, and characterization with other narrative genres (as *El castigo sin venganza* shares some of these things with Bandello's fourty-fourth *novella*). Yet the medium of the play is not words, but the voices and bodies of actors moving on a stage. The text of the play, therefore, as opposed to its script, is not the dialogue alone, but the sum of its words plus all the 'concrete visual actuality' of scenery, props, gestures, and stage-business which the playwright uses to tell his story – 'the drama of action', 'the uplifted hand or tense muscle' which signifies the 'particular emotion'.[9]

By this I do not mean the visual elements of a particular performance; I am referring to staging which is integral to the authorial text, not to a director's realization of it. When a character is made to say 'Dadme los pies Vuestra Alteza' we may postulate a significant gesture in the text, regardless of what an actor may do with it. To take an example, *El castigo sin venganza*

---

9. The quotations are from T. S. ELIOT, 'Seneca in Elizabethan Translation' (1927), rpt in his *Selected Essays*, 3rd enlarged edn (London: Faber, 1951), 65–105 (68). The point is eloquently made for Spanish by John E. VAREY, 'The Essential Ambiguity in Lope de Vega's *Peribáñez*: Theme and Staging', *Theatre Research International*, n.s. 1 (1976), 157–78, rpt, tr. Esther Berzosa, as 'La ambigüedad clave en *Peribáñez*, de Lope de Vega: El tema y la puesta en escena', in his *Cosmovisión*, 113–33.

opens with a night scene, and with Duke Luis carefully hiding his face behind a mask (lines 1–233). As the openings of *Hamlet*, *Macbeth*, and *El burlador de Sevilla* show, the night device was part of contemporary playwrights' stock-in-trade of symbolic or iconographical emblems for moral confusion and deceit; and this is pertinent, regardless of Varey's reminder that the *comedias* were played in daylight, night settings being indicated not by actual darkness but by costume (ladies *medio desnudas*, gentlemen *de noche*, that is, in *capa guarnecida* of red).[10] We should not miss, then, how the connotations of deceitful darkness and disguise are picked up by the first words of the play ('¡Linda burla!'), mirrored in Ricardo's *cultidiablesco* Gongorist jargon (compared to a conjurer's pulling ribbons from his mouth), and picked up in the extended metatheatrical conceit of the stage as an *espejo* of truth (by which is meant, as so often in classical usage, not a mirror but a *katoptron*, a device for reflecting a true image of a distorted original).[11] In the course of the *cuadro* the Duke receives two lectures, one from a courtesan and another from an actress: Cintia's telling speech is delivered *en alto*, from the balcony or upper stage, another visual conceit (degree o'erturned),[12] while the unseen Isabella Andreini's song wafts musically from the discovery-space *dentro* as the Duke and his pimps spy on her pruriently through the curtain ('RICARDO. Pon a esta puerta el oído', line 176; 'DUQUE. ¡Valiente acción! FEBO. Estremada', line 206), a potent image of the voyeurism which is to play so important a part in the drama, and one which will provide a chilling resonance

---

10. J. E. VAREY, 'The Staging of Night Scenes in the *comedia*', *The American Hispanist*, nr 15 (February 1977), 14–16, reworked as part of 'Valores visuales de la comedia española en la época de Calderón' in his *Cosmovisión*, 227–47 (241–45). It is nevertheless tempting to suppose that the *toldo* or awning (*vela*) which shaded the *patio* (see N. D. SHERGOLD, *A History of the Spanish Stage from Medieval Times until the End of the Seventeenth Century* (Oxford: Clarendon Press, 1967), 184, 186, 246, 400) is alluded to in Ricardo's frigid *conceptista* comparison (5–16) between the Duke's *disfraz* and the heaven's *velo* of cloaking night, 'una guarnecida capa con que se disfraza' with stars for *pasamanos* ('lace trimmings of a cape', but also the threaded rope rigging of the *vela* in the theatre). There are further useful discussions of the iconography of deceit in our play in WILSON, 'Quando Lope quiere, quiere', 157–59, and in the useful pages of Donald R. LARSON, *The Honor Plays of Lope de Vega* (Cambridge, Mass. & London: Harvard University Press, 1977), 131–58 (133).

11. The point about metatheatre is developed by William C. MCCRARY, 'The Duke and the *comedia*: Drama and Imitation in Lope's *El castigo sin venganza*', *Journal of Hispanic Philology*, 2 (1978), 203–22.

12. See, for example, the similar scene in Lope de VEGA, *Peribáñez y el comendador de Ocaña*, ed. J. M. Ruano & J. E. Varey (London: Tamesis Texts Ltd, 1980), 44 (lines 1534–1633, with the editors' comments); also VAREY, *Cosmovisión*, 227–36, 291–301.

at the other end of the play, when the Duke peers behind the same curtain to spy on another no less gripping piece of melodrama: 'DUQUE. Aquí lo veré; ya llega; | ya con la punta la pasa' (lines 2972–73).

The whole 'text' of this *cuadro*, in the extended sense I have defined above, thus reveals itself as a little masterpiece of controlled unity; dialogue combines with sound, space, blocking, and movement to convey the atmosphere of deceit and confusion. The *cuadro* which follows, the meeting of Federico and Casandra (lines 234–651), uses deliberate contrasts of setting, costume, sound-effects, and atmosphere to suggest the conceptual antithesis of the dark confusion of the opening: it takes place in a sunlit verdant country pleasance by a stream, and the four principal actors, instead of being separated by balconies or doors, fall into each others' arms (lines 340–57).[13] And yet here too, things are not what they seem: Albano wonders whether the ladies' predicament may not be a *burla* (line 334, compare line 1), and indeed the beautiful young girl whom Federico rescues turns out to be his future stepmother. The contrasts with the first *cuadro* are thus pointed by significant parallels; it is hardly fortuitous that whereas the Duke was arrested from his rake's progress by offstage singing, Federico is aroused from his reverie by the offstage 'voces' of the distressed ladies in the river (lines 323–24), or that whereas the result of the Duke's encounter is to affect him with drowsy melancholy ('Más oyera; pero estoy | sin gusto. Acostarme voy', lines 207–08), the result of Federico's is to jolt him out of drowsy melancholy ('BATÍN. Desconozco el estilo de tu gusto', line 234; 'FEDERICO. Mi disgusto | no me permite, como fuera justo, | más prisa y más cuidado; | antes la gente dejo, fatigado', lines 237–40). Hence the theme of confusion is not absent from this *cuadro*, despite its setting, and it is powerfully represented in the stagecraft by the device of having groups of actors move apart in simultaneous and secret parley at two points: «*Hablen quedo, y diga Batín*», at line 411, of Federico and Casandra, and «*Hablen los dos, y aparte Casandra y Lucrecia*», at line 581, of Federico and the Marquis).

---

13. It is debatable, of course, whether painted flats would have made visually explicit the change of mood implied by lines 242–45: 'al dosel destos árboles que . . . a las dormidas ondas deste río . . . mirando están sus copas' (by 1631 such *mutaciones* were at least possible: see for example SHERGOLD, *A History of the Spanish Stage*, 215–35 on the *corrales*, and 275–76 on Cosimo Lotti's court designs for Lope's *La selva sin amor* in 1629); but the contrast between Federico's wayfarer's costume of top-boots and travelling cape («*de camino, muy galán*») and the Duke's *disfraz* would be quite sufficient. For sunlight see 525–27 ('aquel divino crisol' is epideictic).

Again, the last *cuadro* of the Act (lines 652–993), set before a richly appointed pavilion under the walls of Ferrara – and here, at least, the text requires the actual presence of scenery in the *dosel* and thrones (at line 862), as well as «*grande acompañamiento y bizarría*» (at line 808) – marks another shift of tone and atmosphere, one well summed up by the stage direction «*Todos se entran con grandes cumplimientos*» (at line 926): the showy and deceitful pomp of the court is embodied in sight and sound by the rich costumes and music, by the elaborate stage-business and gesture of ritual bowing, etiquette, precedence, and protocol ('Dadme ... los brazos', lines 836–37; 'Sentaos ... ¿No se sienta el Conde?', lines 858 and 862; 'primero | ... os ha de besar la mano. | Perdonad, que no consiento | esa humildad', lines 863–66; 'CASANDRA. Teneos. FEDERICO. No lo mandéis. | Tres veces, señora, beso | vuestra mano ... | CASANDRA. De tan obediente cuello | sean cadena mis brazos', lines 870–72, 887–88), and by the glittering gold chain which the Duke ceremoniously hands Batín as the *albricia* for his message-bearing (line 807).

To appreciate the structure of Act I even at the most elementary level, then, we can hardly confine our analysis to the dialogue; we must study the dramatic totality of the text, and also its 'scenic form'.[14] The bedrock of scenic form, and the fundamental concern of the dramatic critic, is the question of who is on stage during a scene; it would not be far from the mark to affirm that the study of exits and entrances is the first and indispensable operation of all dramatic criticism. I have already suggested examples of the importance of this topic in my remarks on the Marquis's exit to kill Federico in line 2996, and of the secret parleys in the second *cuadro* of Act I. Another small illustration may throw light on Batín's famous remark, towards the end of the last act, that the Duke is a 'santo fingido' (line 2800). The line has been taken, notably by May in his remarkable article, to show that Ferrara's conversion is a hypocritical fake, and consequently to support the notion that the Duke is the real villain of the play.[15] What seems to me to be important about the context of the line, however, is that it occurs just after the climactic scene where the

---

14. I borrow the term from Emrys JONES, *Scenic Form in Shakespeare* (Oxford: Clarendon Press, 1971).

15. T. E. MAY, 'Lope de Vega's *El castigo sin venganza*: The Idolatry of the Duke of Ferrara', *Bulletin of Hispanic Studies*, 37 (1960), 154–82, rpt in his *Wit of the Golden Age: Articles on Spanish Literature*, Teatro del Siglo de Oro: Estudios de Literatura 2 (Kassel: Reichenberger, 1986), 154–84.

Duke has been spying on Casandra and Federico, who in turn have been arguing wretchedly about the latter's plan to end their affair by staging a marriage with Aurora (lines 2720–29). As these characters exit there is a pregnant pause and the stage is momentarily empty (line 2775). Enter Aurora herself, and Batín with her, secretly negotiating behind his master Federico's back for a change of situation because he has heard that Aurora is to marry the Marquis of Mantua. The two are alone; Batín wishes to wheedle Aurora into taking him with her to Mantua because he is aggrieved at the lack of prospects of advancement in his present employment in Ferrara:

> BATÍN.   Servir mucho y medrar poco
> es un linaje de agravio
> que al más cuerdo, que al más sabio
> o le mata, o vuelve loco.
> . . .
> Fuera desto, está endiablado
> el Conde: no sé qué tiene;
> . . .
> La Duquesa, pues, también
> insufrible y desigual;
> . . .
> El Duque, santo fingido,
> consigo a solas hablando,
> como hombre que anda buscando
> algo que se le ha perdido.
>
> (lines 2784–2803)

As Wilson remarks (178), this speech is 'rich in innuendoes'; Batín is a devious character, and Aurora, as we have seen, is not a simple one. What is certain is that Batín is not speaking straight: he knows what has bewitched his master the Count and made the Duchess moody, and he must suspect that Aurora knows it too, else why her marriage to Mantua, and why his request to enter her employ? As for the Duke, Batín is well aware of the *algo* which makes him behave like a sleep-walker – so much is clear from the insinuating *double entendre* of his earlier conversation with the still unsuspecting Duke on the very subject of the relationship between his wife and son (lines 2401–66: note especially 'BATÍN. No se ha visto, que yo sepa, | tan pacífica madrastra | con su alnado: es muy discreta | y muy virtuosa y santa', lines 2416–19). But that dialogue in turn, we will recall, follows immediately on Ricardo's

announcement, 'el Duque es un santo ya' (line 2362). If Batín greets this with
his accustomed cynicism ('la que es gata será gata, | la que es perra, será
perra, | in secula seculorum', lines 2389–91), the context has made it clear
that his doubts refer not so much to the Duke's conversion itself – there is no
suggestion that he will return to his whoring ('RICARDO. ... que traemos
otro Duque: | ya no hay damas, ya no hay cenas, | ya no hay broqueles ni
espadas, | ya solamente se acuerda | de Casandra', lines 2357–61) – as to
the new and dreadful situation which is likely to convert him, in spite of his
unexpected uxoriousness, into something far worse than he was before.
Hence, when the Duke, still unaware, cheerily informs Batín of his reformed
life, the wily *gracioso*'s retort is to express pious wonder at this 'miracle' that
can turn a duke into a Camaldolese monk (lines 2443–48), and to end with a
dark (and, as he and the spectators already know, hopeless) prayer that
heaven reward his services to the commonwealth with eternal fame (lines
2462–66).

Between that conversation and the one where Batín calls the Duke a 'santo
fingido' comes, as I have said, the Duke's reading of the anonymous letter, his
spying, and his decision to plot a secret but final solution (lines 2744–59).
But Batín is not party to this (he exits at line 2466), even if his description of
the Duke 'consigo a solas hablando, | como hombre que anda buscando |
algo' and of the whole house as lost (lines 2801–04) shows that he knows the
crisis is about to break. Surely, therefore, all he now means by calling the
Duke a feigning (not counterfeit) saint is that the man's ominous patience and
affability is just a lull before the storm.[16]

My point is that the complex entrances and exits in these linked and interweaving dialogues of intrigue serve to build up a tense atmosphere of lowering
catastrophe and pervasive dramatic irony (in the strict sense that the audience, and some of the characters, know things which make what is said untrue
or only partially true). Hence the function of the secret interview of Aurora
and Batín in lines 2776–2810 is not to show us that Batín has some special
knowledge about the sincerity of the Duke's conversion, but the opposite: to
show that nobody quite knows what is going on or what the others are think-

---

16. It may be another argument for not laying too much weight on the words 'El duque,
santo fingido' that Lope first wrote 'El duque, ymaginativo' (VAN DAM, *ed. cit.*, 268, note *ad
loc.*). In his note *ad loc.*, KOSSOFF cites *Dicc. Autoridades*, VI (1739), 43b, 'SANTO. Se toma
muchas veces por sencillo, poco avisado, ù omisso para sí ', to argue that *santo fingido* means
no more than 'pretending not to know what is going on'.

ing, but that each is conscious of an impending doom, which in Batín's case produces an irresistible urge to be somewhere else. It may be true that the Duke's conversion is hypocritical, but if it is Batín does not know it – and neither, for that matter, do we. If a dramatic speech worked like a piece of narrative, we should be justified in asking whether what it said cast light on the story at other points; but in fact a dramatic speech is not a narrative, but something which a character says in a particular scene, so that why it is said, and to whom, are no less important to the meaning – and often much more important – than what it says. The sincerity of the Duke's conversion is a question which neither the dialogue under discussion nor any other scene in the play is designed to address, and one which the context of Batín and Aurora's dialogue renders impertinent.

These, then, are some of the things which reading the play as a play will involve: attention to the special pragmatics of dramatic dialogue and its difference from everyday discourse, sensitivity to the visual and spatial mechanics of the full dramatic text, and a care to grasp the architecture and structure of the play (as a whole and in its parts) through the dynamics of scenic form. In coming thus far, I have tried to illustrate, through my examples, the ways in which a dramatic critique tends to cut free from a purely anagogical moral reading, and to defeat the inductive programme of the thematic approach; if nothing else, it appears to reveal some important formal differences between a play and a theological treatise. We are in a position to appreciate the significance of Pring-Mill's remark to the effect that Lope sought, in *El castigo sin venganza*, to illustrate the moral issues proposed by the title 'with at least as great a concern for its theatrical as for its moral potentialities'.

Now, if we press forward with a dramatic criticism of *El castigo sin venganza*, and particularly of its scenic form, one feature of the play is bound to strike us. It is a well-known fact that MSS and early printed editions of Golden-Age plays (and in this case we are fortunate enough to have both an authorial autograph and a *suelta* first edition overseen by the author) did not indicate scene divisions; and modern editors rightly spurn the lamentable practice of lumbering the text with artificial divisions at each entry or exit.[17]

---

17. Albert E. SLOMAN, 'Scene Division in Calderón's *Alcalde de Zalamea*', *Hispanic Review*, 19 (1951), 66–71, traces the latter practice back to Hartzenbusch. As JONES notes in his introduction to *El castigo sin venganza* (*ed. cit.*, 5), 'nineteenth-century editions . . . produced divisions which were artificial and inappropriate. Entries and exits were indicated in Lope's manuscript by the placing of a cross in the margin as well as by stage directions, and usually

For the purpose of analysing scenic form, therefore, it falls to the critic to determine correctly the internal articulation of each *jornada* into *cuadros*. Luckily, this is an easy matter: for a scene may be defined as beginning every time actors enter an empty stage, and ending when the stage is left (not necessarily by the same actors) empty once again. I have already analysed Act I in this way: the first *cuadro* is defined by the entry and exit of the Duke and his servants at line 1 and line 233 respectively, and takes place in the streets of Ferrara (even though no stage directions indicate either their exit or the setting); the second *cuadro* by the riverside begins with the entry of Federico and Batín in line 234 (though the word *Salen* appears neither in the MS nor in the *suelta*), and the stage is not cleared again until line 651 (although once again there is no indication of an exit in the MS, and no fewer than seven further characters and an accompaniment of *criados* have entered and exited in the course of the *cuadro*); and the last *cuadro* under the walls of Ferrara begins when the Duke and Aurora enter the empty stage at line 651, and does not end until Federico and Batín leave the stage at the conclusion of the Act. It is true that each of these divisions is marked by a change of verse form, but this is not the determining factor; what matters is the pause marked by the clearing of the stage, and this pause can indicate, as in the present cases, both a change of setting and a passage of time. The resultant *cuadros* have a structure and shape which can be analysed, whereas the old method of marking scene-divisions at every entrance and exit reduces the present Act to an arbitrary chaos of seventeen meaningless fragments.

Now the remarkable feature of scenic construction in *El castigo sin venganza*, if we apply our criterion to Acts II and III, is that in all the two thousand remaining lines of the play there are only two places where the stage is cleared: the end of Act II itself (line 2030), and the moment just before the final denouement which we have already examined, when Federico and Casandra leave the stage before Aurora and Batín's secret interview («*Vanse los dos*», at line 2775). That is to say, the whole of Act II is a single *cuadro*; it takes place in a single room within the palace and in a single sinuous stream of interlocking time and movement. Likewise the last Act may be considered

---

coincide with a change of verse-form'. On the MS (Boston Public Library, Ticknor Collection D.174.19) and *suelta* (Barcelona: Pedro Lacavalleria, 1634, in Madrid, Biblioteca Nacional R.4021) see VAN DAM's edition; also useful for study of Lope's use of the marginal cross and stage directions is Henryk ZIOMEK, *A Paleographic Edition of Lope de Vega's Autograph Play «La Nueua Victoria de D. Gonzalo de Cordoua»* (New York: Hispanic Institute in the United States, 1962).

as a single movement, for when the stage is left empty at line 2775 there is no change of setting or time (the break between Acts II and III, by contrast, indicates the passage of four months); the moment is thus more in the nature of a pause than a real division of *cuadros*. In other words this Act, too, takes place within the selfsame room in the palace, and it too preserves a strict classical unity of time.

The articulation of these two Acts into what are in effect single *cuadros* is, I believe, almost unparalleled.[18] The scale of Lope's conception in *El castigo sin venganza* certainly makes the longest scene in Shakespeare, the 600-line 'pastoral' in *A Winter's Tale*, look modest – and English critics have usually treated that as a unique and baggy monster. If Lope, therefore, at the very height of his powers and experience decided to abandon any division of his last two Acts, relinquishing the opportunities which discrete *cuadros* offer for spacing climaxes and contrasting atmospheres (as we saw them doing in Act I), we are entitled to ask the reason why.

Lope's purpose becomes clear, I believe, if we examine the scenic form of the two acts in detail. The exits and entrances are contrived, as I have said, to confine the whole action to a single room in the palace at Ferrara. Observe what happens. When Casandra and her confidante Lucrecia enter, at the beginning of Act II (line 994), they are privately discussing the Duke's scandalous behaviour; he has spent only a single night in his new bride's bed, and has now gone back to his old libertine ways. Casandra is most unhappy. But these intimate confidences are interrupted by the entry of the Duke himself, who is in private conversation with Federico and Batín (line 1114). The ladies, note, are still present; but the Duke studiously ignores them ('CASANDRA. Aun apenas el Duque me ha mirado', line 1132). When Casandra does leave, the three men are left alone for a confidential talk on Federico's marriage to his cousin Aurora (line 1138); when the Duke exits in anger (line 1195), Federico and Batín are left for a confabulation of their own. They are still talking on stage when Casandra re-enters, this time in conference with Aurora about her relationship with Federico (lines 1248–95). Once again, this second pair does not notice the first until Aurora leaves and Casandra catches sight of Federico moving across the stage (line 1296). Batín is dismissed, leaving the two lovers alone for the ironic tête-à-tête in which

---

18.   There is something similar in the first act of Calderón's *El alcalde de Zalamea*, but the effect is less striking because scenic form is not strictly bound by unity of place and time, as shown by SLOMAN, 'Scene division', 67–69, and because there are two cleared stages.

each tries to conceal the truth from the other by talking, once again, about Aurora (lines 1315–1531). When Federico rushes desperately from the stage, unable to keep up the pretence, Casandra stays to deliver her Euripidean monologue (lines 1531–91), but she is interrupted by Aurora and also exits emotionally.

And so it goes on: when Rutilio and the Marquis enter at line 1618 Aurora is still on stage although they do not notice her at once ('MARQUÉS. Calla, Rutilio, que aquí | está Aurora', lines 1621–22). An even more remarkable example of blocking occurs when the Duke, Federico, and Batín re-enter in line 1682: they speak for some moments, but when the Duke stamps off, Batín points out to Federico that Aurora and the Marquis have been present in private conversation throughout ('Mientras con el duque hablaste, | he reparado en que Aurora, | sin hacer caso de ti, | con el Marqués habla a solas', lines 1709–12). From lines 1715–47 these two pairs of actors are on opposite sides of the stage, not communicating, but observing each other's conversation (this elaborate stage-business is helped by the use of a striking prop, Aurora's *banda* or favour, which can be flaunted for Federico's benefit; and Aurora is given an aside to the audience in lines 1722–23 to make the nature of her deception clear). When Aurora and the Marqués at last move off to the garden (line 1747), Batín and Federico remain; when Batín leaves, Federico delivers his famous sonnet monologue '¿Qué buscas, imposible pensamiento?', and Casandra enters at line 1811 without noticing him to deliver her monologue in *quintillas*. It is only when the two catch sight of each other across the stage ('Éste es el conde, ¡Ay de mí!', line 1856; 'Ya viene aquí | desnuda la dulce espada | por quien la vida perdí', lines 1858–60) that the scene is finally set for the climax of their long-delayed embrace.

We need not extend this inquiry to follow every twist and turn of Act III, several parts of which have been discussed already.[19] Suffice it to say the unique scenic form of the two acts, with their constant interweaving of exits and entrances, has been contrived as a sort of complicated charade: groups of characters merge and dissolve, ignoring each other, overhearing each other,

---

19. The analysis is simpler than Act II: only note that in lines 2141–60 Aurora and the Marquis remain in the background when Federico and Batín enter, as in the parallel scene in Act II, so that Federico may angrily catch sight of them in line 2161; and that the Duke is left alone in line 2467 to make his awful discovery among the papers (from which he is disturbed by none other than Federico, line 2552), has a further monologue at lines 2612–35, re-enters «asechando», backstage and unseen, to spy on Federico and Casandra at line 2707, and has a last monologue at lines 2834–2914. The rest is straightforward.

play-acting to each other, spying on each other, fencing and lying and plotting with each other. The whole is a concrete visual icon which extends the themes of deceit and confusion which we saw already adumbrated in Act I; each individual is trying to size up the others, trusting some, distrusting others, sometimes left alone to express real thoughts, sometimes putting up elaborate fronts. The confessional monologues are vital for the effect: juxtaposed with the complex dumbshows of the ensemble scenes, they serve to flesh out the theme of deceit by the contrast of public and private emotion. This, then, is the court: an elaborate and gilded sham of confusions, lies, and treachery.[20]

But the fact that all this happens in a single room adds a further and vital dimension which takes us forward from the atmosphere of Act I. It is no mistake that Casandra sets the tone at the very start of Act II by comparing the brooding and shuttered atmosphere of the palace to the carefree openness of a peasant's cottage where the sun shines through the cracks in the wall on a couple happily entwined in their humble bed (lines 997–1023); or that later she calls it a prison ('el Árgel de su palacio', line 1383). By abolishing all scenic divisions in the two last acts, Lope has created a notable dramatic metaphor of claustrophobia, a theatrical Cretan labyrinth. And what is the Minotaur that lurks at its centre? May's answer was that the monster is the Duke, but the scenic form of the play (quite apart from the Duke's absence after 1708, which is unnecessary for the plot) suggests more powerfully that it is no single person, but an awful secret which entraps all the characters in its toils: the unspeakable passion of incest. The audience knows, of course, that Federico and Casandra will become lovers from the second *cuadro* of Act I, where they have already seen the pair in each other's arms («*Federico sale con Casandra en los brazos*», at line 339), and from Batín's broad hints (e.g. lines 977–91); and the progress of their disastrous passion is charted by a simple but effective visual conceit, the progression from kneeling to kissing hands, from that to embracing, and from that to kissing on the lips, from the most formal *tratamiento* to the most intimate.[21]

---

20. McCRARY, 'The Duke and the *comedia*', noted this connexion between scenic form and the expression of, as he puts it, 'chaos and demoralization': 'Federico, Casandra, and Aurora literally wander around, come and go with little sense of purpose and direction . . . creating fictitious roles which are either unwanted, or created to conceal' (211). In a note he adds: 'The second act . . . is essentially one long scene located in the palace. The absence of traditional smaller dramatic units effectively generates a sense of uncoordinated activity seeking unknown purposes.'

21. WILSON has an excellent analysis, 'Quando Lope quiere, quiere', 165–66. As soon as

The question that concerns me here, however, is not to chart further the devices of the playwright's stagecraft, but to ask whether the particular scenic form of these acts is truly designed to raise those minute moral concerns about the individual characters which the anagogical-thematic approach would seek to determine. Are we really tempted, when Aurora uses the ancient trick of *el desdén con el desdén*, to reflect how a casuist might judge her in the confessional? More pertinently, are we supposed to be drawing up the charge-sheet against Federico and Casandra? My contention is that the scenic form does not invite us to do so, and even that it strongly conspires to prevent us from doing so. What the seamless, unpausing action of Acts II and III makes us see instead is a situation which emerges from, and is carried along by, the particular confusions and intricacies of the circumstantial action. The lovers' surrender to their passion at the end of Act II is immoral, certainly, and they know and confess it to be so – hence the drama of their prolonged and desperate struggle to resist its onslaught; but the point that Lope seems to be making, first by the setting of the pastoral second *cuadro* of Act I and then by the skilfully managed pace and atmosphere of Act II, is that the passion is also natural ('BATÍN. ¿No era mejor para ti | esta clavellina fresca, | esta naranja en azar . . .? | ¡Pesia las leyes del mundo!', lines 638–44), and that the lovers' surrender to it is not the result of a latent criminal streak or radically immoral bias in their characters so much as the tragic outcome of the

---

the two young people recover from the spontaneous proximity of rescue from the river and realize their true relationship (lines 366–95) their physical attitudes to each other become fraught with formality and peril: Federico drops Casandra from his arms, falls to his knees, and asks to kiss her hand as son and vassal ('dé la mano . . . Vuestra Alteza', lines 396–402 – with a rapid change of *tratamiento* from *vos*), while she insists on embracing him as a mother ('Dadme los brazos', ignoring his change of *tratamiento*, line 407). But she will not give her hand and he will not give his embrace, so they stand off with only a heartfelt look ('El alma os dé la respuesta', lines 408–11). The same farce is re-enacted before the Duke in the last *cuadro* of Act I, with notable excess of courtly hyperbole (lines 862–88); and the whole action of Act II may be said to be nothing but the inevitable crescendo of this *mano* vs *brazos* conceit, Casandra leading in what she assumes is merely a flirtatious game to flout her husband (e.g. lines 1296–1310, where she already calls Federico *tú*), until the powder-keg blows up in her face (Federico accuses her of leading him on, and simultaneously uses *tú* for the first time, lines 1520–31 – and note Casandra's horror at seeing how far beyond her control the game has run, and how dangerous it has become to herself, in the following monologue, lines 1532–91). From here on, Federico is the one to force the pace, so that when Casandra tries to draw back from the brink he can once again ask, in a parody of the courtly usage, for her hand in leavetaking ('Sola una mano suplico | que me des; dame el veneno | que me ha muerto', lines 2006–08), knowing that she is powerless to refuse this, or any part of herself. I cannot agree with Wilson (169) that at the end of all this the two exit by separate doors; the whole logic demands that they swoon, embrace, and kiss (lines 2021–25).

hothouse intrigues of the imprisoning court, whose intertwined deceits conspire to throw them together. The emotion which Act II is designed to produce in the theatre is not moral disapproval, but pity and horror.[22]

If this analysis is correct, the incest of Federico and Casandra is not a theme which is supposed to admit of simple moral judgment; and this in turn suggests that their murder in the denouement can hardly be presented as an example of poetic justice. This point has been generally agreed, especially since Parker turned the search for a moral scapegoat upon the Duke; but, though we may accept that Ferrara is no less responsible for what happens than the others, and that 'at the end . . . his life lies in ruins around him', does this have to be his 'punishment' for anything?[23] Parker asserts that 'in interpreting the theme of a play we must not rely on comments, or presume that what any character may say necessarily represents the dramatist's opinion' (18), which is true, but disingenuous; it invites us to suppose that the dramatist has an 'opinion', an unexamined and gratuitous assumption, and also calls upon us to imagine an audience which, though confronted with insistent repetitions of the word *castigo* from the moment of the Duke's discovery of the crime (line 2747; compare lines 2836, 2842, 2854, 2886, 2898, 3012, 3014, and 3019), nevertheless remains undistracted by the rushing alarums on stage, the howls of the dying from behind the curtain, and the climactic discovery of the lovers' corpses, delivering itself up instead to the cool calculus of blame and relishing the infantile conceit of a *castigo* which has nothing to do with these things, but is somehow being inflicted on the punisher.

Faced with such propositions, one can only wonder, with Pring-Mill, 'whether the full range of such equivocation could possibly be appreciated in

---

22. I find wholly convincing the argument of Amado ALONSO, 'Lope de Vega y sus fuentes', *Thesaurus: Boletín del Instituto Caro y Cuervo* (Bogotá), 8 (1952), 1–24, rpt in José Francisco GATTI (ed.), *El teatro de Lope de Vega: Artículos y estudios* (Buenos Aires: Eudeba, 1962), 193–218, who shows by a comparison with the source in Bandello that Lope tones down any moral outrage against the characters by his finely-drawn account of their gradual surrender. Alonso also takes the view that the Duke's papal campaigns and change of heart are designed to 'cerrar a la parcialidad del público todas las salidas', so that by the end we may feel sympathy for all the parties and hence recognize 'en cada palabra y en cada paso la voz y los pasos implacables de la tragedia' (212 of the rpt).

23. A. A. PARKER, *The Approach to the Spanish Drama of the Golden Age*, 2nd edn, Diamante 6 (London: Hispanic & Luso-Brazilian Councils, 1971), 16–19 (first published in 1957). PRING-MILL, *Five Plays*, xxxii–xxxiii, is broadly in agreement, though with an important qualification to be mentioned in a moment; so too are MAY, 'Lope de Vega's *El castigo sin venganza*', and LARSON, *The Honor Plays*.

the theater' (*Five Plays*, xxxvi). Far more reasonable is Pring-Mill's own suggestion, that the whole action (dramatic text and scenic form) comes to rest at the end upon the conflict between justice and vengeance expressed by the play's title. That conflict lays upon the Duke a terrible dilemma: an inescapable duty of punishment, and an absolute interdiction against vengeance – the equal impossibility of acting out of hate, or of refusing to act out of love. It will be recalled that the melodramatic trick by which the denouement is accomplished is Lope's own invention, deliberately contrived (in Bandello the executions are public and judicial); the carefully constructed atmosphere of deceit within the play seems designed to show that such an ending is inevitable, that it is everybody's fault, and that each must bear their own portion of the blame.[24] As Pring-Mill's subtle and intricate analysis of the multiple ironies in the Duke's secret solution implies, there is no simple justice, poetic or otherwise; no restoration of order, but only the tragedy of human error and weakness. If we are to be moved by all this, it is not by sitting in judgment on the characters, but by relating the events 'outward to the framework by . . . analogical correspondences' – which, in one sense at least, means entering the theatrical life of the play, sympathizing with the people in it, and realizing that, but for the grace of God, there go we. Or, to put it another way, it means taking this 'individual drama' – no general paraphrase or moral summary – not as a peg for anagogical theodicies, but, as the epilogue invites us to do, as an *asombro* and an *ejemplo*.

JEREMY LAWRANCE

University of Manchester

---

24. This is also the conclusion, reached by different routes, of ALONSO, 'Lope de Vega y sus fuentes', JONES ('all the three main characters [are] clearly guilty yet worthy of the sympathy and understanding which Lope accords them', *ed. cit.,* 9; 'the play, then, is a "raro caso" demonstrating human behaviour . . . with a considerable measure of impartiality', 14) and WILSON, 'Quando Lope quiere, quiere', 182–83 ('Lope's treatment of the whole subject is detached. He does not apologise for Duke, Count or Duchess; here, he says, is what happens when we do not recognise the confusions and deceptions that lie around us . . . Vanity of vanities, all is vanity').

CALDERÓN'S *LA VIDA ES SUEÑO*:
A MORE THEATRICAL APPROACH

IT IS WITH SOME FEAR that I venture into the well-charted territory of a play generally thought to be the greatest of all Golden-Age dramas, and described in one recent study as 'la obra más discutida del teatro español'.[1] Fear turns to trepidation in the knowledge that Robert Pring-Mill has himself so keenly analysed and carried forward the work of English-speaking *calderonistas*.[2] But, as his successor at St Catherine's, it seemed perhaps appropriate that my own tribute to him for this volume should follow in his footsteps. It has been principally inspired by the experience of teaching undergraduates, through following his own example of close attention to text. It contains no radical new interpretation of the play, nor does it seek to overturn the work of other critics. But there would be no point in approaching *La vida es sueño* if I did not feel that in so much excellent work that has been done on this play, some-thing is missing – the dimension of theatre.

Critics often mention the theatricality of Calderón's plays, though they rarely explore its implications. One of the most recent editions, which I shall use here, wavers between reader and audience in a way which rather uncom-fortably but bravely tries to acknowledge the experience of both.[3] Though Morón Arroyo writes (18) of a 'serie de alusiones que el lector debe recordar en su lectura consiguiente' in the opening scene, he also (23) acknowledges that 'empobreceríamos la obra si no pusiéramos de relieve esos elementos

1. Kurt REICHENBERGER & Juventino CAMINERO, *Calderón dramaturgo*, Teatro del Siglo de Oro: Estudios de Literatura 8 (Kassel: Reichenberger, 1991), 44.

2. See his 'Los calderonistas de habla inglesa y *La vida es sueño*: Métodos de análisis temático-estructural', in *Litterae Hispanae et Lusitanae: Zum Fünfzigjährigen Bestehen des Ibero-Amerikanischen Forschungsinstituts der Universität Hamburg*, ed. Hans FLASCHE (Munich: Max Hueber, 1968), 369–413, and 'La «victoria del hado» en *La vida es sueño*', in *Hacia Calderón: Coloquio Anglogermano, Exeter 1969*, ed. Alexander A. PARKER & Hans FLASCHE, Calderoniana 6 (Berlin: Walter de Gruyter & Co., 1970), 53–70.

3. *La vida es sueño*, ed. Ciriaco MORÓN ARROYO, Letras Hispánicas 57 (Madrid: Cátedra, 1991).

teatrales y la redujéramos a la pura tesis filosófica o teológica'. He deals with
some of these elements, notably Rosaura's sword and the portrait of her
Astolfo has in his possession (41–42), but prefers to argue about the possible
Freudian significance of the first than to follow up his assertion that it
'permite al auditorio conocer el secreto que Rosaura ignora' (42), and devotes
just five lines to the second. Paul Julian Smith, rejecting Parker's hierarchical
vision, writes of how drama offers direct access to the visual and material
presence of the human body sought in vain by readers of lyric, and stresses
both the fact that the actor (unlike the author) is present to the audience and
the subversive nature of 'drama as institution'.[4] But his concerns are more
theoretical and do not directly engage with how a particular moment in a play
might be performed. Nor do I mean theatricality quite in the sense in which
Cascardi uses the idea, as he seeks to reclaim the Calderón who creates illusions on stage from the Calderón who is read primarily as a dramatist who
treats great metaphysical themes. His chapter on *La vida es sueño* is more
concerned with the deceptive illusions of a Basilio and the way in which, on
the other hand, 'the self-aware use of illusion is one of the keys to the process
of healthy social self-imagining'.[5]

    One branch of critical study has taken theatre seriously and has yielded
much valuable information about the way in which Calderón's plays were
staged, and although scholars have been reluctant to move from stage design
into questions of interpretation, their findings do assist the process of imagining the play as performance.[6] In particular, John Varey has drawn attention to

----

4. Paul Julian SMITH, *Writing in the Margin: Spanish Literature of the Golden Age* (Oxford:
Clarendon Press, 1988), esp. 127–29 (128).

5. Anthony J. CASCARDI, *The Limits of Illusion: A Critical Study of Calderón*, Cambridge
Iberian and Latin-American Studies (Cambridge: Cambridge University Press, 1984), 13.

6. See J. M. RUANO DE LA HAZA, 'The Staging of Calderón's *La vida es sueño* and *La dama
duende*', *Bulletin of Hispanic Studies*, 64 (1987), 51–63, which revises Norman D. SHERGOLD,
'*La vida es sueño*: Ses acteurs, son théâtre et son public', in *Dramaturgie et Société: Rapports
entre l'oeuvre théâtrale, son interprétation, et son public aux XVIe et XVIIe siècles, Nancy, 14–21
avril 1967*, ed. Jean Jacquot, 2 vols (Paris: CNRS, 1968), I, 93–109. He writes (58): 'Calderón
maximized the visual impact of his play while at the same time reinforcing some of its key
symbols. Text and staging are thus seen to complement rather than hinder one another.' But
this conclusion is left tantalizingly undeveloped. The most recent contributions are from John
E. VAREY, '«Sale en lo alto de un monte»: Un problema escenográfico', in *Hacia Calderón:
Octavo Coloquio Anglogermano, Bochum 1987*, ed. Hans Flasche (Stuttgart: Franz Steiner,
1988), 162–72; and John J. ALLEN, 'Staging', in *The Prince in the Tower: Perceptions of «La
vida es sueño»*, ed. Frederick A. de ARMAS (Lewisburg: Bucknell University Press & London
and Toronto: Associated University Presses, 1993), 27–38.

the fact that local bye-laws demanded that plays be staged during daylight hours, which had implications for the way scenes in darkness were played. These could be indicated to the audience through the actors' words and dress (e.g. black cloaks), but also through hesitant and stumbling movements to simulate darkness. The inner stage or 'discovery space', both by its position at the back of the stage and by its orientation, away from the sun, could make a particularly effective contrast to the broad daylight elsewhere. He points out how setting, staging, and dress frequently gave visible representation to the more abstract elements in the drama, and calls for a greater emphasis on them as part of a critical approach to Golden-Age theatre.[7]

I am not here so much concerned with the status of *La vida es sueño* as a text to be read or the search for a coherent theme which will bring the extraordinary richness and allusiveness of the story it dramatizes into some kind of unity as with developing a new sensitivity to certain details which seem to me fundamental to the theatrical experience of the play and therefore to the way we might encourage our students to approach it. I am concerned with questions which might interest the would-be director or the actor engaged in creating the illusion of objective reality on stage, and with how this is communicated to an audience, for whom reading the play as text is at best a secondary activity. And therein lies a dilemma. To read a play first and foremost as if it were a novel, a poem, or a treatise is to put the cart before the horse.[8]

---

7. John E. VAREY, 'Valores visuales en la comedia española en la época de Calderón', in *Edad de Oro*, V, ed. Pablo Jauralde Pou (Madrid: Ediciones de la Universidad Autónoma de Madrid, 1986), 271–97; 'The Use of Costume in Some Plays of Calderón', in *Calderón and the Baroque Tradition*, ed. Kurt Levy, Jesús Ara, and Gethlin Hughes (Waterloo, Ontario: Wilfrid Laurier University Press, 1985), 109–18; and 'Cavemen in Calderón (and some Cavewomen)', in *Approaches to the Theater of Calderón*, ed. Michael D. McGaha (Washington, DC: University Press of America, 1982), 231–47. All three studies are reprinted (the last two, in translations by Esther Berzosa, as 'Calderón y sus trogloditas' and 'La indumentaria en el teatro de Calderón'), in VAREY, *Cosmovisión y escenografía: El teatro español en el Siglo de Oro*, Nueva Biblioteca de Erudición y Crítica 2 (Madrid: Castalia, 1987), 227–47, 249–61, and 263–72 (see esp. 232–33, 237–38, 252–53, 266–68).

8. A searching analysis of a similar dilemma facing students of the English stage is provided in three articles by the American scholar Richard LEVIN: 'Some Second Thoughts on Central Themes', *Modern Language Review*, 67 (1972), 1–10; 'Third Thoughts on Thematics', *Modern Language Review*, 70 (1975), 481–96; and 'Performance-Critics vs Close Readers in the Study of English Renaissance Drama', *Modern Language Review*, 81 (1986), 545–59. Robert PRING-MILL has himself published analyses of plays which take into consideration the staged or acted dimension: see, especially 'La estructura de *El gran teatro del mundo*', in *Hacia Calderón: Séptimo Coloquio Anglogermano, Cambridge 1984*, ed. Hans Flasche, Archivum Calderonianum 3 (Wiesbaden & Stuttgart: Franz Steiner, 1985), 110–45 (131–42).

But given that very few of us (myself included) have any experience of theatrical production, how are we to encourage ourselves and our undergraduates to read the drama we study as a text which needs to be brought to life on the stage so that the audience can suspend disbelief and enter the illusion?

Calderón's plays tell stories, contain fine poetry, and may have important things to say about the human condition. But the specifically theatrical elements, such as dress, stage settings and directions, and the modulations of speech, the movements and even gestures of the actors which have to be imagined when we read a play, ought not to be left out of consideration. If we make some effort to follow the clues the dramatist has given us, words which speed by on the page when it is read, whether a brief phrase or exclamation, or the nuances of delivery within a longer speech, can yield fresh insight into the significance of the moment. It is difficult, but worthwhile, to try to read a play as performance, hearing the words spoken at different speeds and volumes, or imagining pauses and silences unmarked in the text, which can have a profound effect on the audience's reaction. Sometimes, too, the visible world of the stage will be in harmony with the words its inhabitants utter; but, at other times, what the audience hears and what it sees will exist in a state of ambiguity or contradiction which may pass a reader by.

If we begin as readers looking for themes and for coherence, we may find ourselves constructing philosophical, theological, or psychological interpretations which will come to govern our reading and especially our re-readings, and we may become so concerned with fitting the play into these extra-dramatic issues that we miss many of the most telling nuances within it. The issue was clearly grasped with regard to the honour plays by my old tutor Cyril Jones, whose pioneering work suggested that Calderón was more concerned with exploring the dramatic possibilities of the extreme situations the conventions of the honour code could be used to produce than he was with constructing a moral critique of them.[9] Two recent interpretations, for example, have looked at the play in the context of contemporary Polish history or have connected it with the breaking of the closed circle of predetermined events which is so much a part of Calderón's mythological plays, while the latest collection of essays on *La vida es sueño* offers a variety of contemporary theoreti-

---

9. Especially C. A. JONES, '*Honor* in Spanish Golden-Age Drama: Its Relation to Real Life and to Morals', *Bulletin of Hispanic Studies*, 35 (1958), 199–210, and 'Spanish Honour as Historical Phenomenon, Convention, and Artistic Motive', *Hispanic Review*, 33 (1965), 32–39.

cal approaches.[10] Hence the emphasis on themes – predestination and free will, the nature of reality, the autonomy of the individual, moral and ethical choices, kingship and rebellion, sons and fathers – or the proliferation of scholarly studies of style and versification, background, sources, and parallels.

I do not wish for a moment to suggest that these or their many predecessors are fruitless exercises. They have all enriched our reading of Calderón. All I suggest is that alongside them there is room for another approach, one which begins with the audience as the play begins and with what it sees and hears on perhaps the only occasion it attends a performance of *La vida es sueño*. As drama the play must work immediately and without assumption of repetition.[11] However, it would be disingenuous to suppose that a would-be producer does not have some overall interpretation of the play as theatre in mind, in order that each detail can contribute to the desired overall effect. I shall therefore look at a number of moments which seem to me to illustrate this more theatrical approach, and then turn to the beginning of the play.

There are many examples in the play of moments which pose problems of interpretation for director and actor; that is, when Calderón's rhetoric is taken seriously as a text to be acted. I remember precisely why I first insisted on this in tutorials: a sense of frustration at the repeated failure of undergraduates to hear the arguments Segismundo has with himself when responding to Rosaura's plea in Act III for him to restore her honour. Rather than respond to her directly, he questions himself on the significance of this moment in the light of his previous struggles to distinguish between illusory and real experience. His first reaction is, as before, to take advantage of the situation and possess her (lines 2950–65), but he suddenly checks himself when he realizes that earlier dreams turned sour: 'Esto es sueño, y pues lo es, | soñemos dichas agora, | que después serán pesares' (lines 2964–66). Unless the reader pauses after line 2965, when Segismundo is still in the grip of sexual temptation, and follows him as he draws a conclusion which calls into question what he has just decided, a significant moment of change, marked textually only by a comma, but in performance by a quite different

---

10. G. A. DAVIES, 'Poland, Politics, and *La vida es sueño*', *Bulletin of Hispanic Studies*, 70 (1993), 147–63; Teresa S. SOUFAS, '*La vida es sueño* as Forerunner of Calderón's Mythological Dramas', *Bulletin of Hispanic Studies*, 70 (1993), 293–303; ARMAS (ed.), *The Prince in the Tower, passim*.

11. It would have been unusual in any case for a play to be performed more than two or three times – and well-nigh impossible to get in to see it more than once, at least in Madrid.

tone of voice, is missed. The same sort of point could be made about lines 2986–93.

Having noticed this, I began to look for other occasions on which my reading of the play might be enhanced by paying attention to how actors might perform their lines. Three examples occur in Segismundo's unfolding responses to his new situation when he awakes in the palace early in Act II. They have in common a certain flatness or matter-of-factness of tone on Segismundo's part. Reichenberger and Caminero, in their generally well-judged analysis of 'los pretendidos crímenes de Segismundo', suggest (60) that the second servant's comment about the Prince, '¡Qué melancólico está!' (line 1248) is an 'observación muy curiosa' because the audience has just heard and seen 'con qué energía tan entusiasta y alegre el joven príncipe se apresura a enterarse de las posibilidades de la nueva dignidad'. They are anxious to establish the character of the second servant as argumentative and antagonistic towards the new Prince (which he may well become), and they interpret this aside, addressed to the other courtiers (and to the audience), as deliberately misleading or undermining.

But Segismundo's speech as he wonders at his new surroundings, all luxury and self-indulgence where before he had known only the harshest of imprisonments (lines 1224–47), is not self-evidently 'la alegre admiración de un niño' nor the speech of someone who is rapidly learning to dominate whatever circumstances come his way (which Segismundo certainly does shortly afterwards).[12] The servant's remark may equally well refer to the tone of doubt and hesitancy the actor uses to articulate the series of exclamations, questions, and imperatives uttered by Segismundo as he rubs his eyes, takes in the unexpected scene, and concludes that he might as well play it for what it is worth (lines 1246–47). It acts as a kind of verbal stage direction, suggesting how the actor is to play the speech. The fact that the first servant and Clarín both appear to support the view that Segismundo is 'melancólico' (lines 1249–51) lends weight to this interpretation, while Clotaldo himself refers to the state of confusion and doubt into which Segismundo has been thrown (lines 1268–71). Only when Segismundo has learnt the truth of his own identity does he round on Clotaldo and demonstrate that rapid adjustment to new circumstances which these critics have noted (lines 1295 ff.). The first time he appears to impose his will, by refusing the offer of more music (lines 1253–54), is likely

---

12. REICHENBERGER & CAMINERO, *Calderón dramaturgo*, 58.

to be less a shout of defiance than as straightforward a reply as a dazed man can manage to the question, and may best be spoken quite softly and without aggression.

The series of dramatic and violent encounters with Clotaldo, Astolfo, Estrella, Basilio, and Rosaura which this scene initiates, incorporating attempted murder and rape, as well as the defenestration of the second servant, forms an extraordinary piece of sustained theatrical tension which raises fresh questions of interpretation for director and actors. When Segismundo replies to Astolfo's greeting, which may contain veiled insults beneath its courtly hyperbole, is his 'Dios os guarde' (line 1351) a deliberate snub, the rather gruff response of a still uneducated Prince to a form of flattery he does not like, or simply the polite best Segismundo is able to manage?[13] He can hardly be expected to have an innate knowledge of court etiquette. It is more likely that Astolfo and the second servant are provoking and antagonizing Segismundo by making no allowance at all for his strange history, which makes sense, since it is in Astolfo's political interests that Segismundo should fail. Shortly afterwards, when Basilio demands to know '¿Qué ha sido esto?' (line 1440), Segismundo's response may not be a defiant assertion of his actions in defenestrating the servant but spoken in the flat tones of a sulking child who knows he has done wrong and wants to make the offence sound as insignificant as possible (Clarín's aside in line 1443 makes it plain to the audience that Segismundo recognizes who Basilio is): 'Nada ha sido; | a un hombre, que me ha cansado | dese balcón he arrojado' (lines 1440–42). The pattern is repeated when Basilio upbraids him for his behaviour and he replies: 'Díjome que no podía | hacerse, y gané la apuesta' (lines 1446–47). Indeed, a tone of rage or defiance sustained by Segismundo throughout these scenes would be a dramatic disaster; the audience would quickly tire of continuous bravado, whereas tension is constantly released and recreated by the variety of tones employed by the actor.

---

13. REICHENBERGER & CAMINERO, *Calderón dramaturgo*, 65, suggest that Astolfo's rhetoric is two-edged. Interestingly, in the first version of the play a stage direction absent from the second has Segismundo turn his back on Astolfo after speaking these words; see *La primera versión de «La vida es sueño»*, ed. J. M. RUANO DE LA HAZA, Hispanic Studies Textual Research and Criticism 5 (Liverpool: Liverpool University Press, 1992), 171. Ruano notes (9) that this version 'fue . . . escrita para ser vista y oída', while the 1635 version for the *Primera parte* of his *comedias* was 'primordialmente, para ser leída'. Yet such an action can hardly be counted a deliberate insult on Segismundo's part, given his bewilderment and inexperience.

Another example of spoken language as a means of dramatic revelation which may be lost in reading occurs in the central *narratio* section of Basilio's long speech to the Polish court (lines 589–856):

> Yo, acudiendo a mis estudios,
> en ellos y en todo miro
> que Segismundo sería
> el hombre más atrevido,
> el príncipe más cruel
> y el monarca más impío,
> por quien su reino vendría
> a ser parcial y diviso,
> escuela de las traiciones,
> y academia de los vicios;
> y él, de su furor llevado,
> entre asombros y delitos
> había de poner en mí
> las plantas, y yo rendido
> a sus pies me había de ver:
> ¡con qué congoja lo digo!
> siendo alfombra de sus plantas
> las canas del rostro mío.

(lines 708–25)

The national implications of Segismundo's foreseen crimes, which might be expected to dominate the discourse and form its climax, though appalling and many, are dealt with briefly: four lines outline his tyrannical character (710–13), and a further four describe the civil war, treachery, and vice of his reign (714–17). The personal implications for Basilio, on the other hand, require eight lines (718–25), and the logic of their rhetoric implies that they affect Basilio more deeply than the national disasters he foresees. What requires repetitions and an aside to make verbally explicit the emotion the actor must already be projecting, is the fact that his white hairs should be trampled under Segismundo's feet. These lines contain four first-person pronouns and three references to the trampling ('plantas', 'pies', 'plantas'), and therefore convey the distinct impression that the ultimate outrage for Basilio is not the violence and tyranny which he believes will be visited on others, but that he, so wise and caring a King, should be so humiliated by his son. Even if the King represents the people, the rhetoric of the speech as the actor delivers it lends weight to the view that Basilio, for all his fine words about the pursuit of science and the rule of wisdom, is fundamentally self-centred.[14]

My final example is rather different, since it is intended to illustrate how the sense of spoken words may be modified by what the audience can see. It is easy to dismiss the scene in which Estrella demands to know (lines 573–74) the identity of the woman in the portrait Astolfo is wearing as an entirely conventional piece of theatrical business. But like many such devices in Golden-Age theatre, the portrait, because it is visible to the audience once attention has been drawn to it, acts as an eloquent reminder of the conflict between power and love in Astolfo. Each time Astolfo speaks thereafter it functions as a visible though silent commentary on what he says. It has its own rhetoric of tacit presence, the sense of which becomes explicit following the cynical aside in which he identifies it as a portrait of Rosaura (lines 1774–77). Estrella has already alluded twice to the gap between the courtly language in which Astolfo attempts to woo her and its subversion by the portrait (lines 537–74 and 1750–63), first, perhaps, with a touch of playfulness, but later angrily. Astolfo's duplicity does not require constant restatement, since as long as he is wearing the portrait the audience is reminded of it and judges him accordingly. Once the resourcefulness of Rosaura has caused him (and Estrella) to forfeit it (lines 1994–95), its return to its rightful owner prepares the way both for the restoration of her honour by the man who had caused her to lose it (lines 3277–78) and the loss of the political power he seeks to acquire. The theatrical function of the portrait is therefore much more significant than that of 'un móvil que detiene el avance de los amores entre Estrella y Astolfo'.[15]

These are but a few of the moments in the play where imagining how words are to be spoken and actors appear may modify our understanding of the

---

14. John V. BRYANS, in *Calderón de la Barca: Imagery, Rhetoric and Drama*, Colección Támesis A 64 (London: Tamesis Books, 1977) – a work closely based on an Oxford doctoral thesis supervised by Robert Pring-Mill – notes the brief *exclamatio*, which serves as a useful reminder of the speaker's emotional involvement (94), though not the way in which the climactic moment of the speech imagines Basilio's fears for himself.

15. MORÓN ARROYO, *ed. cit.*, 43. Robert PRING-MILL has studied the complexities of visual imagery in Golden-Age prose in 'Some Techniques of Representation in the *Sueños* and the *Criticón*', *Bulletin of Hispanic Studies*, 45 (1968), 270–84. For Calderón's own use of painting and portraits as a theatrical metaphor, see Alan K. G. PATERSON, 'The Comic and Tragic Melancholy of Juan Roca: A Study of Calderón's *El pintor de su deshonra*', *Forum for Modern Language Studies*, 5 (1969), 244–61, and 'Juan Roca's Northern Ancestry: A Study of Art Theory in Calderón's *El pintor de su deshonra*', *Forum for Modern Language Studies*, 7 (1971), 195–210.

action. I would now like to look more carefully at the beginning of the play, to see if such an approach can yield any further results, since this moment is formative in establishing audience response. What does it first see? A wild, rocky landscape and a young man dressed in travellers' clothes, who speaks as he descends from a rocky height (stage direction at line 14). His opening words make it clear that he has been thrown from a horse which has bolted and left him injured in this dangerous, unknown place. But as soon as the thirteenth line is reached the audience is made to realise, if it has not suspected it already, that the young man is a woman.[16] Nothing it has heard until she applies two feminine adjectives to herself, 'ciega y desesperada', indicates that she is in disguise, but these immediately raise the question 'Why?' Her speech reveals that her external injury is matched by an internal despair; the setting and her dress that she has lost her way in the forested mountains, and forfeited her true identity as well.

The audience is unlikely at this point to be thinking of great philosophical themes, but of why Rosaura is in disguise, what she is doing with her manservant Clarín in this wild and dangerous landscape, and how this all connects with the emotional turmoil she expresses. Her words reinforce what the audience can see; though addressed to the (presumably) invisible beast, they identify the 'confuso laberinto | desas desnudas peñas' (lines 6–7) and 'la cabeza enmarañada | deste monte eminente' (lines 14–15), the location 'Polonia' (line 17), and her status, 'un extranjero' (line 18). More puzzlingly, they allude to some unknown 'destino' and 'suerte' (lines 12 and 21). But they also strongly reflect the setting, violent and disturbed: a world in which disorder is both seen on the stage and heard in the opening words. The horse is a monster and its speed a hyperbole (lines 1–2); it is a chaos of confusions, defined then negated in images drawn from the four elements: 'rayo sin llama, | pájaro sin matiz, pez sin escama, | y bruto sin instinto | natural' (lines 3–6).[17]

---

16. REICHENBERGER & CAMINERO, *Calderón dramaturgo* (90), place this moment of recognition at line 45, when Clarín addresses Rosaura as 'señora' (as he does again in lines 66 and 82); but this only confirms what line 13 has implied. VAREY (*Cosmovisión*, 265) notes that repeated prohibitions on actresses appearing in male costume on the Madrid stage seem to have been generally ignored.

17. The fundamental study of this subject remains E.M. WILSON, 'The Four Elements in the Imagery of Calderón', *Modern Language Review*, 31 (1936), 34–47, repr. in *Calderón de la Barca*, ed. Hans Flasche, Wege der Forschung 158 (Darmstadt: Wissenschaftliche Buchgesellschaft, 1971), 112–30, and in *The Comedias of Calderón*, 19 vols, ed. D. W. Cruickshank & J. E. Varey (Westmead, Hants: Gregg International Reprints & Tamesis Books Ltd, 1973), XIX, 191–207, and also in WILSON, *Spanish and English Literature of the 16th and 17th Centuries:*

But what the audience also hears in Rosaura's first speech is more than the initial violence of her outburst to the horse (lines 1–10), in a compressed *culto* style. There is also a quieter, more reflective, introspective voice as she addresses herself and her plight (lines 11–14 and 21–22). A third tone enters with the bleak, colloquial humour of the *gracioso*, whose appearance is delayed until Rosaura's despairing '¿dónde halló piedad un infelice?' (line 22). Without this variety, hard to sense by reading the play as text, the opening would degenerate into a shouting-match. That Calderón can convey so much information of an expository kind and encompass such a range of feeling in a bare thirty lines is a tribute to his dramatic powers. But the reader has to imagine all this; has to hear Rosaura's voice change its tone in lines 11 and 22, and feel the tension created by the opening outburst subside into a more resigned form of protest before being undercut by Clarín's 'Di dos' and the ironies of his proverbial wisdom and chivalric metaphor (lines 23–27).[18]

It is true, of course, that the more educated members of a Golden-Age audience might have detected a number of ideas which have been given dramatic expression in these opening lines. A fall from a horse is virtually a *topos* of the drama of the age: other famous examples occur at the beginning of *El príncipe constante*, *El médico de su honra*, and Lope's *Peribáñez y el comendador de Ocaña*. The bolting horse represents unbridled passion, as the reference to Phaeton (line 10) suggests, and has a more distant Platonic ancestry in the myth of the charioteer in the *Phaedrus*.[19] Rosaura's fall is a double one in theatrical terms – not only from the horse, but also by her entrance, as the first stage directions indicate: «*Sale en lo alto de un monte* ROSAURA *en hábito de hombre de camino y en representando los primeros versos va bajando*». A physical fall may represent a moral or spiritual one; being lost in a hostile landscape, a moral or spiritual confusion; disguise, the loss of personal integrity; the shedding of blood, the stain of dishonour through the loss of female virginity, which is a kind of living death. But the action and dialogue

---

Studies in Discretion, Illusion, and Mutability (Cambridge: Cambridge University Press, 1980), 1–14 (with corrections), and, in an unauthorized translation, as 'Los cuatro elementos en la imaginería de Calderón', in *Calderón y la crítica: Historia y antología*, ed. Manuel Durán & Roberto González Echevarría, 2 vols, Biblioteca Románica Hispánica: Estudios y Ensayos 238 (Madrid: Gredos, 1976), I, 277–99.

18. MORÓN ARROYO, *ed. cit.*, 20, perhaps makes too much of the parallel with Don Quixote and Sancho; the chivalric reference is a general one, and fits the black humour of the *gracioso*.

19. MORÓN ARROYO, *ed. cit.*, 20, notes how the opening 'se sitúa . . . en la atmósfera mítica de los héroes griegos'.

are so rapid at the start that an audience hardly has the leisure of the reader
to detect all the allusions. What is important to the dramatist is the creation
of an impression or series of impressions and moods, all of which will in due
course reappear and be given fuller form and purpose. The fact that the first
hundred or so lines of the play contain the germ of what is to follow, not just
in terms of action but also of image and visible sign, is less important at this
stage than Calderón's evocation of violence, confrontation, pain, distress, and
loss.[20]

Yet something more than passion out of control is also suggested by the
opening. Rosaura's arrival takes the form of a dramatic irruption into the
landscape which associates her in the audience's mind with action and confrontation, and not only with her status as victim (as she descends the rock,
she must be showing signs of her fall and consequent injury). It is blind destiny which has impelled her to this place – or, more accurately, a destiny she
does not understand or see – but she arrives with such theatrical impetus that,
fallen though she is, she appears as one driven by a past she cannot fully
understand (symbolized by her sword) or control (her lost honour) to seek a
remedy for her plight. Whereas, as the audience will learn, almost all the
other protagonists are in some way or another running away from their past
responsibilities and taking refuge in dreams of power and status (Clotaldo,
Basilio, Astolfo) or safety (Clarín), Rosaura, by contrast, is revealed as initia-
tor and confronter, willing to assume a variety of disguises (male traveller,
female courtier, male-female soldier) in order to reach her goal. The opening
scene, therefore, does not only use the *topos* of the fall from the bolting horse
to symbolize passion, but also violent confrontation, an element in the drama
which Segismundo will so memorably replay in his clashes with Clotaldo,
Astolfo, and Basilio. He too, once he is no longer trapped into the role of
passive victim of another's actions, will confront his past, in the shape of his
tutor and his father. In this sense Segismundo and Rosaura will be seen to be
fighting the same kind of battle for assertion of their rightful humanity, though
any expectation that their relationship will surmount tribulation and lead to
marriage will ultimately be frustrated by Segismundo's *discreción* as a ruler.[21]

---

20. For example, Rosaura's double reference to destiny and fortune (lines 12 and 21) will
acquire a new significance when the audience hears Basilio's exposition of his astrological
observations and their consequences.

21. Calderón seems to be suggesting such an outcome by his repeated references to Segismundo's feelings for Rosaura. Sometimes these act as a brake on his violent tendencies (e.g.

The essential role of Rosaura in Segismundo's awakening forms a standard element of critical approaches to the play, but undergraduates continue to think of their relationship in terms of plot and sub-plot. Parker may be right when he envisages unity existing at the level of theme but not action, but this makes little dramatic sense when the opening scene brings them so powerfully together and establishes so many connections between them (each is in disguise, voluntarily assumed or imposed; each is the victim of another man's actions; each is 'infelice' and trapped in a living death).[22] Indeed, can one really distinguish so sharply between a theme which is somehow outside the action and the action itself, when Parker derives 'theme' from the chains of causality which constitute the theatrical action? [23]

Clarín's second speech introduces a further piece of information: the sun is going down in this wild place where they are alone and lost (lines 45–48; compare Rosaura's words 'abrasa' and 'sangre', lines 16 and 18), and darkness threatens, with its unknown terrors. The audience's attention is focused again on the predicament of the pair after a brief verbal tussle about the supposed consolations to be found in complaining of one's lot (lines 29–44) has momentarily lessened the tension. The danger shifts from the general (hostile wilderness) to the particular (the prison-tower). Rosaura is the first to spot it in the fading light (lines 50–54) and then to describe it (lines 56–64 and 69–72).

Now, the audience's attention is drawn away from the characters towards an object, on to which the stage lighting in a modern performance might cast a

---

lines 190–242, 1580–81, 1593–1617, 2134–37); at other times they spur it on (e.g. the attempted rape, lines 1638–45, 1659–66). In their final encounter his struggle continues, as I have tried to show. But the reversal of such expectations at the end is perhaps meant to leave the audience to reflect further on what it has seen (as no doubt the imprisonment of the rebel soldier is too).

22. I agree with Albert E. SLOMAN, in his edn of *La vida es sueño* (Manchester: Manchester University Press, 1961), when he writes (xiii): 'Structurally these two plots are so interwoven that it would be impossible to disentangle them without destroying the play.'

23. In his *The Mind and Art of Calderón*, ed. Deborah King (Cambridge: Cambridge University Press, 1988), A. A. PARKER writes (19): 'These two plots are unified in what becomes a separate story with two separate strands, but their unification depends upon the relevance of one life-history to another. The relevance itself depends entirely on the theme of the play.' He traces the chains of causality back to Basilio's horoscope and Rosaura's decision to confront her past; but surely in this second case it is Clotaldo's abandonment of Violante which is the correct parallel. Thus, both Segismundo and Rosaura are the victims of their fathers' irresponsibility (and Rosaura in addition of Astolfo's). See also Robert PRING-MILL's criticism of Parker's principle of the primacy of theme over action in 'Los calderonistas de habla inglesa', esp. 383–88.

faint glow. Whereas even such a hint of the presence of civilization (hence Rosaura's use of 'palacio tan breve', 'rudo artificio', 'arquitectura', 'edificio') ought to be a welcome sign to lost travellers, as Clarín suggests (lines 65–69), Rosaura's words immediately undermine such hope, for they are words associated with death – the entrance is a 'funesta boca' out of which 'nace la noche' engendered from within. Out of the blackness comes the chilling sound to which the stage directions allude: «Suena ruido de cadenas». Sunset and fear outside, night and death within, where a presence awaits them, whose cry is heard (line 78) but who remains unseen for nearly thirty lines (73–101) of mounting tension for the audience. Rosaura and Clarín react predominantly with fear, tempered by Clarín's attempts at humour (lines 75–76), though Rosaura's first response to the cry is to note its sadness (line 79). An attentive member of the audience may already have heard a verbal connection established between her and this unseen prisoner: her '¿mas dónde halló piedad un infelice?' (line 22) and his '¡Ay, mísero de mí, ay, infelice!' (line 78) – another small sign of the close parallels between them established from the beginning and reinforced by Rosaura's response to Segismundo's account of himself (e.g. lines 250–52).

At line 85 Rosaura's reaction changes from fear to curiosity, and expressions of anxiety give way to rhetorical question and tentative description. The shift between lines 84 and 85 is remarkable but may well be missed in reading. Rosaura wants to flee, Clarín is petrified; but their rapid exchanges give way to her *culto* style, as she begins to describe the prison cell: 'No es breve luz aquella | caduca exhalación, pálida estrella . . . ?' (lines 85–86). Rosaura has seen something she has not noticed before and has, for the moment, forgotten her terror, herself, and her problems. It is an important transition, which prepares for the revelation of Segismundo in line 102. Its language of light and darkness, life and death, builds on what we have already heard and will be further developed, but for the moment the antithetical discourse confirms the continuing confusions and uncertainties which the audience is experiencing through the actors' reactions to their situation.

Answering her own question, Rosaura describes the light paradoxically as one which 'hace más tenebrosa | la oscura habitación con luz dudosa' (lines 89–90). She must be peering at something which the audience too is beginning to see as her words and actions suggest the gathering twilight. She and it glimpse for the first time the real nature of the place and its inhabitant: 'una prisión obscura | que es de vivo cadáver sepultura' (lines 94–95). Out of the shadows emerges the outline of what she describes: 'en el traje de fiera yace un hombre | de prisiones cargado | y sólo de la luz acompañado' (lines 96–98). The stage direction which follows confirms her words: «*Descúbrese* SEGISMUNDO *con una cadena y la luz, vestido de pieles*». The images Rosaura uses and the picture the audience now sees before it form a perfect match. The language is made visible; the word, flesh. But I have been surprised at how often undergraduates fail to grasp this, perhaps because they do not read the stage directions carefully. What the audience has been told through Rosaura's tentative then fuller description it can now see before it: a man dressed in animal skins, chained up, in a dark prison lit by a light, or, as Calderón twice insists, 'la luz'.[24] The fact that Calderón uses speech as well as staging to prepare for the first revelation of Segismundo – that is, two distinct forms of theatrical communication – suggests that the moment is of great significance. We have already witnessed the deceptiveness of our senses, when a man is revealed to be a woman, in a world in which everything is described in terms of something else. Now we see a further puzzle: a man dressed as a beast ('en traje de fiera' – the skins cover his body externally but he is still recognisably human). The oxymoronic image is reinforced by the verbal oxymoron of 'vivo cadáver'. The presence of both chains and the light is a further visible sign of the puzzle. Images of death have prepared us for the living corpse; images of wildness (the landscape, the bolting horse, the 'brutos') for the wild man; the 'confuso laberinto' of the setting has yielded to the even more oppressive 'prisión obscura' and its chains. But the fading light of day 'outside' is replaced 'inside' the prison by a light which burns steadily in the darkness, and its physical proximity to the 'pieles' and the 'cadena' is important and emblematic.

The audience may not be able to make sense of all this verbal and visible information, but it can judge that the identity of this mysterious person is a complex one. His exterior is bestial, his humanity is chained, but against all these images of death there remain the light and the cry of pain. It is hard not to think of John 1. 5 – 'et lux in tenebris lucet'. The over-simplified view of

---

24. MORÓN ARROYO, *ed. cit.*, 48, associates this with 'la luz natural del entendimiento, agente capaz de recibir todas las especies que da el arte', and believes that Segismundo and Rosaura represent Adam and Eve (18). I would not dispute that the play has a universal significance or that Segismundo, at least, is a kind of Everyman. But this is a fallen world, not an Edenic one, as the images of wilderness make clear. Morón Arroyo's view, however, would make it difficult to think in terms of a main plot (Adam) and a sub-plot (Eve).

Segismundo as one who progresses from 'fiera' to 'hombre', which undergraduates so often repeat, is not supported by his first appearance, even though the chains and the skins are attached to his body, whereas the light is separated from it, suggesting a realm of possibility rather than actuality. His journey, unlike Caliban's, will be from humanity chained to humanity unbound.[25]

All these impressions are being borne in mind and assimilated as we hear Segismundo's opening speech. One of the problems of these *décimas* is that they are so beautiful that they have become an anthology piece. The only production of the play I have seen began with them, and robbed it of its dynamic opening.[26] The action has paused for the first time and we are invited to concentrate on a strange amalgam of man and beast who is laying bare his soul. In some sense, his words must be enjoyed for themselves, as a fine aria in an opera catches our full attention for a moment. But, like the aria, they have a dramatic function as well as great poetic beauty. It is not just that they reverse the pattern of disorder in the elements which Rosaura's opening outburst identifies, by evoking a world of nature in which each element with beauty and grace fulfils its allotted role. It is that lines of such beauty and power and intelligence and pathos are being spoken by a man 'en traje de fiera... | de prisiones cargado', from the darkness of a tomb-like prison. We have to see him as he speaks to feel their full force. Their whole structure and argument show that Segismundo is capable of belonging to the realm of order and reason which the light visibly and symbolically represents. They begin with questions about an unknown crime which has bound him here, but move out into a world full of space and light and movement in all its parts, the very antithesis of the world he inhabits. How does he know of this world? How can he speak so movingly of it? His capacity to reason and to create beauty out of words does not fit the place or his condition, and we are

---

25. On the connections between *La vida es sueño* and *The Tempest*, see Susan L. FISCHER, ' "This Thing of Darkness | I Acknowledge Mine": Segismundo, Prospero, and Shadow', in *The Prince in the Tower*, ed. Armas, 147–64; a study of particular interest, since it refers to modern productions of both plays.

26. In contrast, the adaptation by Adrian Mitchell and John Barton for the Royal Shakespeare Company production of 1983 conveys the shifting tones of the opening very vividly: see *'Life's a Dream'*, in *Three Plays by Pedro Calderón de la Barca*, tr./adapted Adrian MITCHELL & John BARTON, Absolute Classics (London: Absolute Press, 1990), 91–158. Eric Southworth also praises in this respect José Luis Gómez's fine French-language production at the Théâtre de l'Odéon in Paris, April–June 1992.

not yet in a position to speculate that it may be the natural consequence of his royal condition. He cannot be 'naturaleza sin arte' because his *décimas* are so artful.[27] He is an imprisoned beast for reasons as yet unknown to the audience or to him; an enlightened human, protesting, finally angry, as the language bursts into the element of flame (line 164), at his exclusion from liberty in spite of possessing 'alma' and 'albedrío'.[28]

It is important, once the violent side of Segismundo asserts itself, as it does so soon after his lament has flared into anger at his discovery of witnesses to his degradation (lines 180–85), that we recall what we have just seen and heard, especially when a new element of human tenderness is revealed in Segismundo's reply to Rosaura's plea (lines 190–92). It is equally important that a little later, as we hear his father expound the reasons which led him so to imprison his son, we carry this picture and the effect of his words in our minds, and are unable to accept Basilio's self-justification, because we have been privileged to see and hear what through the illusion of theatre and in his own dream of wisdom Basilio cannot, until he allows the feared horoscope to be fulfilled and learns, to his astonishment, that prophecies are ambiguous and that the future is open, not closed.

Alongside the traditional and new critical approaches to Calderón there ought to be room for one which takes the text of the play seriously from the point of view I have outlined. Many other moments in *La vida es sueño* could fruitfully be examined from this perspective and our reading of drama in general can be enriched by it. Dramatists have at their disposal resources and techniques which we do not normally associate with the study of literature. But if we are prepared to argue about particular images and conceits in Golden-Age poetry, or narrative techniques in its prose, we should also be sensitive to the particularities of the stage and encourage our students to imagine themselves as actors and directors as well as analysts of character,

---

27. Compare MORÓN ARROYO, *ed. cit.*, 30, 45.

28. The MITCHELL–BARTON version has Segismundo speak his *décimas* as he looks over pictures of a swallow, a salmon, a stream, and a leopard in a book. This seems to me an intelligent addition to Calderón's sparse stage directions, given that Basilio in due course will explain that Clotaldo has educated his imprisoned son (756–58). The device of the picture-book anchors Segismundo's lament in his experience. Since from birth he has been chained in his dark prison, he could only know what such creatures and phenomena were through such indirect means. It fits well with the first version of the play, in which the stage directions specify that Segismundo is sitting on the ground until he rises to cry out his final *décima* (see RUANO DE LA HAZA, *ed. cit.*, 133, 135).

verse, or theme. Such close attention to the text of the play in its theatrical setting can only increase our sensitivity to the possibilities of its interpretation and therefore to the multiple play of language itself.

COLIN THOMPSON

St Catherine's College, Oxford

SOME PERFORMANCE CONSTANTS IN CALDERÓN'S *EL MÉDICO DE SU HONRA*

ROBERT PRING-MILL's delight in the infinite subtleties of the human mind, and the scrupulous attention to detail which informs his scholarship, may lead some readers of this volume to suppose that his work on the Spanish drama of the seventeenth century pays scant attention to performance criteria. After all, many of his colleagues and sparring partners have, over the years, concentrated exclusively on the close reading of play texts.[1] Yet, right from his very first essay in the 1940s on Chinese Triad societies, his published work shows him deriving evident satisfaction from the discovery of apparently random but actually significant associations and correlations, as witness his investigations of analogical structures, first in Ramon Llull and then in the plays of Lope de Vega and Calderón de la Barca, and, as perhaps only his Oxford pupils can know, he has, year after year, in the form of illustrated talks and minutely annotated lecture handouts, pointed to structural and thematic links between the visual arts and literary and philosophical texts.[2]   His

---

1. On performance values and fashions in drama criticism see, for example, Richard LEVIN, 'Some Second Thoughts on Central Themes', *Modern Language Review*, 67 (1972), 1–10; 'Third Thoughts on Thematics', *Modern Language Review*, 70 (1975), 481–96;   and 'Performance-Critics vs Close Readers in the Study of English Renaissance Drama', *Modern Language Review*, 81 (1986), 545–59.

2. Robert PRING-MILL, 'The Analogical Structure of the Lullian Art', in *Islamic Philosophy and the Classical Tradition: Essays Presented to Richard Walzer by his Friends and Colleagues*, ed. Samuel Miklos Stern, Albert Hourani & Vivian Brown (Oxford: Cassirer, 1972), 315–26, tr. Albert Soler as 'L'estructura analògica de l'Art lul·liana', in PRING-MILL, *Estudis sobre Ramon Llull (1956–1978)*, ed. Lola Badia & Albert Soler, Textos i Estudis de Cultura Catalana 22 (Barcelona: Publicacions de l'Abadia de Montserrat, Curial Edicions Catalanes, 1991), 241–52;   Introduction to *Lope de Vega: Five Plays*, tr. Jill Booty, Mermaid Dramabook 20 (New York: Hill & Wang Inc., 1961), vii–li; 'Estructuras lógico-retóricas y sus resonancias: un discurso de *El príncipe constante*', in *Hacia Calderón: Segundo Coloquio Anglogermano, Hamburgo 1970*, ed. Hans FLASCHE, Calderoniana 7 (Berlin & New York: Walter de Gruyter, 1973), 109–54; 'Estructuras lógico-retóricas y sus resonancias, 2ª parte: *Hermosa compostura y piedad real*', in *Hacia Calderón: Tercer Coloquio Anglogermano, Londres 1973*, ed. Hans Flasche, Calderoniana 10 (Berlin & New York: Walter de Gruyter, 1976), 47–74.

landmark study of techniques of representation in certain Golden-Age writers
– an essay that has been invaluable to generations of students – is as
convincing a demonstration as I know of a rare capacity for visual analysis
harnessed to critical acumen and lucid exposition.[3] To see him among his own
books lovingly handling a rare Llull edition with its volvelles intact, or to
witness his pleasure in Katya Kohn's silk-screen prints of Neruda's poems and
of his own translations of them is to be reminded of the delight given and
enjoyed when a discerning eye (and never a cold one) is cast upon a shifting
artistic world.

An attentive reading of Pring-Mill's writing on the drama, not least his
carefully argued critique of the first recension of his friend Alec Parker's
famous (or infamous) *The Approach to the Spanish Drama of the Golden Age*,
reveals that the visual component of the *corral*-going experience is one that he
has always borne in mind.[4] The present paper, though in a far cruder form
than would be characteristic of its dedicatee, attempts to survey a few of the
more obvious performance criteria that ought properly to define and,
componiendo, viendo el lugar, inform our reading of seventeenth-century
Spanish drama and, in particular, of the plays of Pedro Calderón de la Barca
(1600–81), given that, as Bruno Damiani recently remarked in an essay
dedicated to the pioneering historian of the Spanish stage, John Varey, 'el
teatro es antes que nada arte visual, y esta es la manera en que lo consi-
deraban los dramaturgos del Siglo de Oro'.[5] As it is not the task of study-
bound textual critics to second-guess actors and directors (who are and should

---

3. 'Some Techniques of Representation in the *Sueños* and the *Criticón*', *Bulletin of Hispanic Studies*, 45 (1968), 270–84. This paper, developing approaches first evident in his 'Spanish Golden-Age Prose and the Depiction of Reality', *Anglo-Spanish Society Quarterly Review*, 32/33 (April-June/July-Sept. 1959), 20–31, was based on a paper given in September 1966 under the title 'The Shifting World and the Discerning Eye' at the Strasburg Congress of the Fédération Internationale des Langues et Littératures Modernes.

4. A. A. PARKER, *The Approach to the Spanish Drama of the Golden Age* (London: The Hispanic and Luso-Brasilian Councils, 1957), corr. rpt, *The Tulane Drama Review*, 4 (1959), 42–59; reviewed by Robert PRING-MILL, *Romanistisches Jahrbuch*, 13 (1962), 384–87. PRING-MILL has himself published analyses of plays which address staging and *compostura*: see, especially, 'La estructura de *El gran teatro del mundo*', in *Hacia Calderón: Séptimo Coloquio Anglogermano, Cambridge 1984*, ed. Hans Flasche, Archivum Calderonianum 3 (Wiesbaden & Stuttgart: Franz Steiner, 1985) 110–45 (131–42).

5. Bruno DAMIANI, 'Los dramaturgos del Siglo de Oro frente a las artes visuales: prólogo para un estudio comparativo', in *El mundo del teatro español en su Siglo de Oro: Ensayos dedicados a John E. Varey*, ed. J. M. Ruano de la Haza, Ottawa Hispanic Studies 3 (Ottawa: Dovehouse Editions Canada, 1988), 137–49 (146).

remain the arbiters of performance) the features chosen here are solely those that are dictated by the text and would accordingly be common to performance in the seventeenth-century *corrales* and to revivals in a modern theatre.[6]

I.   Characters as spectacle

In compiling the following summary of Calderón's *El médico de su honra* (ca 1633–35) I have used the model edition by Don Cruickshank, based on QC, the genuine *Segunda parte* of 1637 printed by María de Quiñones for the bookseller Pedro Coello (hence the acronym).[7] When characters make their entrance their name is given in bold; superscript numbers represent the length, in lines, of their presence on stage. For present purposes I assume what is perforce a rough correlation between the number of lines in a scene and the time it takes to play.

Act I

Scene i :   0001–0044[44]

0001–0044[44]   **Enrique**[44] (*unconscious from 0002*) **Arias**[44] **Diego**[44] **Pedro**[26] (*until 0026*) (*all «de camino»; «ruido de caja»; «Llevan al Infante» at 0044*)

Scene ii :   0045–0574[530]

0045–0076[32]   **Mencía**[530] **Jacinta** (*«esclava herrada»*)[73]

0077–0120[44]   Mencía Jacinta (*until 0117*) **Arias**[44] **Diego**[44] **Enrique**[418] (*carried, then seated, unconscious*)

0121–0224[104]   Mencía Enrique (*unconscious until 0155, seated until 0221*)

0225–0314[90]   Mencía Enrique **Arias**[270] **Diego**[13] (*0229–0242*)

0315–0424[110]   Mencía Enrique Arias **Gutierre**[240] **Coquín**[240]

0425–0494[70]   Mencía Enrique Arias Gutierre Coquín **Diego**[70]

0495–0554[60]   Mencía Gutierre

0555–0574[20]   Mencía **Jacinta**[20]

---

6. The best single volume on the performed aspects of seventeenth-century Spanish drama is John E. VAREY, *Cosmovisión y escenografía: El teatro español en el Siglo de Oro*, Nueva Biblioteca de Erudición y Crítica 2 (Madrid: Castalia, 1987), a collection of studies originally published between 1964 and 1987. Anyone wishing to work on plays of this period ought also to be familiar with the vast arsenal of documentation collected, edited, and annotated by VAREY and by Norman SHERGOLD in the series Fuentes para la Historia del Teatro en España published by Tamesis Books Ltd, London.

7. Pedro CALDERÓN DE LA BARCA, *El médico de su honra*, ed. D. W. Cruickshank, Clásicos Castalia 112 (Madrid: Castalia, 1981; 2nd edn, 1989); useful also is the edition by C. A. JONES (Oxford: Clarendon Press, 1961; rpt Oxford: The Dolphin Book Co. Ltd, 1976).

Scene iii :   0575–1020[446]

0575–0578[4]   **Inés**[28] **Leonor**[418] («*con mantos*»)

0579–0701[122]   Inés (*until 0602*) Leonor **Pedro**[414] **Soldados** and **Viejo**[24] (*0579–0602?*)

0702–0808[107]   Leonor (*hiding*) Pedro **Coquín**[107]

0809–0992[184]   Leonor (*hiding until 0932*) Pedro **Enrique**[208] **Gutierre**[202] **Diego**[208] **Arias**[198] **«La Compañía»**?[208] (*Gutierre and Arias fighting at 0983*)

0993–1006[14]   Arias (*until 0996*) Gutierre (*until 1000*) Enrique (*until 1006*) Diego (*until 1006*) Leonor «La Compañía» (*until 1006?*)

1007–1020[14]   Leonor

Act II

Scene i :   1021–1402[383]

1021–1050[30]   **Jacinta**[24] (*until 1044*) **Enrique**[226] (*both* «*como a escuras*»)

1051–1073[13]   Enrique (*hiding*) **Mencía**[196] (*asleep from 1063*) **Jacinta**[13] **Silvia**[13] **Teodora**[13] (*singing at 1062*)

1074–1170[93]   Mencía (*asleep until 1080*) Enrique (*hiding from 1167*) (**Gutierre** *heard offstage 1143–1144*)

1171–1246[76]   Mencía Enrique (*hiding*) **Gutierre**[232] **Coquín**[232] **Jacinta**?[75] (*1242–1246 only?*)

1247–1293[47]   Gutierre Coquín Enrique (*hiding*)

1294–1309[16]   Gutierre Coquín **Mencía**[109] («*sola, muy alborotada*») Enrique (*hiding*)

1310–1315[6]   Gutierre Coquín Mencía **Jacinta**[6] Enrique (*simulated darkness, with lights put out by* Mencía)

1316–1323[8]   Gutierre Coquín Mencía Enrique (*hiding*) (*simulated darkness*)

1324–1340[16]   Gutierre Coquín Mencía Enrique (*hiding*) **Jacinta**[78]

1341–1354[14]   Coquín Mencía Enrique (*hiding*) Jacinta

1355–1402[48]   **Gutierre**[48] Coquín Mencía Enrique (*hiding*) Jacinta (*play with dagger 1377; scene ends with Gutierre and Mencía leaving stage* «*cada uno por su puerta*»)

Scene ii :   1403–1712[310]

1403–1440[38]   **Pedro**[97] **Diego**[100] (*change of* «*capa*» *from red? to black*)

1441–1485[44]   Pedro Diego **Coquín**[84]

1486–1502[17]   Pedro (*until 1499*) Diego Coquín **Enrique**[94]

1502–1524[23]   Coquín Enrique

1525–1579[55]   Enrique **Gutierre**[188] **Arias**[55] **Diego**[55] (*play with sword and dagger at 1532*)

1580–1712[133]   Gutierre

Scene iii :   1713–1860[148]

1713–1848[136]   **Arias**[148] **Leonor**[136]

1849–1860   Arias

Scene iv :   1861 – 2048[188]

1861 – 1960[100]   **Gutierre**[188] (*in simulated darkness «sale como [quien salta] unas tapias»*)
                    Mencía[188] (*asleep behind curtain, discovered 1897, awakened 1915, does not recognize Gutierre*)
1961 – 1968[8]   Gutierre (*hidden 1964 – 1983*) Mencía **Jacinta**[8] (*simulated darkness continues*)
1969 – 1982[14]   Gutierre (*hidden*) Mencía (*simulated darkness continues*)
1983 – 2048[66]   Gutierre Mencía **Jacinta**[?66] (*possibly only for 1983?*)

Act III

Scene i :   2049 – 2328[280]
2049 – 2179[131]   **Gutierre**[280] **Pedro**[246] «*Todo el acompañamiento*»[4] (*until 2052*)
2180 – 2282[103]   Gutierre (*hidden*) Pedro **Enrique**[103] (*play with dagger 2266 – 2276*)
2283 – 2294[10]   Gutierre (*hidden*) Pedro
2295 – 2328[34]   Gutierre (*dagger at 2306*)

Scene ii :   2329 – 2507[179]
2329 – 2360[32]   **Jacinta**[126] **Mencía**[86]
2361 – 2414[54]   Jacinta Mencía **Coquín**[94]
2415 – 2430[16]   Jacinta Coquín
2431 – 2454[24]   Jacinta Coquín **Gutierre**[50]
2454 – 2479[26]   Gutierre (*reads 2462 – 2464, writes 2474 – 2479*) **Mencía** (*hidden until discovered writing 2458, unconscious 2461 – 2479*)
2480 – 2507[28]   Mencía (*reads 2496*)

Scene iii :   2508 – 2537[30]
2508 – 2537[30]   **Pedro**[30] **Diego**[30] (*music 2525 – 2533; 2537: stage direction: «Vase cada uno por su puerta»*)

Scene iv :   2538 – 2633[96]
2538 – 2565[28]   **Gutierre**[28] **Ludovico**[68] («*cubierto el rostro*»)
2566 – 2568[3]   Ludovico
2569 – 2605[37]   Ludovico **Gutierre**[65]
2606 – 2633[28]   Gutierre

Scene v :   2634 – 2953[320]
2634 – 2648[15]   **Pedro**[320] **Diego**[320] (*music 2634 – 2637*)
2649 – 2656[8]   Pedro Diego **Gutierre**[8] **Ludovico**[63] («*tapado el rostro*»)
2657 – 2711[55]   Pedro Diego Ludovico («*Descúbrese*» *2673*)
2712 – 2723[12]   Pedro Diego
2723 – 2793[71]   Pedro Diego **Coquín**[?231]
2794 – 2813[20]   Pedro Diego ?Coquín **Leonor**[160] **Inés**[160]
2814 – 2871[58]   Pedro Diego ?Coquín Leonor Inés **Gutierre** (*initially offstage 2814 – 2817*)
2872 – 2953[82]   Pedro Diego ?Coquín Leonor Inés Gutierre **Mencía**[82] (*body discovered*).

A survey of the size of the parts to be learnt by each actor – of, that is, the relative importance to the play of each as they tend to 'appear' to the reader rather than the spectator – produces a different picture from that given above. The number of speeches made by each of the main characters, and the number of lines or part-lines he or she utters in each Act is as follows:

Character	Act I	Act II	Act III	Total	(Percentages of text)
Arias	18|089 +	09|072 +	00|000 =	027|0161	(04.4|05.0)
Coquín	15|230 +	24|115 +	14|087 =	053|0432	(08.7|13.5)
Diego	09|025 +	05|011 +	19|041 =	033|0077	(05.5|02.4)
Enrique	33|174 +	28|097 +	16|050 =	077|0321	(12.7|10.0)
Gutierre	32|221 +	65|437 +	41|353 =	137|1011	(22.6|31.7)
Jacinta	06|010 +	13|036 +	10|033 =	029|0079	(04.7|02.5)
Leonor	08|099 +	04|082 +	04|013 =	016|0194	(02.6|06.0)
Mencía	32|211 +	73|201 +	10|086 =	115|0497	(19.0|15.6)
Pedro	38|130 +	13|046 +	68|241 =	119|0417	(19.6|13.0).

Yet our summary shows on-stage appearances of the major characters, in lines, as follows (with percentage of complete text in parentheses): Arias 759 (25.7 %); Coquín ?987 (33.4 %); Diego 824 (30 %); Enrique 1093 (37 %); Gutierre 1529 (51.7 %); Jacinta 419 (14 %); Leonor 714 (24.2 %); Mencía 1191 (40.3 %); Pedro 1133 (38 %).

The comparison gives rise to a number of thoughts. Firstly, Don Arias, on stage for a quarter of the whole play (and over a third of Acts I and II), does not appear at all in Act III. One reason for this is that he is part of Prince Enrique's entourage, as witness his recognition of his master's old flame (Act I, sc. ii, line 92), and Enrique himself leaves town in Act III, sc. i (at line 2282; confirmation in Act III, sc. ii, lines 2508 – 10: 'REY. En fin, ¿Enrique se fue? | DIEGO. Sí, señor; aquesta tarde | salió de Sevilla.'). But there are also practical reasons for his departure, as it allows the actor playing Arias, rather than his more easily recognized (because more prominent) colleague taking the part of the Prince, to double as the blood-letter Ludovico, who does not put in an appearance until Act III, sc. iv. Don Diego's role in Act III is accordingly enhanced to flesh out the royal entourage.[8]

---

8. Calderón had already cut one of the nobles (Don Alonso) from the cast-list in his source play; see Albert E. SLOMAN, *The Dramatic Craftsmanship of Calderón: His Use of Earlier Plays* (Oxford: The Dolphin Book Co. Ltd, 1958), 18 – 58 (21).

Secondly, music (or, more precisely, song), which is central to the spectator's experience of *loa* and *entremés*, appears both in Act II, sc. i, when Teodora sings her mistress to sleep, and, in the final Act, in the form of the *romance noticiero 'futurístico'*, apparently composed by Calderón for this play but reminiscent of many in the public domain with its dark hints of events at and immediately after the battle of Montiel which thoroughly disconcert the King and his right-hand man, Don Diego.[9]

Thirdly, the women are more visible than the reader of this play may assume. Women in Calderón's plays in general, and his wife-murder plays in particular, have attracted considerable attention recently, but published studies have frequently been conducted (and still are) as part of a wider-ranging survey whose purpose it is to demonstrate some supposed larger truth, either about society or about fashionable literary theories. Because of this, they tend to be silent on the questionable status both of the *corrales* as a forum for the debate of such issues, and of actors and actresses as propagandists, and only rarely do they have anything to say about performance values. The conclusions they reach are based on what women say in the plays (and how they say it) and what is said about them (and how that, too, is expressed).[10] Analyses of this kind often also presuppose an absence of extra-textual restraints, turn a blind eye to the age-old tradition of attacking actors and actresses as sexually

9. CRUICKSHANK notes (*ed. cit.*, 124 n.) that neither QC nor Vera Tassis provides text or music for the song whose 'letra y tono' Teodora hopes will please Mencía (lines 1061–62), and that the material included in the editions of Hartzenbusch (1848) and Valbuena Briones (1956) 'no tiene ninguna autoridad'. On music, see Jack SAGE, 'Calderón y la música teatral', *Bulletin Hispanique*, 58 (1956), 275–300, rpt, as 'The Function of Music in the Theatre of Calderón', in *The Comedias of Calderón*, 19 vols, facsimile ed. D. W. CRUICKSHANK & J. E. VAREY (Westmead, Hants: Gregg International Reprints & Tamesis Books Ltd, 1973), XIX, 209–30 (with update at 226–27). For Trastamaran ballads on King Pedro, see *Romancero general (1600, 1604, 1605)*, ed. Ángel GONZÁLEZ PALENCIA, 2 vols, Clásicos Españoles 3–4 (Madrid: CSIC, 1947), I, 61 (nr 81), 195–96 (nr 293), 311–12 (nr 477), 385 (nr 602); also Ramón MENÉNDEZ PIDAL, *Estudios sobre el romancero*, ed. Diego Catalán & others, Obras completas de R. Menéndez Pidal XI (Madrid: Espasa-Calpe, 1973), 28–29, 364; and William J. ENTWISTLE, 'The «Romancero» del rey don Pedro» in Ayala and the *Cuarta crónica general*', *Modern Language Review*, 23 (1930), 306–26.

10. See, if only *à titre d'exemples*, Paul Julian SMITH, *Writing in the Margin: Spanish Literature of the Golden Age* (Oxford: Clarendon Press, 1988), esp. 156–66; Everett W. HESSE, *La mujer como víctima en la comedia y otros ensayos*, Biblioteca Universitaria Puvill (Barcelona: Puvill Libros, n.d. [= ?1987]); and Melveena MCKENDRICK, *Woman and Society in the Spanish Drama of the Golden Age: A Study of the 'mujer varonil'* (Cambridge: Cambridge University Press, 1974). *El mágico prodigioso: A Composite Edition and Study of the Manuscript and Printed Versions*, ed. MCKENDRICK (in association with A. A. PARKER) (Oxford: Clarendon Press, 1992), does review performance (1–6).

promiscuous and ambiguous, and neglect to mention that actresses (usually the wives of *autores de comedias* or of fellow players) were in practice often recruited not so much for their ability to get by heart extended passages of text as for their skills as dancers and singers and for their other physical attributes.[11] Yet, if we look at how often they are on stage in full view of the audience we shall find ourselves taking a rather different view. Jacinta, Mencía's slave, may have little to say (and most of what she does say consists of a servant's one-liners, e.g. 'Ya la luz está aquí ', line 1983), yet she is on stage, usually dancing attendance on her mistress, much more frequently and for much longer than the reader may imagine. Similarly, even if Leonor does have a lengthy set-piece 'aria' in Act I ('Pedro, a quien llama el mundo Justiciero . . . ', lines 609–72), the textual critic might see her more as a dramatic convenience for tying up the loose ends of the play after Mencía's death than as a major player in her own right, since she speaks only one line in twenty in the play as a whole and has practically nothing to say in Act III.[12] Yet, by the time King Pedro restores her to polite society (if he does not guarantee her a tranquil future) by marrying her off to Gutierre at the very end of the play, the spectator in the theatre will be thoroughly familar with Leonor. A lonely supplicant, she has stalked Gutierre and his king throughout the play: it is she who is left on stage to bring Act I to a close with her cries of rage and self-pity and, at the end of the final Act, she it is again who is on stage, this time alongside her future husband. Even Mencía's servant-girl, Teodora, struts her moment upon the stage (Act II, sc. i, at lines 1061–62).

---

11.   Calderón did, however, entrust some extremely lengthy speeches to actresses, as witness Isabel's soliloquy and account of her abduction and rape in Act III, sc. i (lines 1788–1854 and 1884–2057) of *El alcalde de Zalamea*, ed. José María DÍEZ BORQUE, Clásicos Castalia 82 (Madrid: Castalia, 1981), 257–69, Rosaura's speech «con vaquero, espada y daga», to Prince Segismundo in *La vida es sueño*, Act III, sc. iii, ed. Albert E. SLOMAN, Spanish Texts (Manchester: Manchester University Press, 1961, rpt 1965), 81–86, lines 2690–2921, and Serafina «vestida de camino» in Act I, sc. i of *El pintor de su deshonra*, ed. & tr. Alan K. G. PATERSON (Warminster: Aris & Phillips, 1991), 39–46, lines 361–505. On the extent to which playwrights wrote parts with particular actresses in mind, see, most recently, Amelia GARCÍA-VALDECASAS, 'Los actores en el reinado de Felipe III', in *Comedias y comediantes: Estudios sobre el teatro clásico español*, ed. Manuel V. Diago & Teresa Ferrer, Col·leció Oberta (Valencia: Departament de Filologia Espanyola, Universitat de València, 1991), 369–85 (esp. 380–81). The increase, during the seventeenth century, in the number of lines actresses were asked to learn may prove a better indicator than many to the rise in their professional status.

12.   Compare Estrella in *La vida es sueño*, who is given only 121 lines to speak and Sirena in *A secreto agravio secreta venganza* who has 103. They are, however, on stage, making the spectator see them as principals, for 820 and 1207 lines respectively, or a quarter and more than a third of the two plays concerned.

Then there is Mencía herself, 'a virtuous woman who never fails to do the wrong thing'.[13] Condemned by readers of the play who are concerned primarily with *casos de conciencia,* praised by others, she is more frequently sidelined by critics of the play as a mere cipher.[14] Yet she is on stage from as early as Act I, sc. ii (line 45; her husband does not appear until midway through that same scene, at line 315) and she is there, spectacularly, at the end when she is 'discovered' for the third time in as many Acts (*«Descubre a doña Mencía en una cama, desangrada»,* stage direction at line 2872).[15] The three male principals (Gutierre, Prince Enrique, and King Pedro) may have, between them, nearly four times as many lines to deliver as she does, but she is seen by the audience for longer than any other figure in the play save her husband. Furthermore, she is at the centre of some of the piece's most arresting business: hiding (and hiding others), fainting, falling asleep, and, at the last, bathed in her own blood.

In this regard, she has many similarities with the figure of Serafina in *El pintor de su deshonra*: led by the hand on to the stage in Act I, sc. i (*«Sale Don Juan, que trae de la mano a Serafina, vestida de camino»,* stage direction at line 270); fainting later on in that same scene at line 525 and unconscious until line 584; unconscious again for the whole of an appearance on stage towards the end of Act II (stage directions at lines 2012 and 2046: *«Sale Don Juan,*

---

13. I take the phrase from Edward M. WILSON, 'A Hispanist Looks at *Othello*', in his *Spanish and English Literature of the 16th and 17th Centuries: Studies in Discretion, Illusion, and Mutability* (Cambridge: Cambridge University Press, 1980), 201–19 (218).

14. James E. MARANISS, *On Calderón* (Columbia & London: University of Missouri Press, 1978), 69 ('ambivalent and unconsciously incriminatory'); Cesáreo BANDERA, 'Historias de amor y dramas de honor', in *Approaches to the Theater of Calderón,* ed. Michael D. McGaha (Washington, DC: University Press of America, 1982), 53–63 (55: 'La sin par Doña Mencía . . . la más íntegra y admirable de esas malhadadas esposas'); Thomas Austin O'CONNOR, *Myth and Mythology in the Theater of Pedro Calderón de la Barca* (n.p. [= San Antonio, Texas]: Trinity University Press, 1988), 82 ('[a] scapegoat').

15. Compare stage directions at lines 1897 (Act II, sc. iv): *«Descubre una cortina donde está durmiendo [doña Mencía] »,* and 2458 (Act III, sc. ii): *«Descubre a doña Mencía escribiendo»* (*ed. cit.,* 163, 192). On discovery, see John E. VAREY, 'Valores visuales en la comedia española en la época de Calderón', in *Edad de Oro,* V, ed. Pablo Jauralde Pou (Madrid: Ediciones de la Universidad Autónoma de Madrid, 1986), 271–97, rpt in VAREY, *Cosmovisión,* 227–47 (239); VAREY, 'Staging and Stage Directions', in *Editing the Comedia,* ed. Frank P. Casa & Michael D. McGaha, Michigan Romance Studies 5 (Ann Arbor: University of Michigan, 1985), 145–61 (150); also Geoffrey WEST, '«Cerrar al daño las puertas»: Confining Spaces in *El médico de su honra*', in *Golden-Age Spanish Literature: Studies in Honour of John Varey by his Colleagues and Pupils,* ed. Charles Davis & Alan Deyermond (London: Department of Hispanic Studies, Queen Mary and Westfield College, 1991), 233–39.

con Serafina, desmayada», «*Vanse, llevándola*»); hiding from lines 2348 to
2388 of Act III, sc. ii; re-appearing at line 2499 «*con la mano en el rostro*»;
asleep from line 3018 (in a sitting position, in a reprise of her sitting for her
portrait in the opening scene of Act II); awakening at line 3062 «*asustada*»;
and, finally, dying in the arms of Don Pedro (lines 3084–3091). Doña Leonor
in Act III of another play, *A secreto agravio secreta venganza*, is a further case
in point: after fainting (stage direction at line 2499), she is carried off stage
eleven lines later, only to reappear as a corpse in the arms of Don Lope (line
2674). The dead Mencía is the focus of attention for the spectator at the end
of *El médico de su honra*, as is Serafina in the final *cuadro* of *El pintor de su
deshonra*; Leonor, carried by Don Lope, fulfils a similar role right to the end
of *A secreto agravio secreta venganza*.

   This observation of the importance of women, played on the Spanish stage
by women, was one made by many contemporaries of Calderón.[16]   Women
were cited by puritanical enemies of the *corrales* as one of the incentives
seventeenth-century drama offered to public disorder and private sexual
immorality – along, that is, with the reputation of actresses recruited for their
looks and their abilities to entertain by singing and dancing as well as in more
ancient ways, the amount of leg they revealed when disguised *en hábito de
hombre* (an observation which gives us a less anachronistic angle on *mujeres
varoniles*), and the propensity exhibited by Golden-Age playwrights for making
them collapse on stage, either swooning or asleep or in death.[17] If we look at
other plays, such as *El pintor de su deshonra*, we can find a variation on the
same pattern: whereas Serafina is given about half the lines (and part lines)
spoken when she is on stage (711 of a total of 1450), Porcia, who sings and

---

16.   In Madrid, boys were expressly forbidden to take the stage in female costume: see document 6 (1615), *Reglamentos de teatros*, in J. E. VAREY & N. D. SHERGOLD, *Teatros y comedias en Madrid, 1600–1650: Estudio y documentos*, Fuentes para la Historia del Teatro en España 3 (London: Tamesis Books Ltd, 1971), 55–58 (56). The genesis of this bye-law is discussed by SHERGOLD, *A History of the Spanish Stage from Medieval Times until the End of the
Seventeenth Century* (Oxford: Clarendon Press, 1967), 516–19.

17.   Pedro de Castro, recently enthroned as archbishop of Granada, was one of several cler-
ics to campaign against the *corrales* in the late 1580s and 1590s. When summoning the ancient
authorities in his cause, he selected, above all, texts which stressed the supposed sexual impro-
priety of what went on there, citing (Lisbon, Biblioteca Nacional, MS 1464, fols 168v–179r)
from Cyprian, John Chrysostom, and others, and making great play with Isidore's 'histriones
sunt qui muliebri indumento gestus impudicarum foeminarum exprimebant' (*Etymologiae*,
XVIII, xlviii). Many of the texts critical of the *corrales* assembled in Emilio COTARELO Y MORI,
Bibliografía de las controversias sobre la licitud del teatro en España . . . (Madrid: Tipografía de
la Revista de Archivos, Bibliotecas y Museos, 1904) adopt a similar tactic.

speaks only 345 lines, and whose longest speech is a mere twenty, is on stage for 1277 lines, with her singing (off-stage, lines 1630–33 and 1780–83, and on for lines 1714–17, 1740–43, and 1768–71) and playing of a harp giving her a presence, boosted by her being there at the end of Acts I and III, that is more significant for a visualisation of the play than it can be for any but the most attentive reader.[18]

A fourth consideration to emerge from the text, when we concern ourselves with performance constants, is the sheer quantity of stage-business involved. Financial parameters and the constraints imposed by legislation would, at least in Madrid, lead to much of this business being, by modern standards, under-rehearsed: staged, as Shakespeare's Cleopatra has it, by 'the quick comedians, extemporally'. Practised stratagems would accordingly be transferred by actors and *autores de comedias* from the performance of one play to another.[19] Apart from the repeated play with dagger and sword (lines 1377 ff., 1533 ff., 2266–76, 2307) which interjects echoes of foreboding into both the relationship of Enrique and Pedro and into the principal action involving Gutierre and his wife – albeit in a language that neither Gutierre nor his king can read – there is, in Act III, an extended play on letters (lines 2458 ff., 2496), which recalls the use Calderón makes of this device (and of paintings) in such plays as *El pintor de su deshonra*, *La vida es sueño*, and *A secreto agravio secreta venganza*.[20] He also uses to the full the 'discovery space', or

---

18. On Porcia's songs, some of which reappear in other plays of Calderón, see Edward M. WILSON & Jack SAGE, *Poesías líricas en las obras dramáticas de Calderón: Citas y glosas*, Colección Támesis A 1 (London: Tamesis Books Ltd, 1964), esp. 94–95.

19. See, for example, document 2 (1608), *Reglamentos de teatros*, §4: 'Que dos dias antes que se ayan de representar la comedia, cantar, o entremes, lo lleuen al señor del Consejo, para que lo mande ver, y examinar, y hasta que les aya dado licencia, no lo den a los compañeros a estudiar', in VAREY & SHERGOLD, *Teatros y comedias en Madrid, 1600–1650*, 48. The same bye-law also proscribes the appearance on stage of actresses in male attire: a ruling more honoured in the breach than in the observance: *ibid.*, 92, *Reglamentos* (1641), and VAREY, 'The Use of Costume in Some Plays of Calderón', in *Calderón and the Baroque Tradition*, ed. Kurt Levy, Jesús Ara, & Gethlin Hughes (Waterloo, Ontario: Wilfrid Laurier University Press, 1985), 109–18; rpt, tr. Esther Berzosa, as 'La indumentaria en el teatro de Calderón', in *Cosmovisión*, 263–72 (265). For a discussion of accusations levelled against the *corrales* in Seville, mirroring closely the debate that took place in the capital, see Jean SENTAURENS, *Séville et le théâtre de la fin du Moyen-Âge à la fin du XVIIe siècle*, 2 vols (Lille: Université de Lille III, Atelier National de Reproduction des Thèses, 1984), I, 96–110.

20. For *Pintor* (which also has its own play on letters) see, most recently, Alan K. G. PATERSON, 'Calderón's «Deposición en favor de los profesores de la pintura»: Comment and Text', in *Art and Literature in Spain, 1600–1800: Studies in Honour of Nigel Glendinning*, ed. Charles Davis & Paul Julian Smith, Colección Támesis A 148 (London & Madrid: Tamesis,

small inner stage (*vestuario*) at the rear of the platform stage (Leonor, Mencía, Enrique, and Gutierre all hiding at various times). There is also the much-commented simulated stage-darkness that underpins the imagery of sight and blindness, light and darkness, peppering the text – and *all* darkness on stage in the Spanish *corrales* was simulated (hence extra clues for spectators such as 'a escuras entraré' and 'noche . . . sombra': Act II, sc. i, line 1310, and Act II, sc. iv, lines 1862–63), municipal regulations stipulating that performances finish well before dusk, another regulation reflecting the view of the *corrales* taken by the authorities.[21]

II.   Repeated structures

Calderón's attention to the congruence of multiple semiotic systems when it came to the staging of *autos*, where his remit was wide, is a matter of record.[22] Yet, even in the looser format of writing for the public theatres, there is ample evidence of structural coherence: of an eye for structured spectacle and for what the late Premraj Halkoree termed a 'mastery of his physical medium in [the] exploitation of the resources of the contemporary stage'.[23]

    In each Act of *El príncipe constante*, first published in the 1636 *Primera*

1993), 153–66. In *A secreto agravio secreta venganza*, see Act II, lines 1324–37 and Act III, lines 2197, 2301–14.

21. See document 38 (1641), *Reglamentos de teatros*: 'Que se comienze la comedia en los quatro meses de invierno a las dos de la tarde, y los quatro de primavera a las tres, y las quatro de verano a las quatro, de modo que se salga dellas siempre de dia claro', in VAREY & SHERGOLD, *Teatros y comedias en Madrid, 1600–1650*, 93; John VAREY, 'The Staging of Night Scenes in the *comedia*', *The American Hispanist*, nr 15 (Feb. 1977), 14–16, partly incorporated in his 'Valores visuales', *Cosmovisión*, 227–47 (241–45). Palace performances were not covered by this regulation. As Gwynne EDWARDS puts it, 'It is worth repeating that Calderón's audiences, no less than Shakespeare's, must indeed have had extremely vivid and practised imaginations to have been able to identify with such scenes when they themselves were usually bathed in afternoon sunshine': *The Prison and the Labyrinth: Studies in Calderonian Tragedy* (Cardiff: University of Wales Press, 1978), 85. For a rigorously textual approach to the symbolism of these night scenes, see Alberto CASTILLA, 'El arte teatral de Calderón en *El médico de su honra*', in *Calderón: Actas del «Segundo congreso internacional sobre Calderón y el teatro español del Siglo de Oro» (Madrid, 8–13 de junio de 1981)*, ed. Luciano García Lorenzo, 3 vols, Anejos de la Revista «Segismundo» 6 (Madrid: CSIC, 1983), I, 403–12 (410–12).

22. On his use of the artistic autonomy granted him at Corpus Christi, when he had an authority much like that of a present-day artistic director, see John E. VAREY, 'Calderón's *auto sacramental, La vida es sueño*, in Performance', *Iberoromania*, 14 (1981), 75–86, rpt as 'El auto sacramental, *La vida es sueño*, como obra teatral representable', tr. Esther Berzosa, in his *Cosmovisión*, 363–73.

23. Premraj HALKOREE, *Calderón de la Barca: El alcalde de Zalamea*, Critical Guides to Spanish Texts 5 (London: Grant & Cutler, 1972), 57.

parte (a play whose poetry has been minutely analysed by Robert Pring-Mill), the eponymous hero delivers a major set-piece speech (of 104, 157, and 168 lines respectively). His tête-à-tête at the end of Act II with the virtuous Arab princeling, Muley, echoes an earlier encounter, also ending in music, and charts, through spectacle, the Portuguese Prince's reversal of fortune, as, indeed, do his encounters with Princess Fénix, the first of them replete with the much-anthologized matching sonnets.[24]

El alcalde de Zalamea, probably written in the early 1640s, is, for all its alarums and excursions, rabble army and camp-followers, structured as spectacle around the head-to-head encounters between Pedro Crespo, father of Juan and Isabel, and Don Lope de Figueroa.[25] In the final scene of Act I, lines 777–894 (and, especially, from line 850), the encounter is a markedly imbalanced one: that between an army commander, resplendent («*muy galán*») in his tunic as a knight of Santiago on his way to Guadalupe to an audience with King Philip II, and a man he himself describes at this point as a 'testarudo villano' (*aside*, line 891). By Act II, lines 1077–1200, matters have progressed to a point where the two men can sit in the *locus amoenus* of Isabel's garden, away for a short while from the all-too-predictable problems arising from the billeting of an army upon a small rural community. For all their differences, the two are now in some senses well-matched: each is in his own way both stubborn and self-assured, and they proceed to trade phrase for phrase and gesture for gesture, Crespo now being elevated in his noble guest's estimation to the status of a 'ladino villano' – and, indeed, a prudent one (*aside*, line 1199).[26] Despite the social gulf that separates them, it is the similarity between their personalities which is stressed in stage business when next they meet, emerging on stage at the same moment, each with his shield raised. They fight in unison, and to good effect, before turning their swords against

---

24. Pedro CALDERÓN DE LA BARCA, *Primera parte de comedias* (QCL), nominally ed. by Calderón's younger brother, José (Madrid: María de Quiñones for the booksellers Pedro Coello and Manuel López, 1636), rpt in *The Comedias of Calderón*, ed. CRUICKSHANK & VAREY, II, 281r-v, 286v-287v, 294v-295v (speeches of Fernando), 281r-282v, 291r-v (Fernando and Muley); Robert PRING-MILL, 'Estructuras lógico-retóricas y sus resonancias', 109–54. On the sonnets, see Terence O'REILLY, 'The Sonnets of Fernando and Fénix in Calderón's *El príncipe constante*', *Forum for Modern Language Studies*, 16 (1980), 349–57.

25. On the staging of the play see John E. VAREY, 'Space and Time in the Staging of Calderón's *El alcalde de Zalamea*', in *Staging in the Spanish Theatre*, ed. Margaret A. Rees (Leeds: Trinity and All Saints College, 1984), 11–25.

26. In his note *ad loc.*, DÍEZ BORQUE (*ed. cit.*) cites *Dicc. Autoridades*, IV (1734), 347b, indicating that LADINO is used here in its meaning of 'advertido', 'astuto'.

each other, each under the misapprehension, in the mêlée, that he is dealing with a mutineer (Act II, lines 1321–51). Each is impressed by the other's skill at arms, and this encounter and the conversation that follows it cements their friendship and leads directly to Don Lope's suggestion (lines 1506 ff.), that with Crespo's blessing, his host's son Juan might enlist under his banner.[27] When the two meet for the final time in Act III (lines 2501 ff.), Don Lope's friendly greeting to his ally is quickly forgotten in the heat of events and the two men find themselves on opposite sides of what threatens to turn into open warfare between village and army. Crespo's daughter Isabel has been abducted and raped, and he, as the newly-elected mayor of Zalamea, has put both her assailant and her brother Juan behind bars. Indeed, though neither the audience nor Don Lope knows it (until line 2698, another discovery: «*Aparece dado garrote en una silla el Capitán*»), the rapist has already been executed. We have come full circle, as Don Lope addresses Crespo as a villein ('alcaldillo', line 2528; 'villanote', line 2554). The collision between two very angry men – between the unstoppable force that is Don Lope and the immovable object that is Pedro Crespo ('lo dicho dicho . . . lo hecho hecho', lines 2568–69) – threatens, for all its symmetry, not only to raze the local gaol to the ground but also to put the whole village to the sword.

The textual images, balances, and symmetries underlying this developing relationship (and the unfolding drama reflected and conditioned by it) are scrupulously conveyed by action, gesture, and business. From the social disparities of Act I, underscored by costume, we move through the seated, at times reflective, and unfailingly courteous debate of Act II, to the confrontation between the commander and a mayor holding his *vara de la justicia* (lines 2107, 2117–18, stage direction at 2177) and surrounded on stage by as many of his fellow citizens as the acting company can provide.[28] The two confront

---

27. Díez Borque (*ed. cit.*, 243n.) records Robert Marrast's comparison – in his bi-lingual edition of the play for Éditions Montaigne (Paris: Aubier, 1959), 201 – of Crespo's speech of advice to his son Juan (esp. lines 1612–38) both with the *reproches* of Don Beltrán ('viejo graue') to his son Don García ('galán') in Act II of Juan Ruiz de Alarcón's ca 1619–20 *La verdad sospechosa* (see Juan Ruiz de Alarcón y Mendoza, *Obras completas*, ed. Alma V. Ebersole, 2 vols, Estudios de Hispanófila 5 (New York: Adelphi University, 1966), II, 149) and with Quixote's advice (II, 42) to Sancho Panza. The common ancestry of the advice/blessing speech (see, for example, Polonius to Laertes in *Hamlet*, Act I, sc. iii: 'And these few precepts in thy memory | See thou character') is, however, not investigated.

28. The *princeps* has «*Sale Pedro Crespo con vara, y los que puedan*» (*ed. cit.*, 276), while Vera Tassis gives '*Sale Pedro Crespo con vara, y los mas que puedan con el*», in *Séptima parte de comedias del célebre poeta español Don Pedro Calderón de la Barca . . . corregidas por sus origi-

each other, each certain of his rights, each standing his ground as the audience's eyes swivel from one to the other during a lengthy exchange of short speeches, most of them of two lines only (lines 2570–2637), and the tension, the violence, and the impasse can only be resolved by the arrival, to a roll of drums, of the King himself.[29]

Elsewhere in this volume, the visual structure of Calderón's *comedia, La vida es sueño*, is discussed in some detail. There again, we see Calderón carefully plotting the scenes between Segismundo and Rosaura in such a way that each encounter (as is the case with Segismundo's palace excursions) reflects and reflects upon the image of the previous one, and audience expectations of a final resolution through marriage are both fulfilled and yet frustrated.[30] Despite the double betrothal at the end of Act III, it is a play which sends the spectator away puzzled and every bit as thoughtful as the scholar reading the text in his private study.

In *El médico de su honra*, the dual-strand plot with its double tragedy enables Calderón to design a double pattern to the traffic of the stage, alternating between national and domestic concerns. For his portrait of the agony of the marriage, he composes three scenes during which Mencía and Gutierre are alone for a time, and each of these foreshadows and/or recalls the others. Towards the end of the long second scene in Act I the two snatch a moment away from the maelstrom of events (lines 495–554). The balance of power appears to lie, in this encounter, with the young wife: it is Gutierre, in his desire to attend upon the King, newly arrived in Andalusia, who, 'lisonjero' and

---

nales (Madrid: Francisco Sanz, 1683), 511. On the familiarity of *corrales*' audiences with 'semiotic props' such as the *vara de alguacil*, see José María DÍEZ BORQUE, *Sociedad y teatro en la España de Lope de Vega*, Colección Ensayo (Barcelona: Antoni Bosch, 1978), 224–25.

29. A king employed as *deus ex machina*, reminiscent of plays by Lope de Vega and others, is a very different creature from a king present from the outset, as is Pedro in Calderón's *El médico de su honra*; see, for example, Lope de VEGA, *Peribáñez y el comendador de Ocaña* (ca 1605–8), ed. J. M. RUANO & J. E. VAREY (London: Tamesis Texts Ltd, 1980), 145 (Act III, lines 2908 ff.), and *Fuente Ovejuna* (probably written between 1611 and 1618), ed. & tr. Victor DIXON (Warminster: Aris & Phillips, 1989), 204 (Acts III, lines 2290 ff.) – editions which do look at performance values (42–46 and 24–31 respectively). On the arbitrary ennoblement of *villanos* as an element of what he terms 'retraction', see Frank P. CASA's provocative study 'Affirmation and Retraction in Golden-Age Drama', *Neophilologus*, 61 (1977), 551–64.

30. See esp. indications of dress for Segismundo at lines 102, 1224, 2656, and (unstated) 3136, and for Rosaura at lines 1, 1548, 2690 and (unstated) 3136; also William H. WHITBY, 'Rosaura's Role in the Structure of *La vida es sueño*', *Hispanic Review* (Philadelphia), 27 (1960), 16–27, rpt in *Critical Essays on the Theatre of Calderón*, ed. Bruce W. Wardropper (New York: New York University Press, 1965), 101–13.

'parabólico' (lines 545–46), makes all the supplicatory gestures to accompany his entreaties. The only shadow that lies between husband and wife is, apparently, that of Leonor, the southern belle to whom, as we shall soon learn (Act I, sc. iii, line 649), Gutierre once made a promise of marriage. Mencía's tart observation on male fickleness, '¡O qué tales sois los hombres! | Hoy olvido, ayer amor; | ayer gusto, y hoy rigor' (lines 517–19), only serves to indicate who is in the moral ascendant.

By Act II, sc. iv, when the two next have the stage to themselves, things are very different. Suspicion, soon to be stuffed more fully, lays siege to Gutierre even as he scales the garden wall and insinuates himself into his own house by night. The sequence that follows is punctuated by his discovery of Mencía asleep (at line 1897), her sleep-filled discoveries of dishonour, a fleeting visit in the dark by Mencía's maid Jacinta ('temerosa'), and the surprise, once Jacinta has returned with candles, of Gutierre's reappearance *en clair*, «*por otra puerta de donde se escondió*» (stage direction at line 1983). At the end of the interview, the balance between the couple has been totally reversed from what we saw in Act I, Gutierre bringing the Act to a close, muttering of the grave, while Mencía, awakened thoroughly from the uneasy dream figuring her erstwhile suitor, stares full-ghastly at the 'Miedo, espanto, temor, y horror tan fuerte' which, as she acknowledges, 'parasismos han sido de mi muerte'.

The prominence accorded to this, the last *cuadro* before the interlude (and accordingly the image retained by the spectator) is not fortuitous.[31] When Mencía sees her husband alone and for the final time in Act III, sc. ii, their meeting is so choreographed as to recall this scene from Act II. Again, Mencía is 'discovered' by her husband, and again she is, for some of their time together, unconscious. The gulf between the couple is now unbridgeable, all the affection we saw in Act I seemingly gone. Conversation is conducted remotely, by letter, and sentence of death passed down in writing. When Gutierre sees his wife alive for the last time, fleetingly, in Act III, sc. iv, he casts a cold eye on her as she sleeps – 'un vivo cadáver' (line 2583) – on the same bed on which she will be discovered in the final scene «*desangrada*».

There is, then, a carefully contrived visual pattern to the three scenes involving husband and wife *a solas*. Calderón's skill in constructing such pat-

---

31. There is a concise account of the nature and function of the *entremés* and of other 'elements of interruption' in the seventeenth-century *corrales* in Catalina BUEZO's useful little edition *Teatro breve de los Siglos de Oro: Antología*, Castalia Didáctica 31 (Madrid: Castalia, 1992), 12–26.

terns – his skill, that is, as a dramatist – goes a long way towards explaining that sense of artistic coherence which an audience experiences when watching his plays.

III.   Nested scenes

In *El médico de su honra*, Calderón has recourse to narrower scene-patterning as well, more akin to the simultaneous movement indicated by stage directions in Act I of Lope de Vega's *El castigo sin venganza*. As we have seen, Doña Mencía is repeatedly seen fainting, lying down, and asleep. The concealment of characters and the use of the discovery space are also structurally patterned.[32] But there is one set of scenes in Act III which reflects, in what happens on stage, some of the same concerns scholars have extricated from close reading of the text, and also shows just how, on stage, Calderón weaves together into a single tragedy the dual strands of his play.

An audience's view of the character of Pedro – not, as we have said, a king brought on at the end of Act III as a device but rather a fully-fledged and fully-flawed character in the piece – will condition the view they take of his apparent tolerance of Gutierre's actions ('¡Notable sujeto!', line 2872), and will, by extension, shape their response to the play as a whole.[33] If Pedro should prove to be not simply 'cruel', as witness his play with the *lacayo* Coquín (Act I, sc. iii and Act II, sc. ii), but also unaware of what is afoot – if he should be, in Calderonian poetic shorthand, a *confuso* – then the spectator is not going to set great stock by his apparent endorsement of Gutierre's murder of Mencía, but rather regard him as heaping confusion on his own head and on those of others. And, irrespective of the audience's knowledge of history (of, that is, the murder of King Pedro I by Enrique at Montiel castle in March 1369 some ten days after his defeat on the battle-field), what happens

---

32. Act II, sc. i, lines 1063–79 (asleep); Act II, sc. iv, lines 1897–1915 (asleep); Act III, sc. ii, lines 2461–79 (faint); Act III, sc. v, lines 2872 ff (dead). Act I has a prefiguration of these scenes (sc. i–ii, lines 2–155) in which Prince Enrique is on stage unconscious and Mencía fears for his life, as, later, he affects to himself (Act I, sc. ii, lines 243–45), the irony being that it is he who will be the death of her.

33. See A. I. WATSON, 'Peter the Cruel or Peter the Just: A Reappraisal of the Role Played by King Peter in Calderón's *El médico de su honra*', *Romanistisches Jahrbuch*, 14 (1963), 322–46; Don W. CRUICKSHANK, 'Calderón's King Pedro: Just or Unjust?', *Gesammelte Aufsätze zur Kulturgeschichte Spaniens*, 25 (1970), 113–32; Alexander A. PARKER, '*El médico de su honra* as Tragedy', *Hispanófila*, 2 (1975), 3–23; and Frank P. CASA, 'Crime and Moral Responsibility in *El médico de su honra*', in *Homenaje a William L. Fichter*, ed. A. David Kossoff & José Amor y Vázquez (Madrid: Castalia, 1971), 127–37.

on stage in these scenes, even apart from the motif of the dagger that runs through the early encounters between the half-brothers, sends a clear message that Pedro is a baffled – indeed, a flustered man.[34]

The sequence of *cuadros* I refer to is Act III, sc. iii–v, all of them played at night. Music, responsible in Act II for Mencía's falling asleep, plays, as we shall see, a central role in all of this, though the commonplace that music is the food of love – or, in Calderón's words, an 'antídoto a los males' (line 2529) – is here treated differently: the ballad heard 'off' contains an allusion, indirect on its first appearance (lines 2530–33) and direct on its second (lines 2634–37), to Pedro's death. Small wonder that Pedro is, as he admits when he has heard it a second time without being able to identify the singer (lines 2638 ff.), neither fed nor solaced but thoroughly bewildered.

2454–2507	**Gutierre's** apostophe to *honor*; 'discovery' of **Mencía** writing (2458); Mencía faints (2461); Gutierre reads (2462–2464); writes (2474); Mencía recovers (2480) and reads (2496)
2508–2537	**Pedro and Diego**: 'REY. En fin, ¿Enrique se fue? . . . ¿Y dónde va? DIEGO. Yo presumo | que a Consuegra' (2508, 2514–2515); Music ('off', 2525): 'DIEGO. La música | es antídoto a los males. | *Cantan.* | *El Infante don Enrique* | *hoy se despidió del Rey*; | *su pesadumbre y su ausencia* | *quiera Dios que pare en bien.* | REY. ¡Qué triste voz!'
2538–2605	**Gutierre** leading blindfolded **Ludovico**: 'LUDOVICO. . . . me turba y me suspende . . . | . . . ¿Qué confusiones son éstas | que a tal extremo me traen? | ¡Válgame Dios!' (2558, 2566–2568)
[2606–2633	**Gutierre**: soliloquy]
2634–2648	**Pedro, Diego**: '*Para Consuegra camina,* | *donde piensa que han de ser* | *teatros de mil tragedias* | *las montañas de Montiel*' (2634–2637)
2649–2711	Same plus **Gutierre** leading blindfolded **Ludovico**.

If one looks closely at the rapid-fire exits and entrances that characterise these particular scenes, one can begin to appreciate how adept Calderón is at building up a set of nested images on stage. The series begins at line 2454 in the *cuadro* we have already discussed involving Gutierre and Mencía: Mencía, initially hidden, then 'discovered' writing to Enrique, then fainting when her note is read (or misread) by Gutierre, and finally coming to, only to

---

34. The fundamental work for the War of Succession is Peter E. RUSSELL, *English Intervention in Spain and Portugal in the Time of Edward III and Richard II* (Oxford: Clarendon Press, 1955); see 45–68. On the dagger and the sword as 'symbols of the speechless male world' in a language of 'idioms of silence', see Robert TER HORST, *Calderón: The Secular Plays* (Lexington: University of Kentucky Press, 1982), 92–93.

find a note in her husband's hand, judging and sentencing her in her 'absence'. Her speech is replete with a Calderonian shorthand for emotional turmoil that also frees the actress playing the young wife to extemporise suitable movements and gestures: '¿qué es esto?', '¡Válgame Dios!' (lines 2486, 2496), '¡Qué ilusión! . . . ¿Pero qué veo?' (lines 2492–93), 'nadie en casa me escucha . . . mi turbación' (lines 2500–01); and – in a phrase familiar to those who have seen the end of Act II, and also to those who know the opening scene of *La vida es sueño* featuring another much-exercised young lady – '¿Dónde iré desta suerte | tropezando en la sombra de mi muerte?' (lines 2506–07).[35]

The scene that follows involves the battle royal. The King and his close ally Diego discuss the behaviour of Prince Enrique – the unstated presence looming over the previous exchanges between Gutierre and Mencía. This second scene in the sequence ends with Pedro's sense of foreboding – '¡Qué triste voz!' (line 2534) – on hearing the anonymous street-singer. Pedro and Diego rush from the stage («*Vase cada uno por su puerta*») in what will prove a futile attempt to 'discover' the identity of this voice of history, and it is against the background of the ballad that a third pair emerges on to the stage.

This odd couple proves to be the blind (as Gutierre has, with dramatic irony, referred to himself on more than one occasion, and as the audience has seen him, in Act II, sc. i and sc. iv, groping around his own house in the dark) leading the blindfolded (the bloodletter Ludovico). It picks up not only the exclamations and gestures of the previous two scenes '¡Válgame Dios!' (line 2541) but also the image of a pair of characters on stage, caught up in something they do not understand, as witness lines 2566–68: '¿Qué confusiones son éstas, | que a tal extremo me traen? | ¡Válgame Dios!'.[36]

After a short soliloquy from Gutierre, justifying to the audience (and himself) the deed Ludovico is about to perform, and again referring to the metaphor contained in the name of the play ('Médico soy de mi honor', line 2630; compare lines 1401–02 and the last lines of Act II, sc. i (1580–1712), just as he and Mencía are leaving the stage «*cada uno por su puerta*»; also the last speech of Act II, sc. ii, Gutierre's great 'aria', especially 1659–1712), the spectator is then treated to a reprise of these pairs of *confusos* on stage.

---

35. Compare 'yo, sin más camino | que el que me dan las leyes del destino, | ciega y desesperada', *La vida es sueño*, lines 11–14 (*ed. cit.*, 3).

36. On the imagery of blindness, see Gutierre's speech in Act II, sc. iv, esp. lines 1911–12.

Firstly, Diego and Pedro, having run about the streets crying confusion, dash back in («*cada uno por su puerta*») and confess they have been unable to identify the (blind?) street singer responsible for the ballad (*romance de ciego?*) foretelling the King's fate. This time, their exchanges pick up on the image-cluster *honor/opinión/rumor/viento/aire* at the same time as Mencía is being murdered off-stage: 'REY: Supuesto | que cantan en esta calle, | ¿no hemos de saber quién es? | ¿Habla por ventura el aire?' (lines 2638–41), and Diego, espying two men approaching in the simulated gloom, stresses the importance of identifying them (lines 2648–49). Cue Gutierre and Ludovico «*tapado el rostro*».[37] Lines 2657–65, with their prophecy of doom, summarise the darkness, foreboding, and confusion in the minds of Gutierre, Ludovico, Diego, Pedro (and Mencía, whose candle is even now put out). That darkness and that confusion engulf them on stage. The events at Montiel are foretold once again by the anonymous singer and Diego comments (ostensibly about the odd couple, but for the audience, and with dramatic irony, also about the future of the King himself and his half-brother): 'De los dos, señor, que antes | venían, se volvió el uno, | y el otro se quedó' (lines 2657–59). The King's answer reveals his own state of mind: 'A darme | confusión; que si le veo | a la poca luz que esparce | la luna, no tiene forma | su rostro' (lines 2659–2663), and Ludovico, just before removing his blindfold, chimes in with a by now resonant 'Dos confusiones son parte, | señor, a no responderos' (lines 2669–70). Towards the end of the sequence, Don Diego comments to the King 'Triste has quedado', to which Pedro is forced to comment 'Forzoso ha sido asombrarme' (lines 2714–15). As even the reader of the script can tell, such exchanges throw a cloak of confusion, *tristeza*, and *asombro* over all that is happening, leading up, as they do, to the *coup de théâtre*: the opening of the curtain to the inner stage to reveal Mencía once again, this time asleep for good in a tableau already sketched by Ludovico (lines 2575–82).

Even if we take a worst scenario, and postulate an audience unable to hear all or unwilling to listen to most of what is being said by the characters in this final sequence from the last Act of *El médico de su honra*, the quickfire cutting from one pair of characters to another – Gutierre and Mencía, Pedro and Diego, Gutierre and Ludovico, Pedro and Diego, Gutierre and Ludovico

---

37. For a study of this image cluster, see Daniel L. HEIPLE, 'Gutierre's Witty Diagnosis in *El médico de su honra*', in *Critical Perspectives on Calderón de la Barca*, ed. Frederick A. de Armas, David M. Gitlitz, & José A. Madrigal (Lincoln, Nebraska: Society of Spanish and Spanish-American Studies, 1981), 81–90.

once again – as well as their use of exits and entrances, conveys two things to the audience. Firstly, these sets of characters are all involved with each other: the actions of one group are linked indissolubly to the actions of another, the fate of Mencía to that of Gutierre, but also to those of Diego and King Pedro. The long shadow of Enrique falls on all. And, secondly, the King is terrified by what takes place. He is not, as are many Golden-Age kings, above and outside the main action of the play: he is not wheeled on as in some provincial progress, to dispense justice, marry off the principals, and wind up the action in marriage and dance, but rather is implicated in what takes place, and the audience is being invited to judge his verdict on Gutierre accordingly. It is not just the admiration of one hard man for another, or even of one *justiciero*, one cold fish, for another, but the reaction of one badly rattled individual to the actions of another.[38]

None of this should be taken as an invitation not to read play-texts closely as poetry. The publication of the *partes* texts of Calderón plays may well have been undertaken with a view to their private study by a reading public whose interest in Calderón's plays seems to have lasted, even grown, long after he had himself ceased to write for the public theatres. It was an enterprise that had his blessing, even if not necessarily his active editorial intervention.[39] And, as Jeremy Lawrance reminds us (above, 64), night-settings, even those played in daylight, were 'part of contemporary playwrights' stock-in-trade of symbolic or iconographical emblems for moral confusion and deceit'. This short essay should, rather, be viewed as a corrective to analyses and interpretations that pay little heed to the traffic of the stage: a reminder that, as one contemporary of Calderón put it: 'nempe quae in scena aguntur, viva sunt et animata; quae leguntur, mera ossa et cadavera'.[40] Much criticism of the

---

38. It will be clear that I do not see the King as he is portrayed by Anthony J. CASCARDI, *The Limits of Illusion: A Critical Study of Calderón*, Cambridge Iberian and Latin-American Studies (Cambridge: Cambridge University Press, 1984), 68–81.

39. On the textual criticism of the *partes*, see Don W. CRUICKSHANK, 'The Textual Criticism of Calderón's *comedias*: A Survey', in *The Comedias of Calderón*, ed. CRUICKSHANK & VAREY, I, 1–35. Other Spanish dramatists arranged to publish their plays, sometimes adding a frame-narrative, e.g. Agustín de ROJAS VILLANDRANDO's 1603 *El viaje entretenido* and Lope de VEGA's 1604 *El peregrino en su patria*, and even the less textually-centred 'elements of interruption', such as *entremeses*, were published, at least from the 1640s onwards: Hannah E. BERGMAN, *Luis Quiñones de Benavente y sus entremeses, con un catálogo biográfico de los actores citados en sus obras*, Biblioteca de Erudición y Crítica 7 (Madrid: Castalia, 1965), 24–25.

40. Nikolaus AVANCINI, SJ, *Poesis Dramatica*, 5 vols (Cologne: Johann Wilhelm Friessen, 1674–[86]), I, fol. 4r. A good account of what can be achieved by the application of close-

Golden-Age drama manages to devalue splendidly crafted plays such as this one and turn them not only, in Professor's Levin's words, into ontological essays but, criminally, into extremely dull ontological essays. The public theatres of the seventeenth century were notoriously noisy places, as not a few contemporaries observed.[41] Many a dramatist began his plays by begging a hearing patiently. Some years ago, when questioned about acoustics after an Oxford lecture on the Buen Retiro which included a mention of the various locations where Cosimo Lotti mounted plays for the royal court in the new palace of the Buen Retiro (the *Coliseo*, the small courtyard of the King's quarters, and the Hall of Realms where some of Calderón's plays were staged from 1636 onwards) the art historian Jonathan Brown is reported to have replied: 'You mean, would the audience have heard the *words*? I doubt it, though the palace would have been better in this respect than the public *corrales . . .*' Faced with such problems, actors and dramatists alike were only too well aware, as is Robert Pring-Mill himself, that the *admiratio* of the epic has to be transformed into the *mirabile visu* of the theatre – that is, that the show imports the argument of the play.[42]

NIGEL GRIFFIN

University of Manchester

---

reading techniques developed for the private study of sixteenth- and seventeenth-century poetry is Robert PRING-MILL, 'Los calderonistas de habla inglesa y *La vida es sueño*: métodos de análisis temático-estructural', in *Litterae Hispanae et Lusitanae: Zum Fünfzigjährigen Bestehen des Ibero-Amerikanischen Forschungsinstituts der Universität Hamburg*, ed. Hans Flasche (Munich: Max Hueber, 1968), 369–413.

41. The splendidly jaundiced account by Juan de ZABALETA, printed in 1660 by the same María de Quiñones who produced QC for Pedro de Coello, has fights breaking out in the auditorium while the women, jam-packed into the Madrid *cazuela*, noisily scoff plums, elbow each other in the face, and gossip between mouthfuls at the top of their voices: 'La que está junto a la puerta de la cazuela oye a los representantes y no los ve. La que está en el banco último los ve y no los oye, con que ninguna ve la comedia, porque las comedias, ni se oyen sin ojos ni se ven sin oídos.' A dramatist himself, he insists that, in the *comedia*, 'las acciones hablan gran parte': *El día de la fiesta por la tarde*, ed. Cristóbal Cuevas García, Clásicos Castalia 130 (Madrid: Castalia, 1983), 307–23 (321–22).

42. An interesting recent study is María Alicia AMADEI-PULICE, *Calderón y el barroco: Exaltación y engaño de los sentidos*, Purdue University Monographs in Romance Languages 31 (Amsterdam and Philadelphia: John Benjamins, 1990). I would like to thank my Manchester students, who listened to (and watched) a lecture based on an earlier version of this essay, *perdonando sus muchas faltas*.

THE WIT OF ZURBARÁN:
HIS PAINTINGS OF THE TEMPTATION AND
FLAGELLATION OF SAINT JEROME

BESIDES HIS EIGHT PAINTINGS of illustrious members of the Hieronymite order for the newly built sacristy of the Monastery at Guadalupe, Zurbarán also painted three pictures of the Flagellation, the Temptation and the Apotheosis of Saint Jerome for the small, adjoining chapel.[1]

In this study I shall be concerned primarily with the Temptation and the Flagellation, the first completed in 1639, the second probably that same year. These two paintings, which hang opposite one another, represent respectively the punishment of the saint for his devotion to pagan literature and his temptation whilst doing penance in the desert. I propose to treat the paintings as one unit whose two individual parts are akin to the distinct terms joined in a literary conceit, in so far as they establish a chain of conceptual and compositional juxtapositions. Like much seventeenth-century art and literature, Zurbarán's art appeals to the intellect and, in the case of the pictures under consideration, it does this by deliberately juxtaposing two canvases in such a way as to encourage the viewer to treat them not as self-contained entities but as an integral unit. As with any *conceptista* image, the mind must ponder and evaluate their interaction in order to reach a fuller appreciation of their subject-matter.

---

1. Jonathan BROWN, *Zurbarán* (London: Thames and Hudson, 1991), 29, 105 reproduces both paintings. See also *Zurbarán*, Catalogue to the Prado Exhibition (Madrid: Museo del Prado & Ministerio de Cultura, 1988), 25. The Apotheosis is also reproduced in the catalogue (21). On Zurbarán's sacristy paintings of Hieronymite monks, see Jonathan BROWN, *Images and Ideas in Seventeenth-Century Spanish Painting*, Princeton Essays on the Arts 6 (Princeton: Princeton University Press, 1978), 111–27; and for a contemporary history of the Hieronymite order, first published in 1600, Fray José de SIGÜENZA, *Historia de la orden de San Jerónimo*, ed. Juan Catalina García, 2nd edn, 2 vols, Nueva Biblioteca de Autores Españoles 8, 12 (Madrid: Bailly-Baillière e Hijos, 1907–09), esp. II, 629–39.

FIG. 1. Francisco de Zurbarán, THE TEMPTATION OF ST JEROME (1639)
(The Sacristy, Real Monasterio de Guadalupe, Cáceres, Spain)

FIG. 2. Francisco de Zurbarán, THE FLAGELLATION OF ST JEROME (*ca* 1639)
(The Sacristy, Real Monasterio de Guadalupe, Cáceres, Spain)

When considered as a pictorial conceit Zurbarán's paintings can be interpreted as a depiction of the necessity of renouncing the lure of the aesthetic, and, in so far as they are amongst his most accomplished pictures, they do this paradoxically by aesthetic means. The viewer's aesthetic appreciation thereby becomes an act of complicity in so far as it enacts precisely what the choice of subject-matter seeks to condemn, the sensory appeal of beauty and the potential distraction of art.

The two pictures offer a whole series of contrasts. On the most basic, thematic level, they depict the temptations of the flesh and of the mind. In the Temptation, the canvas is divided between the elderly Saint Jerome and his female temptresses and there is no physical contact between the two halves of the composition: Jerome refrains even from contemplating the female musicians, choosing instead to look obliquely out of the canvas at the viewer. Indeed, the saint's theatrical gesture of rejection enforces the separation and non-interaction between the ascetic and his temptresses. In contrast, whilst the Flagellation is also divided as a composition (between Christ seated on a raised cloud on the left and the kneeling saint on the right), the subject is more dynamic since Zurbarán not only depicts the physical interaction between the young saint and his angelic flagellators but also has the saint looking up at Christ in an attitude of prayer and penance. The two most striking features, however, are the differences in the use of light, and the contrast in the body of the saint as it appears in each picture. Whereas the Flagellation depicts Jerome as a muscular young man and is infused with light such that the canvas's very luminosity, as so often in Zurbarán, serves to signal the presence of the divine, the Temptation is sombre in tone, using light simply to highlight the women's faces and the saint's decrepit and rugged body, especially his outstretched arm, which has the appearance of a bolt of lightning about to strike his temptresses.[2]

In his letters, Saint Jerome describes how he was tempted whilst doing penance in the Syrian desert. Through fear of hell the saint had deprived himself of all physical comforts but, despite these measures, he was assailed by a tempting vision:

> Sabed pues que estando en esta vida que os he dicho, en la qual de mi propria voluntad (por temor del infierno) quasi como en carcel me auia

---

2. Compare Ann LIVERMORE, *Artists and Aesthetics in Spain*, Colección Támesis A 131 (London: Tamesis Books, 1988), 77; and BROWN, *Zurbarán*, 24.

condenado y puesto hecho compañero de solos los escorpiones y culebras y bestias fieras. Avn con todo esto muchas vezes me hallaua con la fantasia presente a los coros y danças que las moças en el siglo suelen hazer.[3]

This vision of young Roman girls dancing clearly represents the temptation of the flesh, and the normal pictoral treatment of this subject depicts it as such by emphasizing the lasciviousness of the dancers. However, in Zurbarán's depiction of the scene the dancing girls are replaced by a static group of chaste young women playing various musical instruments. The total lack of lasciviousness or suggestiveness in the portrayal of a supposed moment of intense temptation has been commented upon by various critics.[4]

Although Zurbarán's portrayal of Jerome's temptresses as entirely chaste can be ascribed simply to the overwhelming sense of decorum which is the hallmark of his style, another interpretation is possible. In terms of Golden-Age aesthetics which define beauty as the embodiment of order, proportion, and harmony, the painting represents two such forms of beauty: the visible grace of the women themselves, appealing primarily to the senses, and their music, appealing to the mind. What tempts the saint is perfect form, beauty itself, in a number of its manifestations. Whilst beauty in its physical form (the women) is relatively easy to shun, beauty in its more abstract or intellectual form (music) provides a more acute source of temptation – that of the mind by art.

---

3. See *Epistolas del glorioso doctor sant Hieronymo*, tr. Juan de MOLINA (Seville: Jácome Cromberger, 1548), 110r. In the Golden Age 'coro' still designated a group of people singing *and* dancing, as Covarrubias makes clear when he translates the noun as a 'multitud de gente que canta y se regocija': Sebastián de COVARRUBIAS, *Tesoro de la lengua castellana o española*, ed. Martín de Riquer, 2nd edn (Barcelona: Alta Fulla, 1989), 361. For the original passage, see JEROME, *Lettres*, ed. Jérôme Labourt, Collection des Universités de France, 8 vols (Paris: Belles Lettres, 1949–63), I, 117.

4. See Enrique VALDIVIESO, *Valdés Leal*, Catalogue to the Prado Exhibition, 1991 (Madrid: Museo del Prado & Junta de Andalucía, 1991), 104; Jonathan BROWN, *The Golden Age of Painting in Spain* (New Haven & London: Yale University Press, 1991), 173; and BROWN, *Zurbarán*, 26–29, 104. For a somewhat different view, see Juan Antonio GAYA NUÑO, *Zurbarán en Guadalupe* (Barcelona: Editorial Juventud, 1951), 23. It is impossible to know whether Zurbarán was following his own interpretation of the Temptation or that of the monastery. Artists were usually given precise iconographic instructions by a religious work's commissioners. Francisco PACHECO, for example, gives detailed instructions on the correct means of depicting various religious subjects – including Jerome in his cardinal's robes and in the desert with his lion, in his *Arte de la pintura*, written between 1634 and 1638: ed. Bonaventura Bassegoda i Hugas, Arte: Grandes Temas (Madrid: Cátedra, 1990), 559–712: 'De advertencias importantes en algunas historias sagradas acerca de la verdad y acierto con que se deven pintar conforme a la escritura divina y santos dotores' (691–94).

Beauty was still perceived in seventeenth-century Spain according to Aquinas's formulation, namely the presence of 'integritas sive perfectio', 'debita proportio sive consonantia', and 'claritas'.[5] Moreover, the notion of 'harmonic proportion' was central to aesthetic theory and provided the point of contact between all the various art forms – music, literature, painting, sculpture, architecture, and even dance.[6]

Music, of course, was frequently conceived as the binding force of the entire universe and hence as a means of transcending bodily confines and of ascending intellectually to a contemplation of God; Fray Luis de León's 'Oda a Francisco Salinas' is the classic literary expression in Spanish of such a notion. As Colin Thompson comments, 'the music of the world below, played in time ... is a distant echo of the music of heaven, out of which it flows in a fragmented and limited measure, retaining only the power to arouse the soul to a memory of its source.'[7]

The sheer weight of this Neoplatonic tradition would seem to rule out an interpretation of music as a source of temptation, yet Jerome's dramatic gesture of rejection of the musicians necessitates such a reading. In terms of contemporary musical theory, what is represented in this painting is instrumental music which, as Francisco de Salinas wrote in his *De musica libri septem*, I, i (Salamanca, 1577), affects both the mind and the senses and has a dual capacity to entertain and instruct ('Nos autem ... delectat ac docet').[8]

As with all art forms which claim to follow the Horatian dictum of 'prodesse aut delectare', the danger inherent in (secular) music is that enjoyment may come to predominate. In the *Confessions* Saint Augustine addresses the way in which the music of hymns can lead to sin in a way which throws some light upon what I am suggesting Zurbarán is depicting in this picture:

---

5. AQUINAS, *Summa Theologica*, I q.39 a.8. Compare AUGUSTINE, *De civitate Dei*, XXII, xxiv. For contemporary Spanish definitions of beauty, see Marcelino MENÉNDEZ PELAYO, *Historia de las ideas estéticas en España*, 2nd edn, ed. Enrique Sánchez Reyes, 5 volumes (Santander: Aldus, 1946–47), II: *Siglos XVI y XVII*, 7–143.

6. For example, Leon Battista ALBERTI, *L'architettura / De re aedificatoria*, ed. Giovanni Orlandi, intro. and notes Paolo Portoghesi, 2 vols, Classici Italiani di Scienze Tecniche e Arti: Trattati di Architettura 1 (Milan : Edizioni Il Polifilo, 1966), II, 823: 'Hi quidem numeri, per quos fiat ut vocum illa concinnitas auribus gratissima, reddatur, hidem ipsi numeri perficiunt, ut oculi animusque voluptate mirifica compleantur.'

7. See Colin P. THOMPSON, *The Strife of Tongues: Fray Luis de León and the Golden Age of Spain* (Cambridge: Cambridge University Press, 1988), 255.

8. Cited by MENÉNDEZ PELAYO, *Historia de las ideas estéticas*, II, 492.

Dum ipsis sanctis dictis religiosius et ardentius sentio moueri animos nos-
tros in flammam pietatis, cum ita cantantur, quam si non ita cantaren-
tur ... Sed delectatio carnis meae, cui mentem eneruandam non oportet
dari, saepe me fallit, dum rationi sensus non ita comitatur, ut patienter sit
posterior, sed tantum, quia propter illam meruit admitti, etiam praecur-
rere ac ducere conatur. Ita in his pecco non sentiens et postea sentio ...
Tamen cum mihi accidit, ut me amplius cantus quam res, quae canitur,
moueat, poenaliter me peccare confiteor et tunc mallem non audire can-
tantem. Ecce ubi sum![9]

In the case of Zurbarán's depiction of the Temptation the music being played
is presumably secular rather than religious. Such secular music is also, of
course, inextricably linked to the musicians who create it; however chaste
they appear to be, the very human agents needed to play the musical instruments serve by their physical presence as a potential means of tempting the
senses.[10]

In this way the painting suggests that all artistic endeavour is flawed because it has the very real potential to occupy and gratify the senses. Furthermore, although Jerome rejects the women, literally keeping them at arm's
length, he is nevertheless connected to them by their music, for the more
insidious temptations of sound unite musicians and saint. Similarly, the two
distinct sections of the canvas are intimately united by an art form which cannot be depicted, music – a union effected by the viewer's mind rather than his
or her eye. The viewer is also placed in a situation immediately analogous to
Jerome's, one in which it is difficult not to succumb to the seductive potential
of artistic beauty, for Zurbarán's style can engage the viewer to the extent that
stylistic appreciation can predominate to the exclusion of a consideration of
the implications of the subject-matter.[11] Zurbarán tempts the viewer visually
just as Jerome is tempted aurally and makes us thus experience the power of
artistic beauty.

9. AUGUSTINE, Confessionum, X, xxxiii.

10. Of the six musicians, one has her eyes raised to heaven in the manner of a saint or martyr, and another looks out of the canvas at the viewer. In this way, Zurbarán is possibly reflecting the two possible ways of considering music being discussed here.

11. On the dangers and enticements of the sense of sight, see AUGUSTINE, Confessionum, X,
xxxiv. Here Augustine writes: 'Quam innumerabilia uariis artibus et opificiis in uestibus, calci-
amentis, uasis et cuiuscemodi fabricationibus, picturis etiam diuersisque figmentis, atque his
usum necessarium atque moderatum et piam significationem longe transgredientibus ad-
diderunt homines ad illecebras oculorum, foras sequentes quod faciunt, intus relinquentes a quo
facti sunt et exterminantes quod facti sunt.'

The effect of changing the dancers into musicians and depicting them as chaste rather than lascivious is that Zurbarán has extended traditional interpretations of the subject by emphasizing the temptation of the mind as well as the body. Moreover the art form which was considered to approximate most to the divine order of the universe is depicted as a potential source of sin. The Temptation thus represents the danger of art, the lure of beauty however abstract. This links the painting explicitly with the Flagellation, in which Jerome is punished for his love of another art form, literature. Indeed, it is the very narrative of the Flagellation which encourages a reading of the Temptation along the lines suggested.

The greatest point of similarity between the two paintings is the depiction of the need to reject human aesthetic values which view literature, music, and the human form as worthy objects of contemplation and enjoyment. The paintings establish a chain of differences based on their contrasting evaluations of pain and pleasure and these serve to reinforce this rejection of purely human values. Such differences again arise from the depiction of Jerome's dancers as musicians, establishing a further point of contact between the paintings: sound, which is then used as the basis for a visual conceit.

The Flagellation depicts Jerome's punishment at the hands of angels, a punishment sanctioned and presided over by Christ.[12] In the Temptation, Zurbarán's expansion of traditional renderings of the subject results in Jerome's gesture of rejection amounting to a rejection of contact with either physical or mental pleasure. In contrast to this shunning of contact, the saint's body accepts flagellation and is restored by it, precisely because such physical contact is painful rather than pleasurable. The difference, then, between acceptable and unacceptable bodily contact lies in the difference between pain and pleasure: the Flagellation illustrates the spiritual value of physical pain and sets such pain above mental pleasure (that is, Jerome's devotion to profane literature). All pleasure – whether of the flesh or the spirit – is suspect: to ensure the eternal pleasure of the soul, the surest route to take is one of physical pain.

---

12. Jerome recounts the following famous interchange in his description of his flagellation: 'Interrogatus condicionem, Christianum me esse respondi. Et ille qui residebat: "mentiris", ait, "Ciceronianus es, non Christianus" ' (Lettres, I, 145; tr. Molina as: 'Estando assi fui preguntado quien era: que condicion de hombre era la mia. Yo prestamente respondi que era Christiano. Apenas oue dado esta respuesta quando el mismo juez que estaua presente me dixo: Por cierto mientes, que tu Ciceroniano eres y no christiano', Epistolas, 118v).

Mortification can be deemed pleasing in so far as it shows a willingness to repent and to subject the flesh to necessary discipline.[13] According to Pedro de Valderrama, an Augustinian friar writing in 1612, mortification of the flesh (albeit this time the work of the individual rather than of angels) was highly pleasing to God:

> Mucho se agrada Dios de la música y alabanza que resulta de que os desolléis las carnes y que de vuestros pieles hagáis instrumento para alabarle a él, que eso es alabarle con los adufes de que él gusta más que de los que se hacen de pieles de animales. Pero si esa mortificación y ese desollaros con las disciplinas y penitencia es en coro, es en comunidad de muchos, es mucho más agradable, como suele ser la música de la vihuela, ya la del órgano, en las cuales de varias cuerdas y cañones diferentes se hace una música suavísima estando bien acordadas.[14]

The conceit here expressed, that the bodies of penitents are instruments whose music is pleasing to God, is something of a commonplace in Golden-Age literature. Thus, Juan de Matos Fragoso in a *romance* on Saint Jerome (1667), writes of the saint's self-mortification with a rock: 'Sagrado Diuino Orfeo, | hizo de su pecho Lira, | para que al compas del llanto | mas acordemente gima.'[15] Zurbarán does not simply transpose this conceit from page to canvas. Rather, the two paintings can be read as portraying two different attitudes to sound. This juxtaposition is the basis for a broader religious conceit whose starting-point is the image employed by Valderrama and Matos Fragoso.

In the Temptation instrumental music created by man is not portrayed as a means of bringing the individual nearer to God, but as a source of temptation. This line of thought is then extended in the Flagellation which substitutes man-made music with music made on man, that is the 'music' of the disci-

---

13. See AUGUSTINE, *De civitate Dei*, XXII, xxii.

14. VALDERRAMA, *Ejercicio y platica para las cofradias de los disciplinantes*, in *Ejercicios espirituales para todos los dias de la cuaresma*, 3 parts in 1 (Zaragoza: Carlos de Lavayen, 1605), III, 90v. Compare VALDERRAMA, *Teatro de las religiones* (Seville: Luis de Estupiñán, 1612), 153–54. Francisco de QUEVEDO employs a similar conceit in *La vida del Buscón llamado Don Pablos* (written 1603–08), to describe Pablos's uncle whipping five men: ed. Domingo Ynduráin, 10th edn, Letras Hispánicas 124 (Madrid: Cátedra, 1989), 181.

15. 'Romance, que se canto al maximo doctor de la iglesia san Geronimo, año de 1667', in *Ociosidad entretenida, en varios entremeses, bayles, loas y jacaras, escogidos de los mejores ingenios de España* (Madrid: Andrés García de la Iglesia, 1668), 127v–128v, cited in *Textos dispersos de autores españoles*, ed. José SIMÓN DÍAZ, I: *Impresos del Siglo de Oro*, Cuadernos Bibliográficos 36 (Madrid: CSIC, 1978), 187.

plined body. Hence, in a reversal of purely human priorities, what is painful for the body ultimately brings pleasure to the soul (and, according to Valderrama, to God), in so far as pain, by keeping the body from pleasure, keeps it also from sin. The implications of Zurbarán's conceit are that aesthetic order and harmony are to be shunned, to be replaced by the apparent 'disorder' and irrationality of pain and deprivation. In schematic terms, music – harmonious sound – is a source of sin, whilst the body being whipped – a noise devoid of aesthetic intention and discernible harmony – is a potential source of redemption. This does not simply effect a paradoxical reversal of human aesthetic values; these two paintings, in other words, do not simply amount to an exercise in *desengaño*. They go further by suggesting that art and beauty *per se* are beyond artistic and human recuperation because always and inevitably they harbour a potential for sin.

Pain and suffering can also be 'recuperated' and assimilated as part of an aesthetic which inverts purely human formulations of beauty and artistic pleasure. This aesthetic recuperation of pain has its roots in theodicy. Although theodicy is obviously little concerned with aesthetics, Augustine's recourse to an analogy taken from painting in his attempt to explain the presence of evil in the world does nevertheless draw aesthetics into the debate. Augustine's argument is that sin serves to enrich and beautify God's creation by providing points of antithetical contrast which emphasize all that is beautiful within it. This point of view is summed up by Augustine (*De civitate Dei*, XI, xxiii) thus:

Quoniam sicut pictura cum colore nigro, loco suo posita, ita universitas rerum, si quis possit intueri, etiam cum peccatoribus pulchra est, quamvis per se ipsos consideratos sua deformitas turpet.

Augustine's argument that sin can be viewed as a divine means of enriching the universe, thereby providing an explanation for its existence, has been aptly described as an 'aesthetic theodicy' by one theologian.[16] His suggestive pictorial analogy is taken up and developed by Abelard who uses it to argue that the beauty of the universe is intensified by the existence of evil. Evil thus becomes a necessary component of the divine, providential aesthetic.[17]

This 'aesthetic of antithesis' allows a place in the aesthetic – and indeed the divine – order to what is often considered cruel, violent or ugly so that it

---

16. See John HICK, *Evil and the God of Love*, 2nd edn (Basingstoke & London: Macmillan, 1988), 82–89.

17. See ABELARD, *Epitome theologiae christianae*, cap. xx.

functions as a point of oppositional contrast.[18] In seventeenth-century art and literature such an 'aesthetic of antithesis' is apparent in both the form and content of many works.[19] Most obviously, the theological justification of evil as an enriching aesthetic factor serves to pave the way for the Baroque portrayal of mortification, pain, and suffering as beautiful *per se* and as affording a unique sense of pleasure in and for themselves. Lavish depictions of pain are thus justified and encouraged and presented on canvas as an intense and exquisite experience for the sufferer portrayed. They also become so for the viewer in so far as he or she finds the artistic treatment of such subjects both beautiful and, therefore, pleasurable. To the extent to which they are considered beautiful as objects of art, therefore, viewers will themselves experience the divinely sanctioned 'inverted aesthetic' of Augustine. It is precisely this presentation of pain as something beautiful and hence desirable which makes Baroque art so powerful and disturbing. Zurbarán has encouraged the viewer to interpret pain as attractive, or appealing (in both the spiritual and the physical sense), by the way he portrays Jerome's body. This has not yet been flagellated and, in contrast to many Baroque depictions of torture, martyrdom and physical pain, thus displays a marked absence of the effects of pain (broken skin, blood, and so on). Moreover, in contrast to the sombre use of light in the Temptation, the entire composition is infused with soft and gentle light, with warm colours, which draw attention to the saint's semi-naked body. The effect of this marked lack of graphic realism is not so much to render Jerome's body vulnerable as to make the act about to be committed (flagellation) attractive because sensorially beautiful. The body which is on the point of having pain inflicted upon it is thus offered up to the viewer as an object of attraction, as a means of rendering the act of discipline itself attractive.

---

18. Sin can also play a heuristic role. Diego de Saavedra Fajardo, for example, writing in the late 1630s, employs a similar analogy to this end: 'Más debemos algunas veces a nuestros errores que a nuestros aciertos, porque aquéllos nos enseñan, y éstos nos desvanecen. No solamente nos dejan advertidos los patriarcas que enseñaron, sino también los que erraron. La sombra dio luz a la pintura, naciendo della un arte tan maravilloso': SAAVEDRA FAJARDO, *Empresas políticas*, ed. Francisco Javier Díez de Revenga, Clásicos Universales Planeta, H 161 (Barcelona: Planeta, 1988), 453, nr 65. Saavedra's attribution of the invention of painting to the intervention of shadow refers to Pliny's well-known account in his *Natural History*, Book XXXV, an account which Calderón in turn develops in his defence of painting; see Stelio CRO, 'La «Deposición» de Calderón y la poética del barroco', *Cuadernos para Investigación de la Literatura Hispánica* (Madrid), 9 (1988), 35–51 (43).

19. See the remarks of Robert PRING-MILL, 'Some Techniques of Representation in the *Sueños* and the *Criticón*', *Bulletin of Hispanic Studies*, 45 (1968), 270–84.

Zurbarán's depiction of Saint Jerome's flagellation is certainly muted in comparison with, say, many of Ribera's paintings and drawings of human torture and suffering. It is this non-dramatic quality which fosters a meditative, rather than an emotional response. The existence of various 'líneas de ponderación y sutileza' (to employ Gracián's phrase) between the Flagellation and Temptation, which suggests that the paintings are deliberately juxtaposed and that the viewer is intended to consider them as one pictorial unit consisting of two distinct but interrelated facets, links Zurbarán's art with the aesthetic of wit in which the artistic object deliberately provokes the intellect into active exegetical engagement.[20] Zurbarán possesses a visual wit as acute and powerful as any seventeenth-century writer's verbal wit. It is thus possible to consider Zurbarán's art, with its primary appeal to the intellect rather than the emotions, as no less Baroque than his more exuberant contemporaries.

The Flagellation and Temptation are two physically distinct paintings best viewed and understood as two terms of a single visual conceit based on sound. If my interpretation of the paintings is justified, just as Jerome must renounce all aesthetic pleasure in order to reach God, so similarly must the viewer, whose intellect, which has been instrumental in seeking out this meaning, is intended to pass beyond the surface serenity of the paintings, despite all their attractions. In other words the lure of the aesthetic represented both in and by Zurbarán's canvases must be resisted. This process of resistence is itself replicated in the setting, for the viewer moves forward from the Temptation and Flagellation to the third painting in this series – the Apotheosis of Saint Jerome, which is placed over the altar and which depicts an act of ascent away from Earth towards Heaven. Both the religious setting and the paintings suggest that the viewer is intended to do likewise, leaving behind Zurbarán's art and letting the mind rise, like Jerome, to heaven.

JEREMY ROBBINS

University of Edinburgh

---

20. Baltasar GRACIÁN, SJ, *Agudeza y arte de ingenio*, ed. Evaristo Correa Calderón, 2 vols, Clásicos Castalia 14–15 (Madrid: Castalia, 1969), I, 64.

THREE

TWENTIETH-CENTURY

SPAIN AND

SPANISH AMERICA

THE COHERENCE OF MACHADO'S 'LA TIERRA DE ALVARGONZÁLEZ'

'LA TIERRA DE ALVARGONZÁLEZ' may not be one of Machado's finest poems: within *Campos de Castilla* alone, most readers would probably agree that texts such as 'Campos de Soria', 'A un olmo seco' or 'A José María Palacio' are the more significant creative achievements.[1] Even so, critics have not always treated Machado's long *romance*, or *romancero*, as sympathetically as it deserves, and that is perhaps in part because of a continuing tendency to judge it by comparison with the *romancero viejo*, despite the poet's own warnings against so doing. In the 1917 Prologue to *Campos de Castilla*, which principally concerns itself with 'La tierra de Alvargonzález', Machado put this clearly:

> Muy lejos estaba yo de pretender resucitar el género en su sentido tradicional. La confección de nuevos romances viejos ... no fue nunca de mi agrado, y toda simulación de arcaísmo me parece ridícula.[2]

The influence of Pidalianism has been strong, however, and Machado's commentators have been prone to regret the presence in the poem of such 'untraditional' elements as supernatural happenings and lyrical evocations of the natural world, elements whose role the poet increased between the first version of the *romance* published in the periodical *La lectura* and its longer final redaction in *Campos de Castilla* itself.[3]

---

1. Robert Pring-Mill has long been interested in the transmission of both learned and folk poetry within a twentieth-century Spanish-American context. The present article in complementary fashion seeks to discuss the case of a cultivated Peninsular poet's engagement with his native ballad tradition. The text in question is one which Robert knows well as a tutor of undergraduates, since it is one that all first-year Oxford students reading Spanish are required to study.

2. Antonio MACHADO, *Campos de Castilla*, ed. Geoffrey Ribbans, Letras Hispánicas 10 (Madrid: Cátedra, 1989), 274.

3. Most notably by the addition of lines 183–280 to the section 'Otros días' (nearly 14 per cent of the total).

Arthur Terry could perhaps seem to reflect assumptions of a Pidalian sort
in his Critical Guide to *Campos de Castilla*: '[Machado's] subjective intervention . . . is somewhat at odds with the rest of the poem, and it seems to indicate a basic uncertainty in [his] intentions.'[4] Terry's remarks here are immediately prompted by the narrator's apostrophe to Alvargonzález's blighted
lands as 'pobres campos de mi patria' (576) but he goes on to comment on the
text as a whole as follows:[5]

> In spite of many fine passages, these never quite cohere into a single
> convincing pattern. The 'evocation of Castile' is superbly accomplished,
> but in a way which cannot help but interfere with the narrative itself . . .
> The ballad, because of its dramatic nature, entails a kind of objectivity
> which is hardly possible in the lyric. Where the poem fails . . . is precisely
> in its refusal to limit itself to what is inherently dramatic, however
> impressive the non-dramatic elements may be in themselves.[6]

That was written some twenty years ago but similar doubts have much
more recently been voiced by Geoffrey Ribbans in the Introduction to his
edition of *Campos de Castilla*:

> Para mí sus mejores momentos y sus mayores defectos tienen que ver con
> el estilo narrativo . . . Hay buenos episodios, . . . pero no se mantiene de
> manera consistente el empuje narrativo en las secciones medias . . .
> donde algunos episodios difusos e innecesarios impiden la acción . . .
> Sobre todo, Machado se deja llevar por su impulso descriptivo.

For Ribbans too, lines 563–66 and 575–76 of the poem introduce a personal
note that is 'inoportuna en un texto narrativo'.[7]

The present article seeks to address such criticisms levelled against 'La
tierra de Alvargonzález'. It will be argued that not only did Machado proceed
in a very deliberate manner in the elaboration and revision of his text but also
that the poetic result of so much labour is coherent and (in the main)
compelling. In consequence, doubt may be cast on the claim that 'one's
difficulties in coming to terms with the poem come . . . from the problem of
deciding where its central interest lies'.[8]

---

4. Arthur TERRY, *Antonio Machado, 'Campos de Castilla'*, Critical Guides to Spanish Texts 8
(London: Grant & Cutler, 1973), 51.

5. Numbers in parentheses refer to line numbers in the poem, as printed by Ribbans.

6. TERRY, *Antonio Machado*, 51–52.

7. *Campos de Castilla*, 57–58.

8. TERRY, *Antonio Machado*, 50.

* * * * *

Machado elaborated his successive versions of the Alvargonzález story with characteristic care, and the main lines this evolution took are now familiar. In the course of 1912, he published first a prose version of the story (in *Mundial Magazine*, in January), then a shorter *romance* version (in *La lectura* in April), then the longer *romance* included in *Campos de Castilla*, which is more or less the poem we read now. The most important divergences are three-fold and are between the prose story, or *cuento* as it is usually called, and the two *romances*: first, the *cuento*, unlike the *romances*, has a prolegomenon in which the narrator relates the circumstances in which he initially heard the story of the *tierras*; second, whereas in the *cuento*, Alvargonzález's parricidal sons murder their youngest brother also, in the *romances* Miguel survives to redeem the curse on his father's lands; and third, the poems, and especially the final version, devote more space than the *cuento* does to ambiguously presented supernatural happenings and to lyrical evocation of the Castilian countryside amidst which events unfold. It follows from this that if the poem contains lyrical and supernatural elements, this was because Machado very consciously wanted them there, accentuating their presence in successive versions of the story, and also because he was uninterested in simply pastiching the *romances viejos*.

In 'La tierra de Alvargonzález' Machado has constructed, at least in part, a parable diagnosing a national malaise. However, whereas in his original *cuento* the poet was pessimistic about the chances of Spain's recovery, by changing the plot in his *romances* so as to make Miguel, the youngest son, survive and redeem the curse on his father's lands, the poet suggests ways in which Castile might conceivably, but not necessarily, regain both its material and psychological health.[9] The contrasting optimism of the *romance* versions of the Alvargonzález story may well find some explanation in the evolving

---

9. This assumes it is correct to think that the successive versions of the story were written in the same order as that of their publication. Macrì certainly still inclines to this opinion: Antonio MACHADO, *Poesía y prosa*, ed. Oreste Macrì, 4 vols (Madrid: Espasa-Calpe & Fundación Antonio Machado, 1988), II, 889–91, and concurs with the arguments of Helen F. GRANT in *Atlante*, 2 (1954), 139–58. Amongst other poems in *Campos de Castilla*, 'Por tierras de España' [XCIX], first published in 1910, reflects the pessimism of the *cuento*, both as to its analysis of Castile's major ills and as to its envisaging no relief from them. 'Un criminal' [CVIII], first published in *Campos de Castilla* in 1912, is similarly pessimistic. It relates a parricide, in outline like that of 'La tierra', but there, the 'Miguel figure', an ex-seminarist who develops a taste for a pretty girl, is not a redemptive force but the criminal of the poem's title.

political circumstances of the period, centring on the prime-ministership of Canalejas, who, but for his assassination in November 1912, might have become 'the Lloyd George of Spanish liberalism'.[10]

Evocations of the Castilian landscape are prominent in the poem. They are found at greatest length in the sections 'Otros días', 'La casa' and 'Los asesinos', although they are not confined to these places.[11] One finds repeated echoes of other poems from *Campos de Castilla*, sometimes with a subtle local appropriateness.[12] Real place-names are used too, although it becomes plain that the *tierras de Alvargonzález* stand symbolically for Castile as a whole. They are 'en el corazón de España' (564), a phrase referring as much to a literal geographical as to a metaphorical emotional or psychological centrality. They are indeed identified by the poet in subjective terms as 'pobres campos de mi patria' (576), this particular phrase (of which some commentators have disapproved) being a textual change in favour of greater explicitness introduced by Machado into the revised second version of the ballad. By recounting the origin, growth, and removal of a curse on Alvargonzález's lands, therefore, Machado is talking about a malaise affecting Castile, itself a synecdoche for Spain as a whole.

The newly-wed Alvargonzález had in the past enjoyed a period of happiness 'en el amor de su tierra' (17–18) and had subsequently dreamt that this happiness might become generally available to his fellow men: 'él pensó que ser podría | feliz el hombre en la tierra' (515–16). What went wrong? What was the source of the *maldición* that settled on his previously prosperous lands, a curse that may by extension be seen to afflict Spain as a whole?

Alvargonzález was murdered by his own two elder sons, their motivation being principally greed, sloth, and envy. They sought the short cut of parricide as a way of coming more rapidly into their inheritance. They were impatient and lazy, preferring to live off the fruits of someone else's hard work. Envy entered the equation because of the youngest brother, Miguel. He had been destined for the priesthood, and hence would not have been a call on family funds once he was ordained, but Miguel was too keen on women and too honest about this penchant of his. In consequence, 'colgó la sotana un día' and,

---

10. See Raymond CARR, *Spain 1808–1975*, 2nd edn (Oxford: Clarendon Press, 1982), 492–95.

11. See particularly 165-78, 183-250, 487-500, 523-76, 627-34, 671-708. These lines alone account for around one third of the total text.

12. As for example between 59–60 and poem CII or between 439–40 and CXXVI.

like many other Castilians of the day whom existing lands were inadequate to support, he emigrated to the Americas.[13] It was to be a *felix culpa*. The detailing here is interesting. We are not told that Miguel asked his father for his share of the estate (as does the younger son in the Parable of the Prodigal Son, Luke 15. 11–12) but, rather, that Alvargonzález himself handed over the money without challenging his son's change of vocation (37–44). The older brothers may be imagined as envying their younger sibling for this, for getting funds they did not think he was going to need and for gaining a freedom that they, continuing on their father's farm, would not enjoy. What is more, they were already married but unhappily so. Alvargonzález's daughters-in-law brought dissent to the family but no surviving children (475–77). A further imaginable consequence of this would be the remaining brothers' little relish for working, as it were 'in trust', lands which another man's children were likely ultimately to inherit.

Perhaps, one might conjecture, the elder sons' childlessness was an element in Alvargonzález's generous gesture towards his youngest boy: perhaps the patriarch hoped that a Miguel free from vows of celibacy would produce for him the heirs that his elder sons so far had not, even if this involved some departure from traditional family hierarchies and expectations. In any case, Alvargonzález long seems to have had a preference for his youngest child. The section 'El sueño' leaves it unclear whether or not the episode the old man dreams about immediately before his murder had actually happened in the precise terms in which it is narrated. This is the incident in which Miguel is praised by his father for lighting 'una hoguera | que alumbra toda la casa' (93–94) when his brothers had not been able to do so. But whether fantasy or factual recall, the dream shows Alvargonzález's awareness at some level that his favouritism towards the youngest had fed envy, resentment, and murderous feelings towards himself, feelings that one day, whether on impulse or as the fruit of greater premeditation, are translated into deeds.

One notices that Machado is content to leave certain things inexplicit. He does not account for the father's apparently early taste for one child rather than the others or explain the influence of that preference on the later attitudes and behaviour of the elder ones. Nor does he make explicit why Miguel develops different attitudes from those of his brothers when it comes to hard work. In any case, the children of the same parents often do from

---

13. Compare the references to emigration in poems XCVIII and XCIX.

their youngest days seem to have very different characters. In the spirit of the *romances viejos* in this respect, much is left to be inferred.

With their father dead, the brothers remaining at home come to no good. They are idle and plagued by guilt, the eldest especially. (Machado differentiates between their characters.) To this is added 'bad luck', circumstances beyond their control: their crops are diseased; there are unexpected late frosts; and their sheep fall sick (281–300). It is this global situation that is described by the narrator as a divinely inflicted curse (297–98).

Machado does not ignore material factors in his account of the curse that weighs on the *tierras*, but his greater emphasis is a moral, psychological one. He writes within a broadly Romantic tradition which believes in a *Volksgeist* (his 1917 Prologue to *Campos de Castilla* speaks of 'lo esencial castellano') and in a Herderian spirit holds that the *Volksgeist* may in part be accessed by reflection on differential geographical factors which to a degree mould and come to reflect the human personalities of a particular region.[14]

In the conduct of his predominantly moral, psychological inquiry into Spain's malaise, Machado writes as a Romantic, and more immediately still, closely follows the example of his mentor Unamuno. This is plain when one reads the essays in *En torno al casticismo*. Yet more specifically, Unamuno, like Maeztu, had identified envy as the quintessential Spanish sin and written, as Machado does, about the 'sangre de Caín' that runs through Spaniards' veins.[15] While the motif of the cursed lands recalls Genesis 4. 10–12, Machado's detailed diagnosis of the national sickness is close to Unamuno's own.

Not only is the diagnosis broadly Unamunian; so also is the therapy. In *En torno al casticismo*, Unamuno had recommended re-establishing contact with the best aspects (as he saw them) of the culture of the Spanish *pueblo*, whilst simultaneously cultivating openness to positive foreign values. Miguel, as a returning *indiano*, represents these things. His other strong suit is having learnt the hard way the importance of work, a value associated with the Institución Libre de Enseñanza that is well characterised elsewhere in *Campos de Castilla* by Machado's elegy on the death of Giner (CXXXIX). The returning *indiano* has achieved independence and self-reliance, works

---

14. See for example Isaiah BERLIN, 'Herder and the Enlightenment', in his *Vico and Herder* (London: Chatto & Windus, 1976), 145–216.

15. For a study of this, see Carlos CLAVERÍA, 'Sobre el tema de Caín en la obra de Unamuno' in his *Temas de Unamuno*, Biblioteca Románica Española: Estudios y Ensayos 10 (Madrid: Gredos, 1953), 93–122.

hard, becomes rich and literally ploughs his profits back into the *patria* (407 – 14; see also 203 – 05).

Machado, though, was not just concerned to write about 'lo esencial castellano', in a late-Romantic parable of national regeneration. He also sought to explore what he called 'lo elemental humano', rather as Unamuno earlier had written that 'la tradición eterna española' was, because 'eternal', more widely human than just narrowly and differentially Spanish.[16] 'La tierra de Alvargonzález' is also intended as a parable of a malaise that can affect any individual human being, one not just confined to Spain or to the later nineteenth century. The poet in any case had more sense than to polarize the individual and the social or the national. He saw how sickness in individuals and in societies is dialectically related.

It is, however, the more universal, human dimension of 'La tierra de Alvargonzález' that has drawn less critical comment than its specifically national aspect. Whilst Machado roots his tale in an identifiably Castilian environment, much symbolic weight is borne by images of things by no means simply locally or idiosyncratically Castilian – earth, fire and water. He also – too self-consciously indeed for some commentators – points towards the wider human implications of his story through Biblical allusion, especially to the book of Genesis, as his 1917 Prologue explicitly states:

> mis romances miran a lo elemental humano, al campo de Castilla y al libro primero de Moisés, llamado *Génesis*.[17]

In addition to the Genesis story of Cain, with God's inscrutably motivated preference for Abel's offering rather than his brother's, and the fratricide and the divine curse which ensues, the tale of Alvargonzález in particular alludes to the Old Testament tales of Isaac, Jacob and Esau, of Jacob's predilection for his youngest son Joseph, with the jealousy to which that gives rise, and of Joseph's experiences in Egypt, separated from his family.[18] Jacob alias Israel is the patriarch *par excellence* of course, and both his earlier life and the life of Joseph were marked by fraternal strife. In both their cases, magnanimity is seen to triumph over ill will and in both their cases, a precondition for that ultimate success is travel, working their passage with ingenuity and hard graft,

---

16. Miguel de UNAMUNO, *Obras completas*, ed. Manuel García Blanco, 9 vols (to date) (Madrid: Escelicer, 1966 –   ), I, 794.

17. *Campos de Castilla*, 275.

18. The poem's Biblical echoes are noted in MACHADO, *Poesía y prosa*, II, 896 – 97.

away from their native lands. The case of Machado's Miguel echoes these archetypal tales.

'La tierra de Alvargonzález' is not just a story about the redemption of Machado's fatherland (*patria*); it is also a story about any human parenting and maturing, that has taken a leaf from Nature's book. Alvargonzález is not simply idealized as a father. He does not get the right results with his first two sons, who grow up resentful, make bad marriages, commit murder, then fall prey to an incapacitating depression that culminates in their suicide. But with Miguel, however indirectly, however unwittingly even, the father does ultimately succeed, to the extent, it is suggested, of perpetuating his race. (The poem in an open-ended way does not inform us that Miguel did finally have children in fact but the inference that he did is strong, given his association with the return of fertility in other respects.)

In the spirit of the *romances viejos* or, for that matter, of the Bible, Machado's poem takes certain things about people's genetic makeup and environment as read. Without discursive explanation of why things turn out thus, the poet shows us in Alvargonzález's dealings with his youngest an object lesson in creative parenting. We do not know why – if the father's dream directly recalls family history – Miguel could kindle fire where his brothers could not, an attribute that has a plain symbolic dimension, but when he does do it, his father celebrates the fact. Again, when the son seeks to change careers, exchanging emigration for ordination, his father does not remonstrate at a such a radical change of plans but is affirmative and enabling: 'diole bendición y herencia' (44).

Curiously enough, it is Juan, the eldest son, who cites the piece of folk wisdom encapsulating the relevant insight: 'a veces, | quien piensa atajar, rodea' (267–68). There are no short cuts to maturity and creative independence. Pedro Salinas put the point well when he described the poem as follows:

> Romance original, de los orígenes, preocupado en lo primero del hombre, en lo primordial de su naturaleza, en su trágico destino de malquerer . . . Lo que [Machado] quería representar en su retablo del hombre era el terrible suceso, siempre sucediendo, eterno . . . : el hombre que mata a lo que le crea y, por condigno castigo, se destruye al hacerlo; la idea de que al matar nos matamos nosotros mismos también.[19]

---

19. See the section devoted to Machado in SALINAS's essay 'El romancismo y el siglo XX', in his *Ensayos de literatura hispánica* (Madrid: Aguilar, 1966), 342–44.

Psychiatrists in the Freudian tradition have claimed that parricide is a powerful temptation, as Sophocles had shown in his story of Oedipus whose murder of his father brought a plague on the lands of Thebes.[20] Fortunately, though, most people avoid Oedipus's literalness. The parricides most frequently performed are of a symbolic sort, but it is Machado's suggestion that all short cuts to independence are self-frustrating. Murdering one's father, whether literally or, as is more common, symbolically, brings not freedom but subjection: rather than acquire an independent identity thereby, one remains stunted by merely trying to assert who one is not, in an act that simultaneously denies another person his being also. And then there is guilt. Human bodies are easier to kill off than the ghosts that linger in the memory and in the subconscious. Murder, rather than freeing the murderer, ties him all the faster to the past, depresses him and alienates him from his human and non-human surroundings. Murder is non-creative for murderer and victim alike.

Against this is set Miguel's way. His route to his inheritance, or maturity and independent personhood, involves hardship, risk, openness to novelty, and the renouncing of dependence. Miguel's relationship with his father seems also to be Nature's way. Thus we are reminded of the storks that amidst scenes of fertility Alvargonzález and his wife had once observed from the room that his youngest son returns to inhabit:

> era allí donde los padres
> veían en primavera
> el huerto en flor, y en el cielo
> de mayo, azul, la cigüeña
> – cuando las rosas se abren
> y los zarzales blanquean –
> que enseñaba a sus hijuelos
> a usar de sus alas lentas.
>
> (489–96)[21]

A further aspect of suggestive links established between human and non-human nature is the way in which the symbolism of the seasons of the year is developed in the text, especially perhaps regarding those transitional seasons

---

20. Perhaps another way in which the work of Sophocles might be present in the poem as a pagan witness to 'lo elemental humano' is through a reminiscence of *Antigone* when the poet insists on the scandal of Alvargonzález's body remaining unburied (181–82, etc.).

21. Storks also figure in 169–72 and 529–32.

of spring and autumn. Comparison is certainly invited with other major poems in *Campos de Castilla* in which the cycles of Nature are in a complex way counterpointed with the apparent linearity of human history. Thus in his evocation of autumn in the section 'La casa', beside imagery of decay, the poet introduces a more ambiguous allusion, involving personification of the River Duero:

> entre las marchitas zarzas
> y amarillentos helechos,
> corren las crecidas aguas
> a engrosar el padre río
> por canchales y barrancas.

(554-58)

These lines, which link the patriarch Alvargonzález with the Duero, contrast the river's fertile fullness with the fading vegetation, while also invoking the Biblical image, echoed by the poet's admired Jorge Manrique, of rivers that run down to the sea of death.[22] Machado was keenly aware of how human continuity depends on a sometimes painful acceptance of the cycles of birth, decline, death and rebirth; how the species survives whereas individuals do not. He sees a sense of history alienated from such basic truths as lacking in genuine vitality.

In consequence, as far as 'La tierra de Alvargonzález' is concerned, whilst it is obviously wrong to hasten Alvargonzález's end as his older sons do, once the patriarch is dead, he needs to be buried, earth to earth. A mysterious *copla* sounds this note four times in the section 'Otros días': 'el que la tierra ha labrado | no duerme bajo la tierra.'[23] The way in which Alvargonzález will be laid to rest and contribute to the fertility of his lands has to be Miguel's way – metaphorically speaking, working alongside and in the spirit of his father, not against him, but as a clearly separate person.

As lines 554–58 show, there is a third paternal presence in the poem: in addition to the patriarch Alvargonzález and in addition to an explicit concern with the 'tierras pobres, tierras tristes' of Machado's *patria*, the reader notices

---

22. The Biblical echo is of Ecclesiastes 1. 7 and for Manrique, see not least Machado's 'Glosa' [LVIII]. Compare with 554–58 the spring scene in 173–76, the associations of which are further enriched if one recalls the poems which precede and follow 'La tierra' in the 1917 *Campos de Castilla*, CXIII. xiii and CXV.

23. Three out of four of these instances were additions made to the second redaction of the *romance*.

a host of references to water, centring on 'el padre río', the Duero, and observes as well, perhaps, the links between this paternal source and the generation of poetry. Machado, as befitted a proud descendant of Agustín Durán,
held Romantic beliefs about folk literature, the *romancero* not least, as a
major repository of the National Spirit, 'lo esencial castellano'. His admiration for Spain's *romances viejos* had a patriotic edge to it. Scrutiny of *poesía
popular*, he thought, could provide a truer picture of the national character,
for better and for worse, than hyperbolic, sanitising, *casticista* propaganda was
likely to do: 'for worse' as well as 'for better', since Machado evidently
realised that some strains of *poesía popular* exploited and indulged recurrent
destructive sentiments that it was important both to recognise and to contain.
Thus the *cuento* version of the story makes it especially plain that it is based
on a *romance de ciego*.[24] 'La tierra de Alvargonzález' investigates and implicitly combats the unhealthy prurience and sensationalism of that popular
genre, prescribing as good medicine the sobriety of more ancient balladry. In
Machado's view, however, the better aspects of the folk tradition purveyed
traditional wisdom and values that subsist beyond the vagaries of fashion.
There was a strong link in the poet's mind between ethics and aesthetics,
between human regeneration and poetic health.

Machado simultaneously entertained certain other ethical/aesthetic concerns, set out in the 1917 Prologue to *Campos de Castilla* (albeit in unhelpfully
obscure terms, which seem to draw on Ortega's *Meditaciones del Quijote* of
1914).[25] In the course of the decade preceding the composition of 'La tierra
de Alvargonzález', Machado had grown to find fault with *modernismo* on the
grounds that it was not modern enough. *Modernismo*, with its self-indulgence
and self-absorption, had come to seem an obsolete survival of a now discred-
ited sensibility, with correlatives in superseded nineteenth-century philosophical fashions of a broadly subjective idealist stamp. Nor did Machado warm to
a nineteenth-century positivism that he judged to be obsolete also; hence the
'doble espejismo' of which his 1917 Prologue speaks, characterising various
forms of philosophical idealism on the one hand and positivism on the other.
Against this, in Machado's view the modern philosophy was like Ortega's and
poets had to catch up with the fact. The famous formula Ortega used in his

---

24. *Campos de Castilla*, 287.

25. For Machado's admiration for Ortega, see poem CXL and the *dedicatoria* to poem
CLXI.

Meditaciones, 'Yo soy yo y mis circunstancias', was a transcending of old-fashioned polarisations between the self and external reality and Machado believed that poets needed to write in a comparable spirit.[26] The point for him, in a paradoxical move recalling Unamuno, was both that the modern sensibility now in question was not some transitory fad but rather more akin to 'eternal' truth and that proof of this could be found in Spain's best *poesía popular*, since the 'correct' dialectical relationship was always respected and preserved in it. A healthy dialectical relationship between the self and the other could be observed in the best of the folk tradition, both between the poet and his work and between the work and its wider audience, a mode of relationship that in turn correlates with the relationship between Alvargonzález and his youngest son Miguel, and between Miguel and his father's lands. Hence the 1917 Prologue's oft-quoted sentence:

> Pensé que la misión del poeta era inventar nuevos poemas de lo eterno humano, historias animadas que, siendo suyas [written by an individual poet], viviesen, no obstante, por sí mismas.[27]

Such a view of the composition and dissemination as well as of the ethos of the *romances viejos* and *poesía popular* more widely is in keeping with the teaching of Bédier about French epic that Machado went to Paris to hear in 1911–12, when we may imagine the Alvargonzález project to be taking shape in his mind. It is in keeping also with the theories of Menéndez Pidal, expounded in *L'Épopée castillane*, based on lectures first given in 1909 but published in Paris in 1910.[28]

Machado believed that his mission of diagnosis and therapeutic response with regard to the spiritual malaise of his *patria* and with regard to diseased relationships on a smaller interpersonal scale, the necessary reconnection with basic sources of emotionally healthy living, involved an independently-conducted recreation of the spirit of the *romancero* in his own time (but not of course an 'envious', 'greedy' mimicry of its stylistic externals).   The

---

26. A later, but arguably more lucid, account of this may be found in the poet's 'Reflexiones sobre la lírica' of 1925, in MACHADO, *Poesía y prosa*, III, 1649–62.

27. *Campos de Castilla*, 274.

28. Menéndez Pidal's scholarly reputation was firmly established before 1912, not least by his editions of the *Primera crónica general* (1906) and the *Cantar de mio Cid* (1908–11). He was elected to the Real Academia Española in 1901, at the age of 33, and became director of the Centro de Estudios Históricos in 1910, the year which saw the appearance of *El romancero español*.

romancero's spirit though, was, he thought, a source of potentially regenera-
tive ancestral wisdom. Poets needed to relate to it in a way comparable to
Miguel's relationship with his own father and his father's lands.

It is instructive to make a link between the scenario of Alvargonzález's
dream and murder and the subject matter of poem CII, 'Orillas del Duero'.[29]
This poem in its opening and closing stanzas presents a fatigued 'pobre caminante' stopping to rest and dream beside what is elsewhere in that text too
called 'el padre río'. 'Orillas del Duero' is as much about the future of
Castilian poetry as it is about the future of Castile more widely. In this poem,
Machado is asking in an open-ended way whether both poetically and nation-
ally decadence will prevail or whether there might instead be a rebirth that is
a reassertion of basic continuities. Implicitly, he sees a link between national
regeneration and a continuing capacity on the part of 'pobres caminantes' to
transmute their cares and 'dream' in the spirit of the *romances viejos*.
Dreaming connotes the activity of a creative imagination; dreaming up poems
that will outlast their immediate stimulus is a synecdoche for, and hopefully a
stimulus towards, the living of creative individual and national lives.

'La tierra de Alvargonzález' is in part a poem about the birth and early
propagation of a legend (although articulated initially in the form of *coplas*
rather than *romances*). Immediately after the patriarch's death, we read that
even as the murderers are running away from their crime, 'cuenta la hazaña
del campo | el agua clara corriendo' (127–28). The murder is next an-
nounced in the form of *coplas* heard by the guilty brothers as they travel
'Duero arriba'.[30] In the final section of the poem, 'Los asesinos', too, it is the
River Duero that confronts the brothers with more *coplas*.[31] The source of the
river is now for them forever associated with their crime.

Rumour of the murder also spreads by way of the *pueblo* that in the traditional way uses *coplas* to denounce misdeeds, and Miguel quite possibly first
learns details of what happened to his father by overhearing one such song af-

---

29. I am especially grateful to Robert Pring-Mill for first drawing my attention to the significance of this poem.

30. Strictly speaking, 179-82 appear to contain a comment made by the narrator, which is
then taken up in the form of *coplas* in 211-14, 229-32, 277-80. These *coplas* emanate from
different sources: the first is from 'una voz lastimera' on the far side of the river; the second is
unattributed; and the third sounds as if it comes from the river itself. The other instance of
what might be narratorial comment or might be an unattributed *copla* is 599-602. If one counts
the two possible narratorial sources, that makes eleven *coplas* in the poem as a whole.

31. Lines 641–44, 647–48.

ter his return.[32] What the *coplas* performed by both water or the *pueblo* have in common is that, like the *romances viejos*, they are essentially anonymous compositions as they begin to transform a crime story into myth. Thus in 'Los asesinos' the Duero, as Machado himself aspires to do, seems to the older brothers as they travel towards its source to relate an old old story:

> El agua clara corría,
> sonando cual si contara
> una vieja historia, dicha
> mil veces y que tuviera
> mil veces que repetirla.

(636-40)

Thus also in a marvellous closing passage, the Laguna Negra, into which the patriarch's corpse was thrown and into which his murderers finally fall in expiation, is associated with the grandeur and the beauty of wild Nature and we read the following platonic statements about it, which echo the moral and aesthetic effects Machado seeks for his own poetry:

> agua transparente y muda,
>
> . . .
>
> agua pura y silenciosa
> que copia cosas eternas,
> agua impasible que guarda
> en su seno las estrellas.

(697, 705 – 08)

Machado seeks to associate 'La tierra de Alvargonzález' with the origins of a balladry which itself deals in human basics. Through the designation 'padre río', the imagery of water, associated with poetry, fertility and continuity but not ignorant of mutability, is linked to the poet's healing concerns for individuals and for larger national groupings and to those eternal truths each age has to discover afresh for itself.

But would the necessary transformations take place? Machado eschewed facile optimism. He knew much depended on whether he could summon the appropriate artistry and become in his own way like the earlier anonymous authors of the *romances viejos*. Essential to any effective process of transformation is an appeal to the imagination. Discursive, didactic methods rarely succeed. But much also would depend on whether there were ears to hear.

---

32. Lines 427 – 36, 443 – 48, 517 – 22.

When it came to the feasibility of release from decadence, the poet was guarded: his characteristic mode was questioning, not assertion.

It may now perhaps be granted that in so far as Machado broke with the descriptive sobriety of the *romances viejos* by deliberately enhancing the presence in his text of much lyrical material, it was in order to remain faithful in his own age to the *romance*'s age-old cultural function as a source of vitality and wisdom. Far from being diversionary and centrifugal, the poem's lyrical passages, of a beauty entirely on a par with that of other texts from *Campos de Castilla* that 'La tierra de Alvargonzález' echoes, may be seen as integral aspects of an unfolding psychological drama with great breadth of import, both individual and social, both specifically Spanish and not exclusively so.

It is important to grasp what Machado was seeking to achieve and not require something different of him, as if a poet's insertion into the ballad tradition had to entail a somewhat literal replication of certain selective features of it, rather than its creative adaptation and development. In Machado's *romance* itself, the River Duero provides a model for his relationship with the older poetic tradition, connoting simultaneously both continuity and change. Alvargonzález's paternal relationship to his last-born son Miguel is, amongst other things, another model for the poet's relationship with the *romancero viejo* too.

The other major respect in which Machado significantly added to the *romance* version of his story concerns its supernatural elements. These additions have been less criticised than the lyrical evocations of the *tierras*, and perhaps somewhat surprisingly so, since Pidalian doctrine had it that a significant way in which the Spanish epic and ballad traditions departed from the French was in their robust rejection of the *merveilleux*. Machado seems to have thought differently and to have held a less tendentious view of Spanish balladry. It would, however, be wrong to give the impression that the poet underwent a thorough-going conversion to Pidalian neo-traditionalism: he seems in fact, in the spirit of Gaston Paris, to relate the origins of the *romance* not to the epic, of which ballads became held to be detached fragments, but to the shorter lyric. Where Pidal's ideas, and Bédier's, appealed to him was arguably rather in the way they posited individual authorship, but of a non-possessive sort.

The central point to establish here, however, is the extent to which the poem's supernatural elements can also be shown to be successfully integrated into it. In the *romance* versions of his story, as in the *cuento*, Machado is in the main careful to suggest that what he narrates is how things seemed at the time to the characters in the drama. Supernatural happenings reflect their states of mind rather than necessarily objective facts. This is as true of the characters' hearing *coplas* as of the ghostly happenings that follow Miguel's return, especially in the poem's two final sections, 'La tierra' and 'Los asesinos': furrows close no sooner ploughed, the earth seems blood-soaked as the spade enters it, the dead father seems to be working his sons' fields at night.[33] Machado indicates how effects of light, especially when the moon is full, are enough to trigger the guilty memories and feelings of the patriarch's murderers, even if they are too distraught to understand quite what is happening to them. Moonlight, after all though, had presided over the murder-scene; a recurrence of the same peculiar lighting, therefore, is enough to evoke the earlier crime, through a kind of Proustian *mémoire involontaire*. The repetition of lines 106–07 from the opening of the section 'Aquella tarde . . . ' as lines 608–09 in 'La tierra' III, immediately preceding Martín's quasi hallucination, makes this especially clear: 'la luna llena manchada | de un arrebol purpurino'. (One notes as well here the larger import of both 'manchada' and of the colour of deathly bruising, 'purpurino'.) It is easier to kill a man bodily than it is to erase his memory and his influence at a less than fully conscious level.

A potentially more difficult instance of a supernatural event, though, is undoubtedly Alvargonzález's return, closely following that of his son, in part V of the section 'El viajero' (391–406). However much the subjective nature of the perception of freakish happenings by unsophisticated people is emphasised elsewhere, no attempt is made at this crucial turning-point in the story to mitigate the miraculous character of what takes place or its symbolic import: on the contrary, and especially in comparison with the prose *cuento*, it is evident that Machado chose particularly to stress the supernatural character of the scene, for all that he stops short of saying that this figure is the murdered patriarch in fact:

> Un hombre,
> milagrosamente, ha abierto
> la gruesa puerta cerrada
> con doble barra de hierro.
> El hombre que ha entrado tiene

---

33. See lines 583–98, 603–14, 649–64. Lines 613–14 perhaps echo Genesis 4. 10–11.

el rostro del padre muerto.
Un halo de luz dorada
orla sus blancos cabellos.

(397–404)

The poet hits us with the supernatural event, and then, this time stylistically indebted to the older tradition, *sabe callar a tiempo*. His prime concern no doubt is that we should grasp the symbolic significance of the *indiano*'s return, even if this creates certain other problems of verisimilitude. The primary symbolic meaning is taken when we relate what happens here to the earlier material in the father's dream, narrated in the section 'El sueño' II, III and IV. As to the psychological dimension of the scene, this is perhaps best thought of as a dramatic means of presenting the older brothers' awareness, on seeing Miguel unexpectedly back amongst them, that they had not succeeded in their earlier vengeance, and that it would take more than parricide to annul the effects of their father's preference for his youngest son. Not every reader, however, is likely to judge that this episode works entirely satisfactorily: it seems to be an externalisation of inner processes and significances with insufficient rooting in the world of actual, plausible sense perceptions.

It must finally be admitted that one's difficulties do not end here, nor do all objections to the poem's supernatural elements arise from Pidalian convictions. In some as yet unpublished notes on the poem, Dr Ronald Truman has argued that the mood of the text as a whole is disconcertingly inconsistent in this regard. The tone of many of the supernatural happenings is, he finds, at odds with the plain, austere, and factual idiom that Machado elsewhere adopts, a tone in keeping with the story's echoing of the Old Testament and one where the poet seems closest to the characteristic manner of the *romances viejos*. The supernatural events, he suggests, are of a piece with an apparent desire on Machado's part to produce an emotional and imaginative impression of a kind quite absent from Genesis, despite his indebtedness to the latter in other respects. Truman draws attention to the cumulative effect of passages that indicate a penchant for the more 'Gothic' side of Romanticism. Some have already been mentioned – the return of Miguel, the ghost of the father, the 'arrebol purpurino', the blood on the spade – and to these may be added the account of the mother's death (151–56), the stormy night when Miguel's brothers are alone with the flickering candle and their guilty consciences (301–30), and the horror of the dark wood as the brothers approach the Laguna Negra (675–86). From all this the conclusion is drawn that although Machado's presentation of such features may permit a reading of them in terms of the perceptions and emotions of the characters involved, that sense is not predominant in the operation of the text and does not in consequence mitigate an uncomfortable imaginative tension between them and the greater sobriety and religious austerity of the poem's Old Testament elements.

Perhaps Machado might have answered that he was indeed attempting to appeal to readers' imaginations through a creative development within the ballad tradition but, furthermore, that the resultant tonal mixture is characteristic of the folk tales and legends that 'La tierra de Alvargonzález' is intended to reflect. The Castilian ethos that the poem seeks to represent is one in which not all is sobriety and in which the imagination is a two-edged weapon, now creative now destructive. If the artistic result jars with some readers, however, one may have simply to respect that fact and admit that in this regard the poem is not flawless.

It is contended here, however, that 'La tierra de Alvargonzález' is coherent in conception, successfully involving and integrating both lyrical descriptions of the Castilian landscape and, in the main, the narration of supernatural happenings. The ways in which Machado sought fidelity to the spirit of the *romancero viejo* and through that, fidelity to 'lo esencial castellano', did not involve eschewing such things. Once readers are at least prepared to set aside Pidalian conceptions about the nature of Spanish balladry and approach the poem on Machado's terms, they may more readily appreciate it as a convincing text both in its design and in its execution.[34]

ERIC SOUTHWORTH

St Peter's College, Oxford

---

34. I am grateful to many fellow members of the Oxford Sub-Faculty of Spanish for their encouragement when an earlier version of this article was read to its Graduate Seminar in January 1994. I particularly wish to mention the kindness of Clive Griffin and Ronald Truman in commenting in careful detail on my text. A longer-standing and deep gratitude is to the late Helen Grant.

MORE SOURCES FOR GARCÍA LORCA'S
DOÑA ROSITA LA SOLTERA

The rose that lives its little hour

AT THE BEGINNING of *Twelfth Night* we learn that Olivia, a countess, has taken a vow of seven years' mourning for her dead brother and father. The Clown considers this course of action to be ill-advised, and reminds her that 'As there is no true cuckold but calamity, so beauty's a flower' – two parallel examples of inconstancy.[1] Later in the same scene Viola arrives, disguised as Cesario, sent to Olivia by Orsino Duke of Illyria to press his suit; Viola/Cesario offers a number of arguments, among them the following:

> ' Tis beauty truly blent, whose red and white
> Nature's own sweet and cunning hand laid on.
> Lady, you are the cruell'st she alive
> If you will lead these graces to the grave
> And leave the world no copy.
>
> (Act I, sc. v, lines 242–46, *ed. cit.*, 33–34)

Orsino is not alone in aspiring to Olivia's hand; Sir Andrew Aguecheek is her most ridiculous suitor, and in Act II, sc. iii, he and his drinking companion, Sir Toby Belch, are entertained by the Clown with a love song:

> What is love? 'Tis not hereafter,
> Present mirth hath present laughter:
>   What's to come is still unsure.
> In delay there lies no plenty,
> Then come kiss me, sweet and twenty:
>   Youth's a stuff will not endure.
>
> (lines 48–53, *ed. cit.*, 46)

---

1. William SHAKESPEARE, *Twelfth Night*, Act I, sc. v, lines 49–50, ed. J. M. Lothian & T. W. Craik, The Arden Shakespeare (London: Routledge, 1991), 23–24.

These three moments from early on in the play give first voice to an inter-related group of ideas that coalesce and achieve greater prominence later in Act II. Here the Duke divines that Viola/Cesario is herself in love, and en-quires about the object of her affection. When informed that the person in question is 'about your years', Orsino responds:

> Too old, by heaven! Let still the woman take
> An elder than herself; so wears she to him,
> So sways she level in her husband's heart:
> For boy, however we do praise ourselves,
> Our fancies are more giddy and unfirm,
> More longing, wavering, sooner lost and worn
> Than women's are.

VIOLA.   I think it well, my lord.

DUKE. Then let thy love be younger than thyself,
>   Or thy affection cannot hold the bent:
>   For women are as roses, whose fair flower
>   Being once display'd, doth fall that very hour.

VIOLA. And so they are: alas, that they are so:
>   To die, even when they to perfection grow!

(Act II, sc. iv, lines 27–41, *ed. cit.*, 57)

Immediately after this exchange the Duke calls for music and song, the latter again to be provided by the Clown:

> O, fellow, come, the song we had last night.
> Mark it, Cesario, it is old and plain;
> The spinsters and the knitters in the sun,
> And the free maids that weave their thread with bones
> Do use to chant it: it is silly sooth,
> And dallies with the innocence of love,
> Like the old age.

(Act II, sc. iv, lines 42–48, *ed. cit.*, 58)

The song itself, that follows, is on a conventional courtly theme, concerned with a rejected lover who now only longs for death.

We do not know if Lorca read *Twelfth Night*, and of Shakespeare's plays it is not one that immediately leaps to mind when one is considering possible influences; furthermore, the initial situation and eventual fate of Olivia and

Rosita bear only the slimmest of resemblances.[2] However, my primary purpose here is not so much to establish a distant though still possible affinity, but more to exemplify, as our point of departure, the widespread use of flower and specifically rose *topoi* in the sixteenth and seventeenth centuries.[3]

Rose of the garden! Such is woman's lot

Most criticism concerned with Lorca's *Doña Rosita la soltera, o El lenguaje de las flores: poema granadino del novecientos, dividido en varios jardines con escenas de canto y baile* (1935) and the play's sources and influences has, justifiably enough, focused on the nineteenth and early twentieth centuries.[4] Numerous analogues have been found, including Zorrilla's *Don Juan Tenorio* (1844) (especially the famous 'sofa scene'), Francisco Camprodón's *Flor de un día* (1851) and its sequel *Espinas de una flor* (1852), Ibsen's *Love's Comedy* (1862), various Galdós novels – *Miau* (1888), *Misericordia* (1897), and so on – Maeterlinck's *L'Intruse* (1890), Chekhov's *Three Sisters* (1901) and above all *The Cherry Orchard* (1904), Benavente's *Lo cursi* (1901), the Álvarez Quintero brothers' *La zagala* (1904) and *Amores y amoríos* (1908), Azorín's novels, Arniches's *La señorita de Trevélez* (1916), and, last but not least, Pirandello's *Enrico Quarto* (1922).[5] Nor are lyric poets to be denied their place, and di-

---

2. Four volumes of an eight-volume set of Shakespeare's *Obras completas* are preserved in what remains of Lorca's library, though it is highly probable that he originally owned the complete collection. *Twelfth Night* figures in one of the missing volumes: see Manuel FERNÁNDEZ-MONTESINOS, 'Descripción de la biblioteca de Federico García Lorca (Catálogo y estudio)', unpublished doctoral dissertation (Universidad Complutense de Madrid, 1985), 103. For a consideration of possible borrowings and influences, see Andrew ANDERSON, 'Some Shakespearian Reminiscences in García Lorca's Drama', *Comparative Literature Studies*, 22 (1985), 187–210.

3. Barbara SEWARD, *The Symbolic Rose* (New York: Columbia Univ. Press, 1960; rpt Dallas: Spring Publications, 1989), 55.

4. 'The search for sources has long engaged critics devoted to the exegesis of Federico García Lorca's theatrical works. No play has invited more speculation about the relationship between the drama itself and pre-existing textual models than Lorca's *Doña Rosita la soltera*': Francie CATE-ARRIES, 'The Discourse of Desire in the Language of Flowers: Lorca, Freud, and Doña Rosita', *South Atlantic Review*, 57 (1992), 53–68 (53). Roberto G. SÁNCHEZ, 'García Lorca y la literatura del siglo XIX: Apuntes sobre *Doña Rosita la soltera*', Ínsula, 26, nr 290 (1971), 1, 12–13 (1), goes so far as to deny any influence from Golden-Age theatre.

5. Alfredo DE LA GUARDIA, *García Lorca: Persona y creación*, 4th edn (Buenos Aires: Schapire, 1961), 369–78; Arturo BERENGUER CARISOMO, *Las máscaras de Federico García Lorca*, 2nd edn (Buenos Aires: Editorial Universitaria, 1969), 147; Daniel DEVOTO, '*Doña Rosita la soltera*: Estructura y fuentes', *Bulletin Hispanique*, 69 (1967), 407–35 (427); SÁNCHEZ, 'García Lorca'; José MONLEÓN SÁNCHEZ, 'Una crónica de la cursilería española', in Federico García Lorca, *Doña Rosita la soltera*, ed. Monleón Sánchez & Antonina Rodrigo

verse points of reference have been noted in Espronceda's *El diablo mundo* (Canto V), Alfred de Musset, Bécquer's *Rimas*, Victor Hugo, Verlaine, Rubén Darío, Juan Ramón Jiménez, and José Muñoz San Román.[6] Most recently, Francie Cate-Arries has added a new and quite different dimension by identifying two dream-texts analysed in Freud's *The Interpretation of Dreams* (1900) that bear surprising resemblances to passages in Lorca's play.

Besides this broad attention paid to other authors and their works, there have also been studies of the rose as it appears in many other texts by Lorca himself.[7] And apart from the strictly literary, critics have delved into documentary sources for rose symbolism and the language of flowers – such as the early nineteenth-century botanical manual quoted by Moreno Villa, almanacs and magazines in the Lorca family attic, or oral information culled from Romero Murube's aunts. Still others have unearthed prototypes for both characters and plot in several members of Lorca's extended family and in several of his family acquaintances.[8]

In what follows, however, I propose to shift the focus of attention to considerably earlier models, by examining in greater detail some representative examples of rose symbolism from the so-called Spanish Golden Age: a symbolism which in turn derives primarily from classical authors.[9]

(Barcelona: Aymá, 1976), 7–38 (23); Gerardo VELÁZQUEZ CUETO, 'Actualidad y entendimiento de *Doña Rosita la soltera* de Federico García Lorca', *Ínsula*, 36, nr 410 (1981), 1, 12–13 (12); Ricardo DOMÉNECH, 'Nueva indagación en *Doña Rosita la soltera*', *Anales de Literatura Española Contemporánea*, 11 (1986), 79–90 (81).

6. DE LA GUARDIA, *García Lorca*, 372; DEVOTO, '*Doña Rosita*', 428; SÁNCHEZ, 'García Lorca', 12; Marie LAFFRANQUE, 'Federico García Lorca: de rosa mudable a la «Casida de la rosa»', in *Lecciones sobre Federico García Lorca*, ed. Andrés Soria Olmedo (Granada: Comisión del Cincuentenario, 1986), 279–300 (284–86); John K. WALSH, 'The Women in Lorca's Theater', *Gestos*, 3 (1987), 53–65 (64–65 & n. 33). To this list I would add Espronceda's sonnet 'Fresca, lozana, pura y olorosa', in José de ESPRONCEDA, *Poesías líricas y fragmentos épicos*, ed. Robert Marrast, Clásicos Castalia 20 (Madrid: Castalia, 1970), 121–22.

7. LAFFRANQUE, 'Federico García Lorca', *passim* ; David CLUFF, 'Rose Symbolism in the Works of García Lorca', *García Lorca Review*, 2, nr 2 (1974), n.p.

8. José MORENO VILLA, *Vida en claro: Autobiografía* (Mexico City: Fondo de Cultura Económica, 1976), 120–21; DEVOTO, '*Doña Rosita*', 411–12; DE LA GUARDIA, *García Lorca*, 365–66; Francisco GARCÍA LORCA, *Federico y su mundo*, ed. Mario Hernández (Madrid: Alianza, 1980), 362; Marcelle AUCLAIR, *Enfances et mort de García Lorca* (Paris: Seuil, 1968), 343; José MORA GUARNIDO, *Federico García Lorca y su mundo* (Buenos Aires: Losada, 1958), 167–71; Antonina RODRIGO, '*Doña Rosita la soltera*: Teatro y realidad', in *Lecciones sobre Federico García Lorca*, 117–28.

9. Rose symbolism is virtually absent from the Bible, save for an interesting occurrence in the Apocrypha ('Let us crown ourselves with rosebuds before they be withered', Wisdom of Solomon 2. 8, quoted by SEWARD, *The Symbolic Rose*, 56).

Rose is a rose is a rose is a rose

The 'rose poem' in *Doña Rosita la soltera* is written in *romance* metre with a stressed 'a' assonance, and contains some conventional tropes ('roja como sangre está', 'es dura como el coral') as well as some other imagery much more redolent of Lorca's personal style. On its first appearance in the play it runs like this:

> Cuando se abre en la mañana,
> roja como la sangre está;
> el rocío no la toca
> porque se teme quemar.
> Abierta en el mediodía
> es dura como el coral.
> El sol se asoma a los vidrios
> para verla relumbrar.
> Cuando en las ramas empiezan
> los pájaros a cantar
> y se desmaya la tarde
> en las violetas del mar,
> se pone blanca, con blanco
> de una mejilla de sal.
> Y cuando toca la noche
> blando cuerno de metal
> y las estrellas avanzan
> mientras los aires se van,
> en la raya de lo oscuro,
> se comienza a deshojar.

$$(47)^{10}$$

Structurally, it is reminiscent of the sonnet, breaking down, in its basic form, into blocks of 4 + 4 + 6 + 6 lines, while in its re-elaboration it is expanded to 4 + 4 + 8 + 6. The fundamental relationship between the flower in the 'rose poem' and the life of Doña Rosita is quite transparent. The rare *rosa mutabilis* that is described passes through all of its phases in the space of one day

---

10. All quotations are from Federico GARCÍA LORCA, *Doña Rosita la soltera*, ed. Luis Martínez Cuitiño, Clásicos Castellanos, n.s. (Madrid: Espasa-Calpe, 1992). The 'rose poem' appears at 76 and 99, later at 139–40, and fragmentarily at 148–49; it is introduced into the text as a quotation from a book from which both Rosita and the Tío read aloud; the Tío, an amateur botanist, has cultivated an example of this rare variety (75–76).

(morning, midday, dusk, night), changing from bud, to bloom, to full-blown, to withered and dropping its petals, while correspondingly turning in colour from bright red to white.[11] The rose's day is figuratively equated to the whole span of Rosita's life, and hence each comes to mirror the other: Rosita's age, her physical appearance, and the colour of her various dresses are paralleled in the symbolic underpinning of the rose leitmotiv.[12] Furthermore, the three acts of the play take place, respectively, during the morning, afternoon, and evening of three separate days in Rosita's life, each many years apart: tele-scoped together into the few hours of the running-time of the play's perfor-mance, they simultaneously suggest a single, composite day and the twenty-five years that elapse according to the text's internal chronology.[13]

The self-evident presence here of ancient and time-worn symbols has led most commentators merely to nod in the direction of a few of the best known examples and rapidly move on, but if we look a little more closely it becomes apparent that there are actually two intimately related *topoi* at work here, both of which probably go back as far as the *Greek Anthology*, but which find their most ready point of reference in a single poem attributed to Ausonius.[14]

The better known topic, 'collige, virgo, rosas', is actually the less immedi-ately operative one here. The other, 'quam longa una dies, aetas tam longa rosarum', is an exact match for the concept of the *rosa mutabilis*. Both tags derive from the same composition:

> quam longa una dies, aetas tam longa rosarum;
> quas pubescentes iuncta senecta premit.

---

11. The flower thus embodies the strict etymological meaning of ephemeral – lasting only one day. It is never explicitly described as passing through shades of pink, perhaps to avoid labouring the analogy.

12. Eleodoro J. FEBRES, 'El problema estructural de *Doña Rosita la soltera*', *Sin Nombre*, 10, nr 2 (1979), 98–111, is the only critic to date to have tackled the apparent mismatch between the four phases of the rose ('mañana', 'mediodía', 'tarde', 'noche' : *Doña Rosita la soltera*, 76) and the three acts of the play. Rosita wears a total of four dresses, three pink, each one lighter than the previous, and appears in white at the very end of the play.

13. Arturo JIMÉNEZ-VERA, 'The Rose Symbolism and the Social Message in *Doña Rosita la soltera*', *García Lorca Review*, 6, nr 2 (1978), 127–37 (128–29); Luis FERNÁNDEZ-CIFUENTES, *García Lorca en el teatro: La norma y la diferencia* (Zaragoza: Universidad de Zaragoza, 1986), 211–43, points out (221) that in addition each is a special day: a farewell, Rosita's saint's day, and a house-moving.

14. SEWARD, *The Symbolic Rose*, 13–14; Blanca GONZÁLEZ DE ESCANDÓN, *Los temas del 'Carpe diem' y la brevedad de la rosa en la poesía española* (Barcelona: Universidad de Barcelona, 1938), 12. See also James HUTTON, *The Greek Anthology in Italy to the Year 1800* (Ithaca: Cornell University Press, 1935), 23.

. . .

> collige, virgo, rosas, dum flos novus et nova pubes,
> et memor esto aevum sic properare tuum.[15]

While 'quam longa una dies' could be thought of as a specific iteration of the more abstract and general Virgilian formulation 'fugit irreparabile tempus', 'collige, virgo, rosas' likewise exemplifies both literally and metaphorically the Horatian injunction 'Carpe diem'; furthermore, the 'logical' relationship between the two – that the one follows from the other – is perfectly clear.[16]

Both *topoi* are relevant to the plot and imagery of *Doña Rosita la soltera*: the first is a primary source for the basic rose leitmotiv and hence the symbolic configuration of the three acts of the play; the second is present, negatively, in the action, in as much as it represents what Rosita never does, despite the urgings of several other characters. However, as in other plays, notably *Yerma*, the 'message' is not as unproblematic as it might first appear: there is actually no easy solution for Rosita's predicament and dilemma, as is made abundantly clear in her long speech towards the end of Act III (*ed. cit.*, 173–177), and hence we should be extremely wary of putting words – above all these particular words: 'collige, virgo, rosas' – into Lorca's mouth.

The rose of yesterday

As has been amply demonstrated, 'los autores de la tardía Antigüedad, decisivos para la formación literaria medieval, eran leídos y gustados en el Siglo de Oro'.[17] Reworkings of Ausonius's two connected *topoi*, often, as in the

---

15. DECIMUS MAGNUS AUSONIUS, *Works*, ed. R. P. H. Green (Oxford: Clarendon Press, 1991), 670-71 (lines 43-44, 49-50). Fernando de Herrera includes his translation of this poem in the *Anotaciones a Garcilaso* (GONZÁLEZ DE ESCANDÓN, *Los temas*, 35-38): see *Obras de Garcilaso de la Vega, con anotaciones de Fernando de Herrera*, ed. facsim. with prologue by Antonio GALLEGO MORELL, Clásicos Hispánicos, serie I, 6 (Madrid: CSIC, 1973), 672–73. The famous distich was also rendered by Francisco de Medina and later by Agustín de Salazar y Torres: see *Poetas líricos de los siglos XVI y XVII*, ed. Adolfo de CASTRO, 2 vols, Biblioteca de Autores Españoles 32, 42 (Madrid: Rivadeneyra, 1854–57), II, 217.

16. Compare Robert Herrick's well-known poem, 'To the Virgins, to Make Much of Time' (from *Hesperides*), that glosses Ausonius: 'Gather ye Rose-buds while ye may, | Old Time is still a-flying: | And this same flower that smiles to day, | To morrow will be dying', Robert HERRICK, *The Poetical Works*, ed. L. C. Martin (Oxford: Clarendon Press, 1956), 84, lines 1–4.

17. María Rosa LIDA DE MALKIEL, *La tradición clásica en España* (Barcelona: Ariel, 1975), 286. Rose imagery of the type that concerns us here seems to have appeared in Castilian poetry in the fifteenth century, but was relatively rare: GONZÁLEZ DE ESCANDÓN, *Los temas*, 49; José MONDÉJAR, 'La brevedad de la rosa en la poesía española del XV y en la lírica de Lope de

original, incorporated into a single text, are common throughout the sixteenth and seventeenth centuries in Spain,[18] and I have no doubt that Lorca had many of these authors at the back of his mind as he laid out the groundwork for *Doña Rosita la soltera.*

Garcilaso provides us with one of the first examples in his Second Eclogue:

> ... como la rosa   matutina,
> quando ya el sol declina   al mediodía,
> que pierde su alegría   y marchitando
> va la color mudando ...

(lines 1254–57)[19]

while his sonnet XXIII, 'En tanto que de rosa y d'açucena', combines the two *topoi* :

> coged de vuestra alegre primavera
> el dulce fruto antes que'l tiempo ayrado
> cubra de nieve la hermosa cumbre.
>
> Marchitará la rosa el viento elado,
> todo lo mudará la edad ligera,
> por no hacer mudança en su costumbre.

(lines 9–14)[20]

Góngora returns to these ideas and images on a number of occasions, as in an attributed sonnet, XLVIII, 'A una rosa':

Vega', *Cuadernos Hispano-Americanos*, nr 161/62 (1963), 391–418 (397, 400).

18. José María BLECUA (ed.), *Las flores en la poesía española* (Madrid: Editorial Hispánica, 1944), 18; MONDÉJAR, 'La brevedad', 401; Norma CARRICABURO & Luis MARTÍNEZ CUITIÑO, 'Los signos del tiempo en *Doña Rosita la soltera*', *Letras* (Buenos Aires), nr 8 (1983), 67–73 (67).

19. GARCILASO DE LA VEGA, *Obras completas, con comentario*, ed. Elias RIVERS (Madrid: Cátedra, 1981), 380; first related to *Doña Rosita la soltera* by DEVOTO, '*Doña Rosita*', 426. See specifically lines 7–8 of the 'rose poem' (*Doña Rosita la soltera*, 76).

20. *ed. cit.*, 128. Rivers's comments (*ed. cit.*, 125–26) are useful here; Garcilaso's model is Bernardo Tasso's 'mentre che l'aureo crin v'ondeggia intorno', from *Rime scelte di diversi autori* (Venice: Gioliti, 1586). Note the agency of the wind in the rose's destruction, and compare with the second version of the 'rose poem': 'tan caliente sobre el tallo, | que la brisa se quemaba' (*Doña Rosita la soltera*, 139) and the comment at the very end of the play: 'Como siga este viento no va a quedar una rosa viva' (184). See also Francisco de la Torre's treatment of the same theme in a short ode: *Poesía completa*, ed. María Luisa CERRÓN PUGA, Letras Hispánicas 207 (Madrid: Cátedra, 1984), 82–83, also quoted in Arthur TERRY (ed.), *An Anthology of Spanish Poetry 1500-1700*, Part I: *1500-1580* (Oxford: Pergamon, 1965), 126–27. Both Cerrón Puga and Terry offer useful annotations.

Ayer naciste, y morirás mañana.
Para tan breve ser, ¿quién te dio vida?
¿Para vivir tan poco estás lucida,
y para no ser nada estás lozana?

Si te engañó su hermosura vana,
bien presto la verás desvanecida,
porque en tu hermosura está escondida
la ocasión de morir muerte temprana.

(lines 1–8)[21]

A sonnet of more dubious attribution, XLIX, 'A la rosa y su brevedad', runs in a similar vein:

Púrpura ostenta, disimula nieve,
entre malezas peregrina rosa,

. . .

[el Sol]

. . .

ofendido de tanta competencia,
fulminando veneno la marchita.

(lines 1–2, 13–14)[22]

In 'Cloris, este rosal, que libre o rudo', a close contemporary of Góngora differentiates between the fate of the bush and the individual blooms:

Nota esta rosa, que aún agora pudo
abrir el paso a su niñez modesta,
pero cuán breves términos apresta
la grana que libró de verde ñudo.

Vive su planta los estivos meses;
mas el honor de los purpúreos senos,
mísera edad, la madurez de un día.

(lines 5–11)[23]

21. GÓNGORA, *Sonetos completos*, ed. Biruté Ciplijauskaité, Clásicos Castalia 1 (Madrid: Castalia, 1982), 312; related to *Doña Rosita la soltera* by DEVOTO, '*Doña Rosita*', 426.

22. *ed. cit.*, 313. See also two *Carpe diem* sonnets by Góngora, both heavily influenced by Garcilaso: 149 ('Mientras por competir con tu cabello'), and 150 ('Ilustre y hermosísima María'), *ed. cit.*, 230–31: Robert JAMMES, *Études sur l'oeuvre poétique de don Luis de Góngora y Argote* (Bordeaux: Institut d'Études Ibériques et Ibéro-Américaines de l'Université de Bordeaux, 1967), 366n.

23. Bartolomé Leonardo de ARGENSOLA, *Rimas*, ed. José Manuel Blecua, 2 vols, Clásicos Castellanos 184, 185 (Madrid: Espasa-Calpe, 1974), I, 212.

Lope de Vega devotes frequent attention to the rose. For instance, in a sonnet from the *Triunfos divinos* he depicts the flower thus:

> Doncella en los pimpollos de Abril nace
> la fresca Rosa de su vida incierta,
> y en su casa de aljofares cubierta
> de cinco trenzas verdes muros hace.
>
> . . .
>
> declina el dia, y en los brazos muerta
> del encendido sol marchita yace.

(lines 1–4, 7–8)[24]

In a second sonnet Lope addresses the 'purpúrea esfera':

> Breve huesped del sol, que el mismo dia
> que te recibe alegre, quando sale,
> te despide veloz, quando se vuelve.

(lines 12–14)

and in a third, 'Por labios de coral la blanca Aurora', he speaks again of a rose that opens with the dawn, is a 'coronel de carmín al mediodía', but on returning at nightfall, he finds it bent and broken.[25] In similar vein, the 'Amarylis' contains the lines:

> Nace la vida, y quando nace muere,
> porque de su principio el fin se infiere:
> cuna es el Alva de la rosa pura,
> la noche sepultura.

(lines 235–38)[26]

and the 'Égloga pescatoria en la muerte de don Lope Felix del Carpio y Luxan':

> Lisonja de la mañana
> sale la rosa rïendo,

---

24. *Coleccion de las obras sueltas, assi en prosa, como en verso, de D. Frey Lope Felix de Vega Carpio, del habito de San Juan*, ed. Francisco de CERDÁ Y RICO, 21 vols (Madrid: Antonio de Sancha, 1776–79), XIII, 93–98 (96–97). The dew motif – 'aljófares', 'rocío' – is common, and also appears in the 'rose poem' (*Doña Rosita la soltera*, 76).

25. 'Sonetos a la rosa', §7, *Coleccion de las obras sueltas*, XIII, 96. Lope devoted a total of twelve sonnets to the rose in the *Triunfos divinos* (MONDÉJAR, 'La brevedad', 404–05); GONZÁLEZ DE ESCANDÓN, *Los temas*, reproduces ten of them (116–25).

26. *Coleccion de las obras sueltas*, X, 147–92 (155), cited by MONDÉJAR, 'La brevedad', 413.

al llanto del Alva abriendo
un libro de hojas de grana:
sacude la noche escura,
y toda su lozania
dura un dia.

(lines 187–93)[27]

In the course of his opening description of Arcadia, in the meadows and among a wide variety of other flowers, we encounter a curious species almost identical to the *rosa mutabilis* : 'aquella rosa, que nació del sudor de Latona, de quien se dice, que al alba está blanca, al mediodía roja, y a la noche verde'.[28]

Finally, in a striking passage from *Jerusalén conquistada*, book X, Lope tells of a fabulous creature:

Nace en la India un animal al alba
que está en su juventud al medio día,
y en trémula vejez helada y calva
cuando sube del mar la noche fría;[29]

to which he then adds:

Así es retrato de la vida nuestra
cada día que pasa, así amanece
la rosa y su color, que al alba muestra,
coronado de perlas resplandece;
así la noche de la muerte diestra
la luz de nuestras vidas oscurece;
no sé quién de esperar ni servir fía
siendo una breve vida cada día.

(lines 353–56, 361–68)[30]

---

27. *Coleccion de las obras sueltas*, X, 362–79 (368), cited by MONDÉJAR, 'La brevedad', 417. For yet another like example, see 'La selva sin amor', in LOPE DE VEGA, *Laurel de Apolo, con otras rimas* (Madrid: Juan González, 1630), 109v., cited in DEVOTO, '*Doña Rosita*', 426.

28. LOPE DE VEGA, *La Arcadia*, ed. Edwin S. Morby, Clásicos Castalia 63 (Madrid: Castalia, 1975), 66; first connected with *Doña Rosita la soltera* by Rafael SOLANA, 'Mapa de afluentes en la obra poética de Federico García Lorca', *Letras de México*, 1, nr 29 (1937–38), 5–8 (6).

29. Compare from the 'rose poem': 'y se desmaya la tarde | en las violetas del mar' (*Doña Rosita la soltera*, 76).

30. Stanzas 45–46 in *Jerusalén conquistada*, ed. Joaquín de ENTRAMBASAGUAS, 3 vols (Madrid: CSIC, 1951), I, 404.

By the time we reach Quevedo, the *desengaño* motif has become even stronger; for instance, in a 'Letrilla lírica' he writes:

¿De qué sirve presumir,
rosal, de buen parecer,
si aun no acabas de nacer
cuando empiezas a morir?

. . .

No es muy grande la ventaja
que tu calidad mejora:
si es tus mantillas la aurora,
es la noche tu mortaja.[31]

(lines 5–8, 19–22)

Similarly, in the sonnet explicitly entitled 'Con ejemplos muestra a Flora la brevedad de la hermosura para no malograrla', 'la ostentación lozana de la rosa' (line 5) is one of a list of items that

reprehensiones son, ¡oh Flora!, mudas
de la hermosura y la soberbia humana,
que a las leyes de flor está sujeta.

Tu edad se pasará mientras lo dudas;
de ayer te habrás de arrepentir mañana . . .

(lines 9–13)

and in 'Ofrece a Lisi la primera flor que se abrió en el año', Quevedo writes:

A corta vida nace destinada:
sus edades son horas; en un día
su parto y muerte el cielo ríe y llora.

(lines 9–11) [32]

Francisco López de Zárate sees in 'el breve minuto de la rosa' the 'tránsito compendioso de la vida', while Francisco de Rioja, a near contemporary, again stresses the standard associations of ephemerality.[33] Thus his Silva VI,

31. Francisco de QUEVEDO, *Obra poética*, ed. José Manuel Blecua, 4 vols (Madrid: Castalia, 1969–82), I, 408; first quoted in DEVOTO, *'Doña Rosita'*, 428.

32. *ed. cit.*, I, 488–89 (nr 295), 642 (nr 446).

33. GONZÁLEZ DE ESCANDÓN, *Los temas*, 145. A third poet, Pedro SOTO DE ROJAS, and his *Granada, paraíso cerrado para muchos, jardines abiertos para pocos*, also comes to mind, when one considers that the action of *Doña Rosita la soltera* is set in a *carmen* in the Albaicín, and that the subtitle mentions 'varios jardines': *Obras de Don Pedro Soto de Rojas*, ed. Antonio Gallego, Biblioteca de Antiguos Libros Hispánicos B 5 (Madrid: CSIC, 1950), 367–417.

'Al verano', runs:

> veloz passa bolando,
> al umano linage amonestando,
> viendo las rosas que su aliento cría
> cómo nacen i mueren en un día: [34]

(lines 71–74)

and in sonnet XXXVII Rioja observes:

> . . . la flor que aparece al nuevo día,
> el crespo seno en púrpura bañado,
> con color se ve en tierra desmayado
> antes que el mismo al mar tuerça la vía.

(lines 5–8)[35]

It comes as no surprise that Calderón inherited this poetic tradition and still found ways to elaborate upon it. In a famous sonnet it is particularly notable that human lives are reduced, figuratively, to the span of a single day:

> Éstas que fueron pompa y alegría
> despertando al albor de la mañana,
> a la tarde serán lástima vana,
> durmiendo en brazos de la noche fría.
>
> Este matiz, que al cielo desafía,
> iris listado de oro, nieve y grana,
> será escarmiento de la vida humana:
> ¡tanto se emprende en término de un día!
>
> A florecer las rosas madrugaron,
> y para envejecerse florecieron:
> cuna y sepulcro en un botón hallaron.
>
> Tales los hombres sus fortunas vieron:
> en un día nacieron y expiraron,
> que pasados los siglos, horas fueron.

(lines 1652–65)[36]

---

34. FRANCISCO DE RIOJA, *Poesía*, ed. Begoña López Bueno, Letras Hispánicas 196 (Madrid: Cátedra, 1984), 192.

35. Compare, from the 'rose poem': 'y se desmaya la tarde | en las violetas del mar' (*Doña Rosita la soltera*, 76), and the return of the fainting motif at the very end of the play (186). For a sequence of four sonnets in a similar vein, see Pedro de CASTRO Y ANAYA, *Auroras de Diana*, ed. M. Josefa Díez de Revenga (Murcia: Academia Alfoso X el Sabio, 1989), 106–08; one of these is quoted in BLECUA, *Las flores*, 145.

36. *El príncipe constante*, ed. A. PORQUERAS MAYO, Clásicos Castellanos 204 (Madrid:

The foregoing survey, though highly selective, nevertheless demonstrates the degree to which these images became deeply entrenched commonplaces.[37] More specifically, we can see how Garcilaso, Lope, Quevedo and Calderón all pick up the Ausonian *topos* of *quam longa una dies* and elaborate upon it further, splitting the rose's single day into some combination of dawn, morning, midday, afternoon, dusk and night;   Lope, moreover, dwells on the corresponding changes in colour.[38] Finally, several related motifs found in Lorca's 'rose poem' – dew, wind, fainting, night and the sea – are also anticipated in these Golden-Age texts.

Coda: If music be the food of love

Following now a very different line of association, *Doña Rosita la soltera* might also put one in mind of Richard Strauss's *Der Rosenkavalier*, premièred in Dresden in early 1911.[39]   Set in eighteenth-century Vienna, the opera anachronistically incorporates a number of Viennese waltzes, is plotted around the ceremonious gift of a silver rose, and is concerned, among other things, with the Marschallin's autumnal thoughts on the passing of her youth ('Die Zeit, die ist ein sonderbar Ding', she sings), reflexions that eventually lead her to encourage Octavian's interest in Sophie.

Acts I and II of *Doña Rosita la soltera*, as its subtitle announces, are shot through with music and song.   The first that we hear is a piano study by the Austrian composer Karl Czerny: off-stage music that frames the farewell scene (*Doña Rosita la soltera*, 94, 98).   Notable here also are some lines spoken by the Primo, 'te digo, porque te quiero, | que me moriré por ti' (96), which closely recall one of the projected but never completed books of poetry

---

Espasa-Calpe, 1975), 75–76 (lines 1652–65);   see DEVOTO, *Doña Rosita la soltera* ('*Doña Rosita*', 426); also SOLANA: 'un soneto inmortal' ('Mapa de afluentes', 6).

37.   See Antonio de SOLÍS, 'A la Rosa, moralidad burlesca', in his *Varias poesías sagradas y profanas*, ed. Manuela Sánchez Regueira, Clásicos Hispánicos 16 (Madrid: CSIC, 1968), 97; Agustín de SALAZAR Y TORRES, 'Con moralidad de la rosa, escribe haciendo donaire', *ed. cit.*, 220; and Sor JUANA INÉS DE LA CRUZ, *Sonetos y endechas*, ed. Xavier Villarrutia (Barcelona: Labor, 1980), 69–71.

38.   As DE LA GUARDIA comments (*García Lorca*, 369): '¿Pero, cómo no encontrar influencia de Lope de Vega en una obra de García Lorca? Aun cuando no sea consciente, surge por cualquier parte, por estar tan imbuido de ella' (see also SOLANA, 'Mapa de afluentes', 6).

39.   The year that Lorca, in one interview, ascribes to Act III of *Doña Rosita la soltera*: Pedro MASSA, 'Estreno de *Doña Rosita la soltera*, nueva obra de García Lorca interpretada por M. Xirgu', *Crónica* (Madrid), 15 December 1935.

that Lorca mentioned during the 1930s: *Porque te quiero a ti solamente. (Tanda de valses).*[40] In Act II the Tío mentions 'el vals de las rosas, que es una de las composiciones más bonitas de estos tiempos' (118), more tunes are mentioned later – 'la tarantela de Popper', 'la plegaria de la Virgen' (131-32), '¡Viva Frascuelo!' and 'La barcarola de «La fragata Numancia»' (137-38) – while eventually Rosita, the Tía, the three Solteronas and the Madre sing 'Lo que dicen las flores' to piano accompaniment (138-41). At the end of Act II «*La* SOLTERONA 3ª *se sienta al piano y toca una polka*» (149).

Given this conjunction of elements, it is surprising that no one, to date, has linked *Doña Rosita la soltera* with Ravel. Debussy and Ravel were two of Lorca's favourite composers; he mentions both several times in his works and letters, and of course would have received up-to-the-minute news of their activities from Manuel de Falla. In 1911, the same year as *Der Rosenkavalier*, the first performance was given of a new composition for piano by Ravel, the *Valses nobles et sentimentales*, written partly in imitation of Schubert.[41] The following year, 1912, the very year suggested at one juncture in the text for the third act of *Doña Rosita*,[42] Ravel orchestrated the suite of eight pieces – seven waltzes and an epilogue – to provide the music for a new ballet entitled, significantly enough, *Adélaïde, ou le langage des fleurs*, for which he also wrote the scenario. The ballet had four (gala) performances, on 22, 23, 25, and 27 April, danced by the Russian ballerina Natasha Trouhanova and her company, with Ravel himself conducting the Lamoureux Orchestra, as part of the 'Concerts de Danse' at the Théâtre Châtelet, Paris. The story runs thus:

Adélaïde, ou le langage des fleurs is set in Paris about 1820, at the home of the courtesan Adélaïde. On each side of the stage, vases are filled with flowers, and as the curtain rises, couples are dancing or conversing quietly. The story centers about the fickle Adélaïde and her rival suitors, Lorédan [a young poet] and the duke [who is old and wealthy]. The various emotions of love, hope, and rejection, are symbolized by the flowers which the dancers exchange.[43]

---

40. Pablo SUERO, 'Crónica de un día de barco con el autor de *Bodas de sangre*', *Noticias Gráficas* (Buenos Aires), 14 October 1933; see also Mario HERNÁNDEZ, 'Música y memoria: Poemas sobre el vals', *Poesía* (Madrid: Ministerio de Cultura), nr 29 (1987), 118–21.

41. This first performance was by the pianist Louis Aubert at a concert organized by La Société Musicale Indépendante in the Salle Gaveau, Paris, on 9 May.

42. «*Entra la* SOLTERONA 3ª, *vestida de oscuro, con un velo de luto* [. . .] *que se llevaba en el año doce*» (182).

43. Arbie ORENSTEIN, *Ravel: Man and Musician* (New York: Columbia University Press,

The flowers in question were a tuberose, a buttercup, a marguerite, a sun-flower, a branch of acacia, a poppy, and, last but not least, a red rose.[44] Al-though the ballet's plot bears no resemblance whatsoever to *Doña Rosita la soltera*, the use of pastiched waltzes, the language of flowers, the red rose of love, the configuration of the title, and the historical setting in a somewhat idealized earlier period, all provide clear analogues for Lorca's play.[45]

Relating works of art to one another can be fraught with difficulty, and even when a plausible connection demonstrably exists, it is often impossible to determine whether one is dealing with a coincidence, an echo, an influence, or a direct source.[46] The continuing effort to identify further points of compari-son (and possible points of departure) for *Doña Rosita la soltera* should not in any way diminish Lorca's original achievement; rather they signal the richness of resonances that accompanied its composition – resonances which, likewise, await recovery by the alert reader or the attentive spectator.[47]

ANDREW ANDERSON

University of Michigan

1975), 176. This whole section is based on material from Orenstein, and from ROLAND-MANUEL, *Maurice Ravel* (London: Dennis Dobson, 1947), Victor I. SEROFF, *Maurice Ravel* (New York: Henry Holt, 1953), and Rollo H. MYERS, *Ravel: Life and Works* (London: Ger-ald Duckworth, 1960).

44. MYERS, *Ravel*, 170–71.

45. ' . . . the graces of the [French] Restoration. [Ravel] was in love with its conceits, its fashions and its furniture – and its frivolities as well, even while he ridiculed them': ROLAND-MANUEL, *Maurice Ravel*, 65.

46. DE LA GUARDIA, *García Lorca*, 371, has a good paragraph on this topic in his chapter on *Doña Rosita la soltera*.

47. WALSH, 'The Women in Lorca's Theater', 59, writes precisely of 'the rebus of all the pieces Lorca wanted us to catch'. My thanks to Monroe Z. Hafter, who was kind enough to comment on this article in draft.

NERUDA'S 'EXPLICO ALGUNAS COSAS':
SOME THINGS EXPLAINED

ROBERT PRING-MILL's writings on the Chilean poet Pablo Neruda are numerous, important, and varied. One of his major contributions has been to analyse individual poems closely while setting them in their historical and biographical contexts in the belief, and with the result, that text and context are mutually illuminating. It is in the spirit of this approach to Neruda's poetry that the following analysis of his 'Explico algunas cosas' is offered.[1]

EXPLICO ALGUNAS COSAS

Preguntaréis: Y dónde están las lilas?
Y la metafísica cubierta de amapolas?
Y la lluvia que a menudo golpeaba
sus palabras llenándolas
5   de agujeros y pájaros?

Os voy a contar todo lo que me pasa.

Yo vivía en un barrio
de Madrid, con campanas,
con relojes, con árboles.

10   Desde allí se veía
el rostro seco de Castilla
como un océano de cuero.
                  Mi casa era llamada

---

1. The text of the poem is taken from Robert PRING-MILL (ed.), *Pablo Neruda, A Basic Anthology* (Oxford: Dolphin Co. Ltd, 1975), 34–36.

la casa de las flores, porque por todas partes
15   estallaban geranios: era
una bella casa
con perros y chiquillos.
                                 Raúl, te acuerdas?
Te acuerdas, Rafael?
20   Federico, te acuerdas
debajo de la tierra,
te acuerdas de mi casa con balcones en donde
la luz de junio ahogaba flores en tu boca?
                                 Hermano, hermano!
25   Todo
eran grandes voces, sal de mercaderías,
aglomeraciones de pan palpitante,
mercados de mi barrio de Argüelles con su estatua
como un tintero pálido entre las merluzas:
30   el aceite llegaba a las cucharas,
un profundo latido
de pies y manos llenaba las calles,
metros, litros, esencia
aguda de la vida,
35   pescados hacinados,
contextura de techos con sol frío en el cual
la flecha se fatiga,
delirante marfil fino de las patatas,
tomates repetidos hasta el mar.

40   Y una mañana todo estaba ardiendo
y una mañana las hogueras
salían de la tierra
devorando seres,
y desde entonces fuego,
45   pólvora desde entonces,
y desde entonces sangre.
Bandidos con aviones y con moros,
bandidos con sortijas y duquesas,
bandidos con frailes negros bendiciendo
50   venían por el cielo a matar niños,
y por las calles la sangre de los niños
corría simplemente, como sangre de niños.

Chacales que el chacal rechazaría,
piedras que el cardo seco mordería escupiendo,
55   víboras que las víboras odiaran!

Frente a vosotros he visto la sangre
de España levantarse
para ahogaros en una sola ola
de orgullo y de cuchillos!

60   Generales
traidores:
mirad mi casa muerta,
mirad España rota:
pero de cada casa muerta sale metal ardiendo
65   en vez de flores,
pero de cada hueco de España
sale España,
pero de cada niño muerto sale un fusil con ojos,
pero de cada crimen nacen balas
70   que os hallarán un día el sitio
del corazón.

Preguntaréis por qué su poesía
no nos habla del sueño, de las hojas,
de los grandes volcanes de su país natal?

75   Venid a ver la sangre por las calles,
venid a ver
la sangre por las calles,
venid a ver la sangre
por las calles!

*   *   *   *   *

'Explico algunas cosas' was written at the height of the Spanish Civil War. The poem is a *pièce d'occasion*, its publication being timed to coincide with the Segundo Congreso Internacional de Escritores Antifascistas which Neruda helped to organize and which he attended during the first fortnight of July 1937 in Valencia, Madrid, Barcelona, and Paris.[2] He must have written it in France, where he had gone to raise support for the Republic after leaving Madrid in November 1936.[3] He would have sent the poem to Rafael Alberti in Madrid where it was first published under the title 'Es así' on the front page of the twenty-second issue (1 July 1937) of the staunchly Republican *El mono azul.*[4] It was later incorporated with its new title in Neruda's collection – or extended poem in parts – *España en el corazón* (1937), which was in turn subsumed into his *Tercera residencia* (1947).

'Explico algunas cosas' is generally considered to mark a turning point in Neruda's development, the events of the Spanish Civil War and in particular the death of his friend Federico García Lorca converting him from an introspective to a militant poet and eventually resulting in his espousal of communism. This straightforward explanation for the transformation of his poetry was given later by Neruda himself on many occasions, but he was notoriously unreliable when rewriting his own past and it has been argued that the change was not as sudden as he maintained and that it was foreshadowed in his earlier writings. Nevertheless, it does appear that the Civil War crystallized Neruda's already changing aesthetic and the more outward-looking and humane perspective which can be traced in some of the later poems of *Residencia en la tierra II* and his 'Sobre una poesía sin pureza' (both 1935; *Residencia en la tierra I* had appeared in 1933). The Civil War provided the catalyst which eventually converted him to left-wing political commitment,

---

2. The congress began in Valencia on 4 July. In his memoirs, *Confieso que he vivido: memorias* (Buenos Aires: Losada, 1974), 176–80, Neruda gives an untruthful account of some aspects of his involvement in this congress. A more reliable source is Manuel AZNAR SOLER & Luis Mario SCHNEIDER, *II Congreso Internacional de Escritores Antifascistas*, 3 vols (Barcelona: Laia, 1978–79).

3. Luis Enrique DÉLANO, *Sobre todo Madrid* (Santiago de Chile: Editorial Universitaria, 1969), 115–16, 128. Délano worked under Neruda in the Chilean consulate in Madrid until November 1936.

4. Reprinted in facsimile as *El mono azul, Madrid, agosto, 1936–febrero, 1939, 47 números* (Glashütten im Taunus: Detlev Auvermann & Nendeln: Kraus Reprint, 1975). 'Es así' was substantially revised before it appeared as 'Explico algunas cosas'. Some of the revisions merely correct the many errata in the version of the poem published in *El mono azul*; more significant changes are pointed out in the course of this article.

and the poem which was to be retitled 'Explico algunas cosas' was an early expression of the change in question.[5] For these reasons, and perhaps because of the poem's apparent transparency, there are few general works on Neruda which fail to make mention of it.[6]

As Robert Pring-Mill has shown, students of Neruda's poetry ignore its historical and biographical background at their peril and, when examining how Neruda seeks to channel his readers' reactions to 'Explico algunas cosas', it is particularly important to bear in mind the context in which the poem was published and the context to which it alludes. For example, lines 7–39 describe the period immediately preceding the Nationalist rising in July 1936, the outbreak of the Civil War, and the death of Lorca the following month, as one of individual and collective well-being. But this is at best an imaginative recreation of the past, for the time depicted was, in reality, one of considerable unrest: while the 'bienio negro' of 1934–36 had seen political turmoil, risings in Asturias and Catalonia and economic havoc, the peacetime Popular Front government presided over a period (February–July 1936) of extreme tension and violence. Similarly, Neruda's personal life (alluded to in lines 7–9 and 13–17 with the intimate references to his home in Madrid) was scarcely less tumultuous: in 1934 his severely handicapped daughter had been born, a source of particular anguish to someone who had longed for a child, and, during the period he nostalgically recreates in 'Explico algunas cosas', his difficult first marriage was falling apart with Delia del Carril's eruption not only into his life but also into his matrimonial home.[7]

Thus, his evocation of the past idealizes and simplifies reality, but it does so for particular purposes: first, that of making the outbreak of the war appear all the more horrific by contrast with an imagined private and public idyll which preceded it; and, second, that of promoting unity at a moment when

5. 'Sobre una poesía sin pureza' is reprinted in PRING-MILL, *Pablo Neruda*, 30–31. Neruda's first committed poem, 'Canto a las madres de los milicianos muertos' appeared in the fifth issue of *El mono azul* (24 October 1936); this poem was published anonymously because at that time he still held his consular post and was therefore theoretically neutral.

6. Surprisingly, no thorough analysis of 'Explico algunas cosas' seems to have been published. The most helpful article on the poem is José Manuel LÓPEZ DE ABIADA, 'Neruda como paradigma: acotaciones sobre su estancia madrileña, su evolución estético-ideológica y su compromiso frente a España', in *Les Poètes latino-américains devant la Guerre Civile d'Espagne (Nicolás Guillén, Pablo Neruda et César Vallejo)*, ed. Olver GILBERTO DE LEÓN & others (Paris: L'Harmattan, 1986), 29–46.

7. Volodia TEITELBOIM, *Neruda*, 5th edn (Santiago de Chile: Ediciones BAT, 1992), 182–89.

the Republic was riven by internal divisions. In May 1937, shortly before the publication of the first version of the poem, the Republican government had ordered the crushing of the revolution which had been taking place in Barcelona. The political stance taken by the communists, to some of whom Neruda was at that time already close, was that all the various anti-Nationalist factions should show disciplined solidarity in support of the legitimate Republican government of Spain (albeit a bourgeois democracy) to defeat the illegal rising of the Nationalist generals. This particular view underlies 'Explico algunas cosas' where there is no hint of division among the Republican forces, unified action is promoted, the Nationalist generals are directly accused of treachery, and it is asserted that they will be punished.[8] There is, then, a specific agenda underlying what might at first appear an innocently transparent poem. Likewise, although Neruda's aim in 'Explico algunas cosas' may well have been to provoke a simple emotion of outrage, he does so by manipulating his reader in particular ways, as we hope to show in the following close reading of it.

The original title, 'Es así', implied that the facts presented in the poem were incontrovertible and spoke for themselves in an uncomplicated fashion. This directness contrasts with Neruda's previous poetry in two ways: first, he had at the time of composing that poetry often been bewildered and, second, the complexity of the poetry had exemplified the difficulty he experienced in expressing that perplexity. Now, on the contrary, he can state things clearly, which implies understanding them, and the directness of what he says and how he says it is in keeping with the straightforward language of *El mono azul* in which he publishes his poem. In the revised version of 'Es así', however, the first word encountered by the reader, 'Explico', shifts the focus from the facts to the poet's own reaction to those facts and to the relationship between poet and reader as Neruda attempts to explain his reaction, persuading us of its appropriateness. The deliberately prosaic 'algunas cosas' of the new title similarly prepares the reader for the interplay between the poetic and the

---

8. For the political background to 'Explico algunas cosas' see Robin WARNER's very helpful 'The Politics of Pablo Neruda's *España en el corazón*', in *Hispanic Studies in Honour of Frank Pierce Presented by Former and Present Members of the Department of Hispanic Studies in the University of Sheffield*, ed. John England (Sheffield: Department of Hispanic Studies, University of Sheffield, 1980), 169–80, rpt in *Pablo Neruda*, ed. Harold BLOOM (New York & Philadelphia: Chelsea House, 1989), 233–41. Relevant also is Mike GONZALEZ & David TREECE, *The Gathering of Voices: The Twentieth-Century Poetry of Latin America* (London: Verso, 1992), 134–42.

non-poetic which is a major feature of 'Explico algunas cosas'. This is the first of several occasions in his career in which Neruda seeks to justify his committed poetry, affecting to enter into dialogue with readers or critics who might take him to task for abandoning poetry for propaganda. As we shall see, 'Explico algunas cosas' relies upon a series of contrasts, the first and predominant of which is between Neruda's former poetry and the new concerns which the Civil War has brought to a head and which demand a different sort of verse. Somewhat surprisingly, then, his first preoccupations when depicting the horrors of war are personal and poetic ones.

'Explico algunas cosas' is a carefully constructed poem, its most obvious structural feature being its simple division into two halves: life before the Civil War (lines 1–39) is contrasted with the outbreak and consequences of that war (lines 40–79). Neruda switches mood at several points as he seeks to persuade and involve the reader and, to this end, has recourse to a range of conventional rhetorical, or persuasive, techniques. For example, in the first five lines he uses the device of putting three surprised questions into his readers' mouths. In doing so, Neruda not only abandons the self-absorbed stance of his previous verse by now addressing others directly – 'Preguntaréis' – but also assumes in those readers a knowledge of his previous poetry. While 'pájaros' had formed a constant element in his early collection *Veinte poemas de amor y una canción desesperada* (1924), 'lilas', 'amapolas' and 'lluvia' hark back to his childhood and adolescent memories of the south of Chile, subsequently appearing in *Residencia en la tierra I* and *II*.[9] These lines not only provide the first of many examples of the rhetorical grouping of three words or phrases, but also introduce a series of further contrasts which will be developed in the course of the poem.

First, Neruda contrasts his homeland (the rain and the particular flowers he associated with Chile) with Spain (aridity and those typically Spanish flowers, the geraniums: lines 11–12 and 15) which, as the title *España en el corazón* suggests, had in the 1930s become his spiritual home. Hence the description of Chile as his 'país natal' (line 74) had appeared in 'Es así' as 'patria natal', an apparently tautological phrase but one which highlights the contrast between Chile, the homeland of his birth, and Spain, the adopted homeland of

---

9. See Hernán LOYOLA's comments on these words in his edition of *Residencia en la tierra*, Letras Hispánicas 254 (Madrid: Cátedra, 1987), 87, 108–9, 354.

his choice.[10] The second contrast is between the present 'I' of 'explico', 'voy', 'Yo', etc. and the 'he' of the poet he was before the Civil War, Neruda, as ever, self-consciously narrating his own biography. These two contrasts come together in a third tacit juxtaposition between a Chilean voice and the Spanish one with its distinctive use of Peninsular forms of the language which the 'I' now adopts: for example, the pervasive 'vosotros' which characterizes the Spanish spoken in the Peninsula and may also reflect the widespread use of that familiar, comradely form of address in the Spanish Republic, and the word 'patatas' (line 38) where a Chilean would normally use 'papas'. Neruda the Chilean identifies so completely with Spain in its agony that he speaks to Spanish readers as if he were a native Spaniard. A fourth contrast is suggested by the word 'metafísica': while he characterizes his previous poetry – doubtless it is *Residencia en la tierra* which he has in mind here – as dealing with abstract intellectual questions, he implies by contrast that 'Explico algunas cosas' will be concerned with a non-intellectual response (the 'corazón' of the title of the collection is again suggestive) to concrete facts (the 'cosas' of the poem's revised title). Indeed, just as this poem heralds a political commitment which will prove an enduring element of his subsequent poetry, so the emotional rather than intellectual roots of that commitment are mirrored in it. A final contrast is introduced by these first five lines, for Neruda writes about his previous poetry in an ostentatiously 'poetic' manner. The natural world and meditations upon the great abstract questions are traditionally poetic subjects, and they are here couched in musical verse.

The poem opens with a traditional sapphic hendecasyllable, an insistent, dignified, slow binary rhythm being established by the stresses on syllables 4, 6, 8, and 10.[11] Although the second line is not an alexandrine, for the first hemistich has only six syllables, it is reminiscent of this metre; it is what we could call a free alexandrine, one of Neruda's favourite forms. The third line is another powerfully rhythmic one, a dodecasyllable composed of three groups of four syllables in each of which the third alone is stressed; this use of a repeated rhythmic foot brings to mind *modernismo*, where Neruda began his

---

10. LÓPEZ DE ABIADA, 'Neruda como paradigma', 36, suggests that Neruda may also have substituted 'país' for 'patria' because in the late 1930s the latter word was used almost exclusively by the Right.

11. We use the system of analysis devised by Tomás NAVARRO TOMÁS, notably in his *Métrica española: Reseña histórica y descriptiva*, Publicaciones del Centro de Estudios Hispánicos 4 (Syracuse, NY: Syracuse University Press, 1956).

poetic career. Line 4 is a traditional dactyllic heptasyllable, stressed on the third and sixth syllables, and line 5 echoes it. Thus the first stanza concludes with a striking rhythmic change, from long slow lines to short quick ones, and from strong binary rhythms to skipping triple time. Loose assonance holds together lines 3, 4, and 5.

Moreover, not only are the rhythms used here by Neruda very 'poetic'; he also includes something that is a feature of most poetry, and is fundamental to his own early collections, the metaphor, here represented by yoking together the concrete and the abstract: 'la metafísica cubierta de amapolas', and 'la lluvia que . . . golpeaba | sus palabras llenándolas | de agujeros y pájaros', the latter possibly referring to the spiritual emptiness ('agujeros') out of which emerged the difficult poetry ('pájaros') of *Residencia en la tierra*. These introductory five lines thus rehearse the subject-matter and expression of his previous verse and, while he draws attention to the metaphorical nature of that earlier poetry, the elusive meaning of the metaphors he uses in these lines recreates the obscurity of the sort of poems in which they had appeared. It soon becomes apparent that 'Explico algunas cosas', by contrast, is very different, for Neruda is now concerned to make his poetry accessible to a wide readership.

After all this line 6 comes as a calculated shock. It is a prosaic line of twelve syllables, although it could be read as another free alexandrine, with a caesura after 'contar' forming a first hemistich of six syllables. Either way, its rhythms are irregular and unpoetic, with the long succession of unstressed syllables in the second half of the line. It stands on its own, isolated from the flow of the previous five lines. Here Neruda is announcing that some events are too serious to be poeticized; he now casts himself in the role of a chronicler who must 'contar', not 'cantar', and the distant 'he' of line 4 who muses about memories and abstractions becomes the 'I' of the here and now about to narrate concrete and contemporary events. The expression of this abandonment of 'poetry' is striking, and Neruda achieves his effect through rhetorical techniques designed to persuade the reader of the sincerity and urgency of what he has to communicate.[12]

The story Neruda recounts in 'Explico algunas cosas' begins with the evocation of pre-war Madrid, his home there, his friends, and the markets around

---

12. He had previously used this same technique in lines 2–3 of poem 20 of his *Veinte poemas de amor y una canción desesperada* where he contrasted his 'authentic' experience of love with a parody of *modernista* verse which, he implied, was empty of all sincere emotion.

his house (lines 7–39). Much underlies this description. In November 1936 the Republican government had been evacuated to Valencia from the capital, which was under attack; it was feared that the city would quickly fall to the Nationalists, but Madrid's resistance during that terrible winter of starvation and siege became emblematic both in Spain and abroad of the struggle against fascism. Neruda's mention of Madrid by name (line 8), his identification with the capital, and his elegiac depiction of life there would thus be charged with significance for pro-Republican readers of July 1937, especially as many would have been aware of the much-trumpeted Segundo Congreso Internacional de Escritores Antifascistas, some sessions of which were about to take place in the capital. This congress also involved numerous famous Spanish and foreign intellectuals visiting the front lines round the besieged capital, as did many other sympathizers who travelled to Madrid once the Nationalist campaign to capture it degenerated into stalemate in the spring of 1937. It would also mean Neruda's return to his adoptive city.

Argüelles, the district of Madrid in which Neruda had lived, is described not with poetic adjectives, but by three concrete nouns, 'campanas', 'relojes' and 'árboles', which encapsulate the normality of the area before it had been so badly damaged in the battle for Madrid during the winter of 1936–37.[13] The first simply alludes to a concrete fact of Spanish life, the sound of bells. However, bells are also constantly used as images in Neruda's poetry, normally with a positive meaning, and here possibly recreate an atmosphere in which, in the poet's picture of pre-war harmony, the Church is not threatening or partisan, as it will be in line 49, but a thread in the weft and warp of normal Spanish life. This interpretation is complemented by the 'relojes': on the one hand simply descriptive and, on the other, suggesting the ordered division, marking, and passing of time before war disrupted the normal flow of everyday activity. The third element, 'árboles', likewise serves two functions, one descriptive and the other allusive. It describes the tree-lined streets of Argüelles which, in the 1930s, was on the very edge of Madrid, half urban and half rural (see lines 10–12). In 1930 a competition had been held for designs for the expansion of that part of the city, the 'Ensanche Norte de Madrid'. One of the most promising projects had been submitted by the architects Zuazo Ugalde and Fleischer, who subsequently built in that area

---

13. Federico BRAVO MORATA, *Historia de Madrid*, 4 vols (Madrid: Fenicia, 1966–78), III, 296.

the innovatory block of flats known as the Casa de las Flores, which still stands today.[14]

This building, with its spacious internal gardens intended as a play area (line 17) and its delicate balconies designed with the cultivation of flowers in mind (lines 15 – 16, 22), was constructed in 1930 and 1931 and was considered not only one of the finest examples of airy residential architecture in the Madrid of its day, but also emblematic of forward-looking urban design under the Republic. Rafael Alberti had found a flat in the building for Neruda and his wife when they returned from Barcelona on Neruda's appointment as Chilean consul in Madrid, and the consulate was subsequently transferred to this flat.[15] The description of his home is therefore closely based on fact but, as well as being shot through with personal reminiscences, it probably once again carried a pro-Republican charge for his contemporary readers. It was likewise suggested above that the word 'árboles' was not merely descriptive: it foreshadows the synthesis of Nature's plenty and urban vibrancy which forms the core of lines 25 – 39 of the poem and implies an organic and productive relationship between Man and Nature – a frequent association of trees in Neruda's later poetry, but here specifically related to life under the Republic. This harmonious relationship is thrown into further relief later in the poem by its antithesis: the disharmony between Nature and the 'unnatural' National-ists, who are rejected by even the traditionally basest, most unproductive and archetypically treacherous elements of Nature: jackal, thistle, and snake (lines 53 – 55).

The proximity of the urban and the rural is mirrored in lines 10 – 12 where the countryside outside Madrid is viewed from Argüelles. Neruda's looking out on to Castile from his home (he lived on the top floor of the Casa de las

---

14. It is bounded by the following streets: Hilarión Eslava, Gaztambide, Meléndez Valdés and Rodríguez San Pedro, and was declared a national monument in 1981. In 'Es así', Neruda had written 'la casa [sic] de las Flores'; the lower-case letter of 'flores' in 'Explico algunas cosas' obscures the link with the building.

15. DÉLANO, *Sobre todo Madrid*, 67, 78 – 79. TEITELBOIM, *Neruda*, 178, 182 – 83, claims that Neruda moved into the Casa de las Flores in 1933 before taking up his consular post in Barcelona, but Rafael ALBERTI, *La arboleda perdida: Libros III y IV de memorias* (Barcelona: Seix Barral, 1987), 137, remembers helping to find the flat when Neruda returned from Barcelona to live in Madrid. Ian GIBSON, *Federico García Lorca*, 2 vols (Barcelona: Grijalbo, 1985 – 87), II, 315, suggests that this would have been in the summer of 1934. By 1936 the inhabitants of the Casa de las Flores could be described in a Madrid newspaper as including 'numerosos republicanos, socialistas y demás elementos adictos al Frente Popular, así como gran cantidad de extranjeros' (*La voz*, 23 July 1936, 2).

Flores) echoes how the war caused him to look beyond personal experience to the collective national tragedy, for the Nationalist troops had reached Madrid in November 1936, attacking through the Ciudad Universitaria from those very lands he had gazed upon from the fragile security of his home.[16] The momentary shift of focus from house to Castile in lines 10–12 also reflects the change in Neruda's writing from a self-centred to a wider public poetry, a change which 'Explico algunas cosas' both rehearses and represents. His readers are by analogy called upon to abandon any interest in his former personal, maudlin, philosophical or exotic poetry (lines 1–5, 72–74) and to become active witnesses of the collective tragedy which caused him to change (lines 75–79).

The rhythms reinforce the shift of focus. Lines 7–10 are regular dactyllic heptasyllables, a continuation of a series begun in line 4 and interrupted by line 6. Their triple time is both insistent and light, because of the shortness of the lines and the avoidance of juxtaposed dactyls; one in the middle of each line is enough to establish the rhythm without over-insistence (in contrast, for example, with line 56). This light triple time adds to the sense of simple, happy harmony in pre-war Madrid. When the focus shifts to Castile, in lines 11 and 12, their length increases to nine syllables and their rhythms become binary and altogether more solemn.

The Castile upon which Neruda had gazed is compared in lines 10–12 both to a face and a leather ocean. These are the first poetic figures we encounter in this description, and they are appropriate to his new determination to write in an accessible manner, for neither are enigmatic metaphors of the sort evoked in lines 2–5. The metaphor 'el rostro seco' is immediately explained by the addition of 'de Castilla', and introduces the personification of Spain which will be important later in the poem. The comparison of Castile to an 'océano de cuero' is not only a straightforward simile, but also draws upon the traditional image of Spain or the whole Peninsula as a stretched bull's or ox's hide.[17] But more lies behind the use of this comparison than is at first apparent: Castile was parched in the hot summer of 1936 when the war broke

---

16. Carlos MORLA LYNCH, then Chilean ambassador to Spain, describes in his diary, *En España con Federico García Lorca (Páginas de un diario íntimo, 1928–1936)* (Madrid: Aguilar, 1957), 419, the magnificent panorama of Castile he saw from Neruda's living room in 1934.

17. The earliest recorded comparisons of the Iberian Peninsula to an ox-hide appear in STRABO, *Geography*, 2.i.3, 2.v.27, and especially 3.i.3. This image was subsequently repeated in much Spanish writing.

out and is fittingly likened to brown leather, but the comparison of the land to hide also suggests activities often considered characteristic of Spain, the breeding of bulls and working of leather, and even the character of the Spain Neruda loved: humble yet strong. Moreover, in this simile Neruda picks up the tacit comparison between Spain and Chile mentioned above. The geography of the land of Neruda's birth means that the sea is ever-present, and this is reflected in his poetry; Chile is also invariably linked in his verse with another form of water, rain (line 3), while in 'Es así' what later became line 74 of 'Explico algunas cosas' mentions the 'grandes ríos' of his homeland. Castile, on the contrary, is landlocked and arid, but is described by a word which, in Neruda's work, we have come to associate with Chile: 'océano'. Yet, while alive to the incongruity of the comparison of lines 11–12, we are also forced to accept its appropriateness for, although Castile viewed from Argüelles is, unlike the sea, as dry as leather, it is nevertheless vast, stretching away into the distance like an ocean complete with the waves formed by the Guadarrama mountains.

Neruda's focus then switches to his house with a description and, again, explanation (the 'porque' of line 14). In this touchingly simple picture of domestic happiness the phrase 'estallaban geranios' of line 15 is arresting, for it is a poetic figure set in a prosaic narrative; on the one hand, it underscores the tranquillity of pre-war Madrid where the only things to explode were flowers; on the other, we shall see this phrase in retrospect as ominous when the city is bombed and the red geraniums come to foreshadow the flames and blood which are mentioned again and again in the second half of the poem. But, in the calm before the storm, Neruda builds up a crescendo as he leads us from the inanimate to the human and from the general to the individual: from his house to flowers, to animals, to undifferentiated children (the colloquial and affectionate diminutive 'chiquillos' adding a suggestion of noise and vibrant life), and eventually to the three particular friends he calls upon as witnesses to the past.

Raúl González Tuñón, the Argentine communist poet with whom Neruda had a long friendship in Argentina, Spain, and Chile, and Rafael Alberti, one of his principal promoters and political mentors in Madrid who would be instrumental in his adoption of a committed stance in his verse, are invoked to recall what, because of the very insistence of his questioning, we realise is a paradise irremediably lost. They are witnesses of that joyous time in which Neruda's home was a centre of discussion and bohemian fun for the talented generation of Spanish poets who had lionized him in the pre-war period during which, after years of isolation in the Far East, he had come to feel that Spain was his real home.[18] Neruda can ask these friends to corroborate his description because, unlike the solitary world which underlies his former poetry (lines 1–5), the experiences he now narrates are shared and verifiable. He here has recourse not only to the use of rhetorical questions but also again to that tried and tested rhetorical technique of the use of threes, but he keeps back until last the third and most important of his old friendships.

He had met Lorca in Buenos Aires in 1933 where they had forged a close friendship which blossomed when Neruda moved to Spain.[19] Immediately prior to the outbreak of the war, Lorca had, indeed, been with Neruda at the Casa de las Flores; one month later he was shot near Granada (line 21).[20] Overcome with emotion, Neruda allows himself momentarily to falter in his determination to express himself clearly: in line 23 we encounter the image 'la luz de junio ahogaba flores en tu boca'. Neruda frequently associated Lorca with light, and this equivalent line in 'Es así' had read: 'la luz de junio jugaba con tu pelo', the verb 'jugar' recalling the childlike playfulness which Neruda frequently mentions as a characteristic of the dead poet.[21] However, the revised line which appears in 'Explico algunas cosas' is more enigmatic. The reference to June 1936 in both versions is full of impending doom, but the revised 'ahogaba flores en tu boca' may well be a delicate homage to his friend, for Neruda here seems to adopt Lorca's own voice, forging an image which is typical in feel of Lorca's and simultaneously associates his utterances

---

18. GIBSON, *Federico García Lorca*, II, 357–58. For González Tuñón's friendship with Neruda and the Spanish poet Miguel Hernández, see Juan CANO BALLESTA, *La poesía española entre la pureza y la revolución (1930–1936)*, Biblioteca Románica Hispánica: Estudios y Ensayos 168 (Madrid: Gredos, 1972), 167.

19. It is no coincidence that in a poem written to be published in July 1937 Neruda should have chosen González Tuñón, Alberti, and Lorca to represent the companionship of his pre-war Madrid years. The first two were to play a key role in the Segundo Congreso Internacional de Escritores Antifascistas, while Lorca would be much on the participants' minds, being celebrated on the first day of the congress by the presentation of a volume of poems, including work by Neruda, entitled *Homenaje al poeta García Lorca contra su muerte*, ed. Emilio PRADOS (Valencia & Barcelona: Ediciones Españolas, 1937); see AZNAR SOLER & SCHNEIDER, *II Congreso*, I, 78–79, 115.

20. Throughout Neruda's Madrid years Lorca was a frequent visitor to his home, and GIBSON, *Federico García Lorca*, II, 329, maintains that a good deal of Lorca's 'Llanto por la muerte de Ignacio Sánchez Mejías' was written there.

21. See, for example, 'Federico García Lorca', in NERUDA, *Para nacer he nacido*, ed. Matilde Neruda & Miguel Otero Silva (Barcelona: Seix Barral, 1978), 68–73.

('boca') with the beauty and – most poignantly in this context – the fragility of flowers which here are ominously smothered or drowned. Once identified so closely with Lorca's poetic style, Neruda cannot stifle an outburst of now unpoeticized grief: 'Hermano, hermano!', but, as so often in 'Explico algunas cosas', he goes on to place the personal against the background of a collective experience.

In the next section of the poem Neruda therefore switches mood and looks outside himself to describe the markets of Argüelles (lines 25–39), but his apparently straightforward depiction is again charged with meaning. The single word 'Todo' of line 25 sums up the plenty which, in Neruda's recreation of the period, was enjoyed before the outbreak of the war, and his description is firmly situated in a social context. Thus, Neruda here seems to be putting into practice ideas he expressed more theoretically in his 'Sobre una poesía sin pureza', where he advocated the examination of objects in their relation to human beings. On a different level this is paralleled by his description of the statue of the nineteenth-century statesman, Agustín Argüelles, after whom the district of Madrid where Neruda lived was named. Argüelles was an emblematic republican figure: he helped to draft the Liberal 1812 Constitution, fought for the freedom of the press, and was an enlightened reformer; the plinth of his statue was constructed from white stone and did, indeed, resemble an ink-stand, Neruda aptly comparing the monument to 'un tintero pálido'.[22] It is also playfully appropriate that an intellectual should be depicted standing on an ink-pot, and this adds to the light-heartedness of this section of the poem. Although surrounded by books, Argüelles was sculpted in the pose of an orator. Neruda similarly depicts him as no ivory-tower intellectual. Like Neruda now speaking out to others rather than to himself in this poem, Argüelles is to be found in the midst of the hurly-burly of the life of ordinary people, a role in which Neruda will henceforth cast himself. The market is characterized by noise and bustle: the loud voices of line 26 and the pulse of life seen in lines 27, 31, and 32. There may appear to be muddle in the 'aglomeraciones' and the 'pescados hacinados', but a measured order

---

22. The statue has been moved from the position in which Neruda knew it at the junction of Princesa, Alberto Aguilera, and Marqués de Urquijo, and its tall white plinth replaced. A photograph and description of the statue in its original state and location can be found in José RINCÓN LAZCANO, *Historia de los monumentos de la Villa de Madrid* (Madrid: Imprenta Municipal, 1909), 243–44. For Neruda's and Lorca's favourite game of 'inaugurating' well-known Madrid statues by delivering speeches at them, see GIBSON, *Federico García Lorca*, II, 358.

underlies it – the 'metros' and 'litros' of line 33 – paralleling Neruda's presentation of pre-war Madrid in terms of a vibrant but ordered collectivity and his advocacy of ordered collective action in 1937.

The food described would have constituted an appetising evocation of plenty for the hungry and war-torn *madrileños* of July 1937.[23] Significantly, Neruda chooses to describe ordinary foodstuffs for ordinary people: salt (although 'sal' may here have another meaning, leading on from 'grandes voces', and implying the good-natured humour of market-place banter), bread, oil, fish, potatoes, and tomatoes. The abundance of this simple food is stressed: the bread is piled up and the fish lie in heaps, the latter being given particular emphasis by being described in a separate line. As had happened in line 23, an emotive memory of the past seems momentarily at odds with Neruda's determination to express himself clearly, for the meaning of lines 35–37 is not immediately apparent. The cold fish with their glistening scales have the visual texture of a cluster of tiled or slate roofs, viewed from above, but the 'flecha' is enigmatic. Perhaps the fishmongers' busy flashing knives and scissors, trimming, scaling, and gutting the fish as they are bought, remind the poet of weather vanes on a gusty summer morning. On the other hand, Neruda's association of the fish with roofs may lead him to use the word 'flecha' in its architectural sense of the height of an archway, to describe how the slippery fish do not form high, arched heaps but have collapsed – 'la flecha se fatiga' – into low mounds. The mention of 'sol frío' may simply refer to the clear light of a cool, early-morning sun in the market-place, but it may equally allude to the round tops of barrels of fish which are likened to the shape of the sun, the word 'frío' modifying that comparison because the silver colour of the fish suggests cold rather than the warmth normally associated with the sun.

This moment of ambiguous imagery soon passes and Neruda switches his attention to the vegetable stalls, the tomatoes being so numerous that they seem to reach to the sea. The mention of the sea, from which of course the fish had come, would have been particularly telling for readers of *El mono azul* in the Madrid of 1937, isolated as they were in the centre of Castile and suffering from near famine. While celebrated for its abundance and its relationship with ordinary people, this food seems to take on a life of its own:

---

23. At this time bread was in very short supply in Madrid, while fish was available only on prescription; see BRAVO MORATA, *Historia de Madrid*, III, 340.

oil flows on to spoons; bread is not only life-giving but is described as itself pulsating with life – 'pan palpitante' (line 27) – a phrase which prefigures other examples in *España en el corazón* and many of Neruda's later poems where bread, the mainstay of the common people, is placed at the centre of a network of imagery of natural fertility and collective labour, creativity, and sustenance. The simple foods described in this section are not only animate but are elevated in a way we shall later encounter in the *Odas elementales* (1954). For example, Neruda likens potatoes to ivory, partly because their colour and texture are similar, and partly because nothing could be more precious than the humble potato which feeds ordinary people and thus can not only appropriately be compared to the most exquisite of treasures but is ironically more valuable than such luxuries, which are available only to the wealthy.[24]

It is on this note of harmony and plenitude that the last section of the first half of the poem ends. Its juxtaposition with the first section of the second half (lines 40–52) is numbing, recreating the shock and subsequent outrage felt in Madrid in August 1936 when the capital became the first city in Europe to suffer modern aerial bombardment. Several striking contrasts are drawn between pre-war and wartime Madrid: the 'Todo' of line 25 is echoed by the 'todo' of line 40 but, while everything had previously pulsated with life, everything is now on fire, the flames caused by the bombing seeming to an unprepared populace to spring from nowhere (lines 41–42), consuming people in an ironic and unnatural reversal of lines 25–39 where people had consumed food. The bells of Argüelles with their peaceable resonances are replaced by 'hogueras' (line 41), with all their suggestions of the darker side of Spanish history and foreshadowing line 49 where representatives of an obscurantist Church – 'frailes negros' – second the forces of darkness. Whereas the markets of Argüelles had embodied continuity and normality, the bombing suddenly – 'y una mañana' (lines 40–41) – banishes that ordered world for ever – 'desde entonces' (lines 44–46). These contrasts are simple ones, and are of a piece with Neruda's desire, which emerges from that attack on Madrid, to write accessible poetry. To achieve this he has recourse to traditional rhetorical techniques involving triads. For example, lines 44–46,

24. In this context see Robert PRING-MILL, 'La elaboración de la cebolla', in *Actas del III Congreso Internacional de Hispanistas* (Mexico City: Colegio de México, 1970), 739–51, rpt in *Aproximaciones a Pablo Neruda*, ed. Ángel FLORES, Colección Ocnos: Serie Ensayos 1 (Barcelona: Llibres de Sinera, 1974), 227–41.

47–49, and 53–55 are again structured in groups of three parallel phrases, while lines 44–46 employ a double chiasmus, its force increased by the absence of verbs.[25] Most of these lines are written in conventional metres: heptasyllables (like those in the preceding section), hendecasyllables, and alexandrines, both free and orthodox, for these are the metres which sound natural to a Spanish ear and which are therefore an effective vehicle for direct communication.[26]

Just as the world depicted has been destroyed by the war, the mood of 'Explico algunas cosas' changes equally suddenly from line 40 onwards, abandoning the elegiac for the denunciatory. Appropriately for invective and propaganda, Neruda speaks clearly and assigns blame. The enemy is categorized simply. It consists, first, of the Nationalist rebel army (line 47) who are, quite literally, outlaws (the 'bandidos' of lines 47–49), with Neruda stressing, as did the Republican media, how the rebels relied upon foreign troops (the 'moros' of line 47), thus being doubly treacherous to their country. The reference to aeroplanes in the same line recalls both the bombardment of Madrid and the key role played on the Nationalist side by air transport at the beginning of the Civil War. The wealthy and aristocratic (line 48) constitute the second element of which the enemy is composed; and the third is the Church (line 49). As ever in war propaganda, children are presented as the principal victims of enemy action (lines 50–52). Considering Neruda's own sad experience of parenthood, however, he may have felt the suffering of children particularly strongly, and he avoids populist cliché in his treatment of them in lines 51–52 where, as we have seen before, he refuses to use conventional poetic language to describe the horrors of war. The 'como' of line 52 appears to announce a simile, but his refusal to elaborate it is deeply moving: no poetic figure can make the shedding of children's blood more poignant than it is, for the fact is shocking enough in itself. But, whereas children are innocent victims, and therefore their blood flows 'simplemente' (line 52), their murderers are du-

---

25. 'Es así' had contained an extra stanza between lines 55 and 56: 'Asesinos de pueblos pobres, asesinos de niños, | asesinos de casas pobres y cercados, | asesinos de madres ya vestidas de luto.' This stanza provided a further example of the use of repetition, but not in a group of threes. Neruda may have felt that it contained superfluous invective and broke the rhetorical patterning of this section of 'Explico algunas cosas'.

26. Neruda's exploitation of conventional verse forms for his committed poetry is best illustrated by the *Antología popular de la Resistencia* (Santiago de Chile: Ediciones de la Resistencia, 1948; rpt as an unpublished hand-out to accompany the Oxford/Warwick Neruda Symposium, 12–16 November 1993).

plicitous; metaphor, the presentation of one thing in terms of another, is only too appropriate for them, and Neruda draws upon a stock of conventional metaphors of invective to heap insults on their heads (lines 53–55).[27] As he had warned us in lines 1–5, this is scarcely what readers who knew his previous work had come to expect of him, but it nevertheless communicates his hatred directly and simply while at the same time implying the bloodthirstiness ('chacal'), hard-heartedness ('piedra'), and, as we have seen, deadly treachery ('víbora') which he attributes to the Nationalists.

The mood shifts once again in lines 56–71 as Neruda warns the Nationalist camp (lines 56–59) and the rebel generals specifically (lines 60–71) of the punishment which awaits them. This is perhaps the weakest section of the poem for, despite the inventive power of its clear metaphors, it is full of wishful thinking. It may even unwittingly convey doubts about any imagined Republican victory in the tentative 'un día' of line 70. Similarly, abstractions such as 'la sangre de España' (lines 56–57) employed to describe the agent of that victory, contrast tellingly with Neruda's all-too-concrete depiction of pre-war Madrid and the real, not imaginary, destruction unleashed on the city.[28] But again he is at pains to support the 1937 policy of bringing anti-Nationalist factions together to present a united and disciplined front – 'una *sola* ola' (line 58) – and to raise morale with a promise of vengeance, however vague and deferred.

The 'vosotros' of line 56 is no longer the Spanish form of address used to his comrades or readers but represents a contemptuous familiarity: for all that they may be generals (line 60), the rebels deserve no respect. Neruda picks up the references to blood of lines 46, 51 and 52, but now turns them against the enemy. They will be drowned in an irresistible tide of blood (line 58) – either the dead children's blood which will ironically engulf those responsible for its shedding, or the metaphorical full-bloodedness of the Republic which has risen up against them as the rebels rose up against it – which forms that united and disciplined wave. This blood is described in terms of a natural force, the sea, because the common people whom Neruda identifies

27. Robert PRING-MILL, 'Both in Sorrow and in Anger: Spanish American Protest Poetry', *Cambridge Review*, 20 February 1970, 112–22.

28. The days of July 1937 were indeed dark for the Republic: in February that year Málaga had fallen, and the loss of Bilbao to the Nationalists in June was viewed with particular apprehension in Madrid because it would release enemy troops to reinforce the besiegers of the capital; see BRAVO MORATA, *Historia de Madrid*, III, 393.

with the Republic are organically associated with Nature whilst the enemy is considered unnatural. It is indicative of the abstract character of Neruda's threat here that it is unclear whether the 'orgullo y . . . cuchillos' of line 59 refer to the dignity of the Republican fighters and their simple knives which will overcome all the Nationalists' superior *matériel* or to the arrogance of rebels who knifed the Republic in the back.[29]   Predictably enough, these tub-thumping statements are expressed in heptasyllabic and hendecasyllabic lines. The *gaita gallega* form – strong stresses on syllables 1, 4, 7, and 10 – of line 56, with its fast ternary beat reminiscent of the *muiñeira*, perhaps indicates an excessive striving for rhythmic insistence, giving an inappropriate result.

The long sentence which forms a separate stanza in this section of the poem (lines 60–71) is somewhat more concrete than lines 56–59. The two single-word lines, 'Generales | traidores', constitute a bald condemnation of the rebel leaders, the impact of the insulting 'traidores' being enhanced by its separation from the 'Generales', for the first word momentarily suggests respect, but that suggestion is dashed after the pause at the end of the line by the damning 'traidores'. These generals are faced with what Neruda would like to convince his readers of July 1937 were, like the wave of line 58, unified and irresistible forces. But those forces are more closely integrated into the patterning of the poem than were lines 56–59, as Neruda returns to three subjects previously described and shows how each will cooperate in the generals' punishment: his home of lines 13–24, the Spain in ruins of lines 40–46, and the dead children of lines 50–52. His home is now personified – 'mi casa muerta' (line 62) – but his private loss is not dwelt upon; it represents, but is rapidly subsumed into, the general destruction of buildings – 'España rota' (line 63) – and lives (line 68).[30]   When seen in this context, his home becomes merely one more ruined dwelling among the many which, now further personified in line 64, will attack the enemy. This parallels how

---

29. In 1937 Neruda associated 'orgullo vital' with Republican Spain in his speech 'Federico García Lorca', in *Para nacer he nacido*, 69.

30. In *Confieso que he vivido*, 180–82, Neruda writes of returning to the Casa de las Flores during the Segundo Congreso Internacional de Escritores Antifascistas and seeing for himself the damage inflicted on his flat, which was on the front line during the battle for Madrid. He claims that it had been intact when he left it in 1936. If this account is reliable, he had therefore not seen this damage when he wrote 'Es así' in France. DÉLANO, *Sobre todo Madrid*, 128, 132, supports this claim, stating that on 8 November 1936 he left Madrid for Valencia with Neruda; when Délano returned alone, on 19 November, he discovered that the Casa de las Flores had received a direct hit in a bombing raid. TEITELBOIM, *Neruda*, 219, asserts, on the contrary, that the Casa de las Flores had been bombed while Neruda was still in Madrid.

Neruda's personal grief for the loss of one named friend (line 24) is set within the context of wider suffering and the death of many (lines 40–46 and 50–52) and leads to his abandonment of a hermetic poetry dealing with merely personal concerns and his turning to an accessible poetry of commitment. But, at the same time, the collective tragedy is made more tangible to the reader because it is exemplified by that very personal grief.

Just as food had come to life to sustain the common people, so buildings now do so to avenge them. But, while buildings – particularly, of course, the Casa de las Flores – should rightly be where flowers are grown (line 65), the war unleashed by the Nationalists has so deformed normality that they are now the source of bullets. Just as his home of line 62 takes the offensive in lines 64–65, in a parallel construction introduced again by the word 'pero', the 'España rota' of line 63 seeks vengeance in lines 66–67: out of the ruins of houses come bullets; out of the ruins of Spain surges the true Spain, Neruda implying here that the more the enemy destroys her, the more Spain will spring back to take her vengeance. The same introductory 'pero' is repeated in line 68 where the third element from an earlier section of the poem joins the hunting down of the generals: the children they killed live on in the weapons which emerge from their corpses, for each rifle is 'un fusil con ojos', and such guns, equipped as they are with their own eyes, are ineluctable. So accustomed are we by now to the use of threes, that the fourth 'pero' (line 69) takes us, like the generals, by surprise. They will be cut down for their crimes by bullets which are ironically an organic product of those crimes – 'de cada crimen nacen balas' (line 69) – and which unerringly find not the generals' hearts, for they are heartless, but 'el *sitio* del corazón' (lines 70–71).[31]

In a final shift of mood, line 72 begins the last section of the poem. The first stanza recalls the questions of lines 1–5, Neruda echoing the 'Preguntaréis' and the 'he' of that opening stanza, but now implying how misplaced are such questions. Three elements represent the former poetry he now rejects, 'sueño', 'hojas' and 'volcanes': selfish introspection, the private appreciation of Nature – possibly that sadness which autumn leaves traditionally inspire in the self-centred poet – and the exoticism of Latin-American geography for his Spanish readers. Chile, his 'país natal', is here referred

---

31. In 'Es así' Neruda had completed line 71 with heavy-handed invective of which he subsequently thought better: 'del corazón, canallas'.

to openly for the first time and is again tacitly contrasted with Spain, now with grim irony: while the volcanoes of his homeland are violent, the destruction they wreak and the fire they belch are natural phenomena; the Civil War in Spain is, by contrast, all the more horrific for being caused by men. The return to the opening questions of the poem is juxtaposed with the death and anger of lines 56–71 and with the final stanza of lines 75–79, its position being contrived to *reculer pour mieux sauter* to the climax of the last five lines of the poem.

The development of the 'Explico algunas cosas' has been one of moving ever outwards from the personal to the public and from the particular to the general. Neruda has led us from his early poetry to his home, his *barrio*, Madrid, Castile, and finally Spain; from self-absorption to a concern for ordinary people and their suffering; from subjective thoughts to verifiable facts and shared experience; and from an apparently neutral narration (line 6) to a climax of pity and invective. The questions of lines 1–5 awaited an answer; when they are posed again in lines 72–74, they are seen in the light of the accumulated evidence of the intervening lines. Yet Neruda does not seek to justify intellectually the transformation of his poetry; rather, he presents selected, representative facts – the 'algunas cosas' of the title – which explain his emotional reaction to the events he witnessed in Spain. The poem has not argued for a change in his poetic perspective, but has shown why such a change was inevitable.

Thus, in the final five lines, which are among the best known he ever wrote, readers are similarly called upon to look on and respond emotionally to the horror which provides a far more eloquent and persuasive explanation than could any argument. And these final lines are enormously powerful. Neruda again employs the rhetorical grouping of threes, this time the same statement, 'Venid a ver la sangre por las calles', being repeated twice; but, as is best brought out in his recorded readings of this very oral poem, he modulates the emphasis by stressing in turn the streets and the seeing and the blood, by their position at the end of lines. Here he picks up the harrowing lines 50–52, from which the reader will remember that this blood is the blood of dead children.[32]

---

32. In 'Es así' line 51 had read 'y por la calle, la sangre de los niños'; in 'Explico algunas cosas' the streets are made plural to reinforce their association with lines 75–79. The description of children dead in the streets once again places Madrid at the centre of Neruda's account of the Civil War and calls attention to the new phenomenon of aerial bombardment of which civilians were the principal victims.

The effect of the double repetition with variation is the powerful crescendo of feeling created by the rhetorical figure once known as *tricolon ascendens*, much used by advertisers ('anytime, any place, anywhere', a triumph of rhetoric over semantics) and politicians ('government of the people, by the people, for the people'), as well as by poets. This figure is as powerful, popular, and durable as it is because a double and thus confirmed repetition is the minimal and therefore most elegant type of pattern incorporating change and growth; in a single repetition the change would prevent the pattern from being noticed, or at least divert attention from it, and a third repetition is usually redundant since the point has already been made (lines 64–71 are the exception that proves that rules are there to be broken by great artists). What is original and subtle about Neruda's example is that the words themselves do not change, only the emphases.

The crescendo reaches its peak in the word 'sangre', followed by the anticlimax of the last line. The intensity of these lines is increased by their parody of another well-known example of *tricolon ascendens*: 'veni, vidi, vinci'. Neruda invites his readers to come and see, too – not victory, however, but the unspeakable suffering, slaughter of the innocents, and defeat which is the reality of war. Further power is provided by the rhythm of the twice-repeated command. 'Venid a ver la sangre por las calles', with its stresses on even syllables (2, 4, 6, 10), is a heroic hendecasyllable, a form traditionally considered appropriate for the elevated treatment of noble and heroic themes. At one level this rhythm complements the sense, by adding weight, authority and gravity to the command; however, at another it makes an ironic contrast to the unheroic vision of war that is presented. Although the effect is carefully calculated, lines 75, 77, and 78 being written in a combination of those conventional heptasyllabic and hendecasyllabic metres which constitute over half the poem, and all but one of the five lines rhyming assonantally, the repetition of the same simple words and syntax and the absence of any overt literary language – no adjectives, no adverbs – are also the final reassertion that Neruda will not attempt to adorn with conventionally poetic vocabulary a reality which speaks so horrifically for itself.

*   *   *   *   *

'Explico algunas cosas' is an accessible but surprisingly complex poem. Even at this distance from the events which gave rise to it, but in a world where civil war is only too frequent, it also remains, with its calculated persuasive techniques, a moving account of war and its effects upon human beings in general and upon an artist and his work in particular. But, whatever it might say to us today, it cannot be fully appreciated unless, following the example provided by Robert Pring-Mill, the historical and biographical context in which it was written is taken into account in any close reading of the poem.[33]

CLIVE GRIFFIN & JOHN RUTHERFORD

Trinity College &
The Queen's College, Oxford

---

33. We are grateful to María Luisa López Vidriero, Julián Martín Abad, Ian Michael and Eric Southworth for their help with this analysis.

UNA CORRIDA EN LOS ANDES

LOS CRÍTICOS QUE HAN ELOGIADO *Yawar fiesta*, la primera novela de José María Arguedas, partían del supuesto según el cual debería existir una coincidencia esencial entre la realidad y la ficción que 'la describe', que una novela está más lograda en la medida en que expresa más fielmente a su modelo, y por eso han subrayado las semejanzas entre la 'fiesta sangrienta' de este relato y la vida de los Andes. Mi supuesto es el contrario: que entre realidad y ficción hay la incompatibilidad que separa la verdad de la mentira (y la complicidad recóndita que las enlaza, ya que la una no puede existir sin la otra), que una novela nace como rechazo de un 'modelo' real y que su ambición es alcanzar la soberanía, una vida autónoma, distinta de aquélla que parece inspirarla y que finge describir. Así, lo genuino de una ficción no es lo que la aproxima sino lo que la aparta de lo vivido, la vida sustitutoria que ella inventa, no lo que refleja de una experiencia ajena y anterior sino aquel sueño, mito, fantasía o fábula que su poder de persuasión y su magia verbal hacen pasar por realidad. Y es precisamente en este sentido que *Yawar fiesta* es una ficción lograda.

El tema de esta corrida de toros india como centro de un conflicto que enfrenta a las razas y clases sociales de un poblado andino rondaba a Arguedas desde julio de 1935, cuando, según confesión propia, hallándose de vacaciones en Puquio, asistió a una corrida como la que describe *Yawar fiesta* y en la que uno de los capeadores indios, apodado el 'Honrao' – como el personaje de su novela – fue destrozado por el toro.[1] En 1937 aparece en una publicación limeña *El despojo*, que figuraría como segundo capítulo de la novela, y ese mismo año, en la *Revista Americana de Buenos Aires*, el cuento *Yawar (Fiesta)*, versión rudimentaria del libro, que había sido escrita el año anterior.[2] El

---

1. Carta de José María Arguedas a Manuel Moreno Jimeno de diciembre de 1940, recogida en José María ARGUEDAS, *La letra inmortal: Correspondencia con Manuel Moreno Jimeno*, ed. Roland Forgues (Lima: Ediciones de los Ríos Profundos, 1993), 101.

2. 'El despojo', *Palabra en Defensa de la Cultura: Revista órgano de los alumnos de la Facultad de Letras de la Universidad* (Lima), 2 (1937), n° 4; 'Yawar (Fiesta)', *Revista Americana*

proyecto de rehacer y ampliar este relato que abrigaba desde entonces se vio interrumpido por el año que Arguedas pasó en la cárcel como preso político, de modo que sólo pudo llevarlo a la práctica en el segundo semestre de 1940, en la provincia cusqueña de Sicuani, donde, recién casado con Celia Bustamante Vernal, se trasladó en marzo de 1939 y donde fue profesor de castellano y geografía en el Colegio Nacional de Varones Mateo Pumacahua hasta octubre de 1941. Fue después de un viaje a México, en 1940, para asistir al Congreso Indigenista de Pátzcuaro, que, aprovechando unas vacaciones de medio año, Arguedas escribió la novela, casi de corrido. A medida que lo hacía iba enviando los capítulos a Lima, al poeta Manuel Moreno Jimeno. La correspondencia de esos meses entre ambos amigos, publicada por Roland Forgues, documenta con detalle el trabajo de Arguedas en ésta su primera novela, que, aunque basada en experiencias personales, como todo lo que escribió (como todo lo que escriben los novelistas) es más un esfuerzo de invención que de memoria, de despersonalización de la experiencia gracias a la fantasía y al lenguaje, para crear un mundo de ficción.[3] Y en esta novela Arguedas acertaría, más aún que en los cuentos de *Agua*, su primer libro, en crear al eje y sistema de toda ficción que es el narrador.

El narrador versátil

Porque el personaje principal, aunque casi en todo momento invisible, de esta intensa y bella novela no son sus 'mistis', sus 'chalos' ni sus indios, esos protagonistas colectivos que parecen actuar al unísono y como obedeciendo una coreografía, ni las pálidas figuras individuales que se desprenden de sus placentas gregarias – el mestizo don Pancho Jiménez, el latifundista don Julián Arangüena, el Subprefecto costeño, el Sargento arequipeño – ni tampoco el

de Buenos Aires (Buenos Aires), 14 (1937), n° 156. Véase también Jose María ARGUEDAS, *Obras completas* (Lima: Editorial Horizonte, 1983), 135, n. 11. Todas las citas de la novela *Yawar fiesta* están hechas a partir de esta edición, que, aunque no exenta de ellas, adolece de menos erratas que las anteriores.

3. ARGUEDAS, *La letra inmortal*, principalmente las cartas de Arguedas a Manuel Moreno Jimeno que van desde agosto de 1940 a junio de 1941 y que contienen valiosos datos sobre la gestación de la novela, el concurso literario al que fue presentada y en el que fue descartada por el jurado (que premió la hoy totalmente olvidada *Panorama hacia el alba*, de José Ferrando) y sobre la publicación del libro y los comentarios y reseñas que mereció. Entre éstas, hubo una del historiador Luis E. Valcárcel, padre del 'indigenismo', quien había formado parte de aquel jurado, el que, según Valcárcel, prefirió *Panorama hacia el alba* porque abarcaba 'costa, sierra y montaña' en tanto que la de Arguedas sólo se refería a una región del Perú y era 'ininteligible' para quien no hubiera 'vivido con los indios' (en ARGUEDAS, *La letra inmortal*, 128).

Misitu, toro a medio camino entre la realidad de la lidia y la mitología de los Andes, con vagas reminiscencias del Minotauro heleno, sino quien los muestra u oculta, desplazándose entre ellos astuta y diestramente, refiriendo ciertas cosas que dicen y acallando otras, retrocediendo en el tiempo para iluminar algunos hechos del pasado que pueden arrojar una luz sobre el presente (la crisis de la minería de la región que avecindó en Puquio a muchos blancos y las exacciones agrarias de que fueron víctimas las comunidades, lo que impondría al pueblo la estructura social y económica que luce al ocurrir los sucesos, en un año innominado de los treinta), o viajando en el espacio, desde los Andes hacia los pobres barrios de Lima donde viven los lucaninos emigrados, y yendo y viniendo sin cesar entre los mundos de blancos, mestizos y comuneros, paisanos o policías, quechua o hispanohablantes, andinos o costeños, el cristianismo y el animismo, la razón y la magia, con una libertad y desenvoltura que nadie fuera de él goza en esta sociedad piramidal y rígida en la que, según su testimonio, cada cual vive confinado en su grupo social, en su raza, en sus ritos y creencias y en su tiempo histórico como entre los barrotes de una cárcel.[4]

El narrador es el más importante personaje de toda ficción, se trate de un ser exterior a la historia y omnisciente – el Dios Padre egolátrico de los relatos clásicos y románticos o el discreto e invisible de los modernos – o de un narrador implicado, protagonista o testigo de lo que narra, el personaje primero que debe inventar un autor para que lo represente en la historia inventada. Y lo es porque de él depende – de sus movimientos, elocuciones y silencios, de sus perspectivas y puntos de vista – que aquello que cuenta parezca veraz o inconvincente, una ilusión que se impone como realidad o desluce como mero artificio. El narrador de *Yawar fiesta* tiene una tarea ímproba, pues, aunque cuenta una historia breve, un relato largo más que una novela, el mundo que refiere está dividido en grupos étnicos radicalmente distintos, en culturas que buscan destruirse, en sociedades distanciadas por abismos de odio e incomprensión. Y, sin embargo, gracias a su versatilidad y recursos, el narrador cumple su cometido eficazmente, presentando este mundo como una indivisible aunque desgarrada totalidad.

¿Quién es y cómo es este narrador? No hay duda de que se trata de un varón y de un serrano (pues para él los costeños son 'ellos' y los serranos los

---

4. En el manuscrito original, la historia sucedía en el año 1931, pero luego Arguedas decidió borrar el '1 de la fecha, y poner dos puntos suspensivos', según le comunicó a Manuel Moreno Jimeno en carta sin fecha (8 de noviembre de 1940): ARGUEDAS, *La letra inmortal*, 94.

'nuestros'), de un blanco o mestizo que se siente anímicamente muy cerca de los indios, a quienes conoce de cerca (de adentro) y cuyas penalidades, fobias y creencias hace suyas. Narra desde la omnisciencia y el presente, pero efectúa mudanzas en el tiempo, para referir la llegada de los blancos a Puquio, hace tres siglos, cuando se arruinaron las minas de los contornos o para rememorar la construcción de la carretera Puquio-Nazca por el trabajo voluntario de los comuneros, unos años antes de esa corrida que es ocurrencia central de la novela, y para evocar las oleadas migratorias de campesinos andinos hacia las ciudades de la costa que esa carretera, y otras como ella, permitieron.

A ratos se acerca a las bocas de 'mistis', de 'chalos' y de indios y, por el instante de unas frases – una exclamación, una canción, un intercambio de insultos, un discurso – les cede la palabra, pero pronto recupera el gobierno de la historia. Tiene una sensibilidad visual muy aguzada y sus observaciones sobre la naturaleza de ese rincón de los Andes – la provincia de Lucanas, el pueblo de Puquio – son vívidas, delicadas y poéticas. Es bilingüe y se expresa, cuando describe el paisaje – los ríos, las quebradas, los árboles, los pajonales, las montañas – en un castellano neutro, elegante y castizo, que, luego, al acercarse a los hombres, se amestiza con vocablos quechuas o con castellanizaciones de quechuismos y colorea con la escritura fonética de las deformaciones del lenguaje popular.

Tiene un espíritu musical, una vocación preferente por las canciones y las danzas, actividades humanas a las que privilegia confiriéndoles un papel principalísimo en la vida social y engalanándolas de un aura religiosa y sagrada, y está dotado de un oído finísimo capaz de registrar todas las diferencias de tono, de acento, de pronunciación entre los grupos sociales, y de una destreza estilística que le permite hacer saber al lector, por la diferente música con que se expresan, cuándo hablan los costeños como el Subprefecto y el Sargento (que, aunque arequipeño, se expresa como si fuera de la costa), los principales alimeñados como don Demetrio Cáceres o don Jesús Gutiérrez, los provincianos aserranados como el latifundista don Julián Aranguena o el comerciante don Pancho Jiménez, los cholos 'leídos' y politizados del Centro Unión Lucanas, o los indios de los cuatro ayllus de Puquio. Este acierto expresivo, la pluralidad de maneras de hablar de los personajes de *Yawar fiesta* según su cultura y condición, ha sido justamente destacado por la crítica como uno de los logros artísticos de la novela, aunque, a menudo, aquellos elogios equivocan el blanco, pues aplauden esos modos de expresarse de los personajes indígenas de la novela por su 'autenticidad', por su carácter 'genuino'. En verdad, esas maneras de hablar son 'auténticas' en un sentido literario, no histórico ni sociológico. Se trata de eficaces artificios narrativos, de invenciones más que de reflejos de un habla viva, de creaciones en vez de documentos lingüísticos.

El habla inventada

En una carta a Manuel Moreno Jimeno, quien al leer el manuscrito de *Yawar fiesta* había hecho algunas reservas sobre el lenguaje de los personajes, Arguedas le respondió así: 'Tengo la idea de que quien pueda escribir en castellano bien cernido, y dominado, desde buena altura del panorama y la vida de nuestro pueblo serrano, no podría, en cambio, describir con la fuerza y la palpitación suficiente, este mundo en germen, que se debate en una lucha tan violenta y grandiosa.'[5] Era más bien al revés. Para inventar un lenguaje como el de los indios de *Yawar fiesta* era indispensable dominar el castellano, además de tener, claro, una experiencia personal del habla real de los indígenas. Pero ambas cosas son sólo materiales de trabajo y no predeterminan el resultado literario: en manos de un escritor menos artista que Arguedas ese lenguaje hubiera podido sonar tan 'falso' como el de tantas novelas indigenistas.

En el tan citado artículo de 1950, 'La novela y el problema de la expresión literaria en el Perú', Arguedas explicó de manera muy sugestiva su 'larga y angustiosa' búsqueda de un estilo que le permitiera hacer hablar en castellano, de manera que pareciera fidedigna, a personajes indios que, en la realidad, se expresaban entre sí en quechua.[6] Para 'guardar la esencia', para 'comunicar a la lengua casi extranjera la materia de nuestro espíritu', luego de múltiples intentos, la solución (que Arguedas llama 'hallazgo estético') vino 'como en los sueños' y consistió en 'encontrar los sutiles desordenamientos que harían del castellano el molde justo, el instrumento adecuado'. Esta solución, literaria, y, más precisamente, retórica, fue 'crearles (a los indios) un lenguaje sobre el fundamento de las palabras castellanas incorporadas al quechua y el elemental castellano que alcanzan a saber algunos indios en *sus*

---

5. Carta mecanografiada, sin fecha (octubre de 1940), en ARGUEDAS, *La letra inmortal*, 90.

6. Publicado en *Mar del Sur: Revista Peruana de Cultura* (Lima), 3, n° 9 (enero-febrero de 1950), 66–72. Hay una versión revisada y corregida por Arguedas que aparece como prólogo a la edición de *Yawar fiesta*, Colección Letras de América (Santiago de Chile: Editorial Universitaria, 1968). Cito por esta última versión.

propias aldeas'. ¿Hablan de este modo los campesinos de carne y hueso de la sierra? El testimonio del propio Arguedas en ese artículo es inequívoco: '¡Pero los indios no hablan en ese castellano ni con los de lengua española, ni mucho menos entre ellos! Es una ficción.'

Sí, ese lenguaje es una ficción y, como tal, entraña una distancia infranqueable entre ella y la realidad – el habla de los vivos – en la que aparenta inspirarse. Es una ficción semántica y sobre todo musical, melódica, un lenguaje genérico, que disuelve a los individuos en categorías gregarias y los hace expresarse de manera despersonalizada, como conglomerados. Ahora bien, toda generalización es una adulteración; ella suprime lo específico individual para destacar lo genérico, la cualidad común, la característica afín del grupo o la serie. De este modo Arguedas crea un objeto verbal expresivo eficaz, pero autónomo, distinto de la realidad lingüística andina. Ni el latifundista, ni el mestizo ni el indio son sólo masa – clase, raza, estrato sociológico; son también individuos, con características propias que distinguen a cada cual de los demás miembros de su propia etnia, grupo social o colectividad. Al suprimir las diferencias particulares y registrar sólo los denominadores comunes en los modos de hablar, el narrador irrealiza la realidad ficticia, la separa del modelo real, la torna representación. Pues, en un escenario, todos los intérpretes de una danza, como ocurre con los practicantes de un rito o una ceremonia, adquieren una transitoria identidad colectiva, sus rasgos individuales son abolidos por el gesto y el movimiento del conjunto al que todos contribuyen y del que todos son parte.

Este lenguaje inventado de los indios de *Yawar fiesta*, de sintáxis desgarrada e intercalado de quechuismos, de palabras castellanas que la escritura fonética desfigura, y en el que abundan los diminutivos y escasean los artículos, no expresa nunca a un individuo sino a una muchedumbre, la que, a la hora de comunicarse, lo hace siempre con una voz plural, como un coro. A diferencia de lo que sucede con muchas otras novelas de la literatura indigenista o regionalista, donde el lenguaje figurado que aparece en boca de los indígenas resulta caricatural y mata la ilusión del lector, en *Yawar fiesta* es persuasivo, parece 'auténtico', no porque sea más verdadero que en aquellas obras, sino porque su coherencia y su factura formal – sobre todo, la musicalidad y el colorido – le confieren categoría artística.

La fantasía de lo social

Es verdad que este lenguaje inventado contribuye de modo muy efectivo a dar consistencia literaria a uno de los rasgos más llamativos de la sociedad india de la novela – su colectivismo, la hegemonía absoluta que en ella tiene la comunidad sobre los individuos particulares – pero esto no impide que ese lenguaje sea un espectáculo en sí mismo, es decir que, además de vehículo expresivo, sea también, cada vez que estalla su rica sonoridad y su plástica original, una realidad autónoma que concentra la atención del lector con prescindencia de lo que quiere comunicar. Cuando los indios de la novela hablan, sus palabras los borran: son ellas las que viven, ellos desaparecen. Ni más ni menos que cuando, en un concierto, el hechizo de la música hace olvidar al melómano que hay unos instrumentos y unos instrumentistas que la producen, o cuando la perfección de las voces de un coro desvanece detrás de la melodía a sus autores. Toda escritura regionalista, construida a partir de esos 'desordenamientos' del lenguaje de que hablaba Arguedas en su artículo de 1950, implica el esteticismo, el formalismo, pues emancipa la forma de la materia narrativa y establece el predominio de la expresión sobre la anécdota. Lo que el personaje dice queda opacado por la manera como lo dice y este exhibicionismo verbal – los disfuerzos, distorsiones, manierismos, anomalías y libertades que se toma con la norma lingüística – pasa a ser, mientras esas bocas pintorescas parlotean, el verdadero tema del relato. Como buen número de esas historias regionalistas persiguen un propósito social, moral o ideológico antes que artístico, el 'formalismo' expresivo de que hacen gala, ese esteticismo que reemplaza en ellas las ideas por lo excéntrico y multicolor del lenguaje en que vienen envueltas, produce una incongruencia que las priva de poder persuasivo, que las delata como fraudulentas. En realidad, se trata sólo – pero ese sólo en literatura lo es todo – de fracasos artísticos, de un desfase insuperable entre medios y fines.

¿Por qué en *Yawar fiesta* no ocurre así? ¿Por qué, aunque el lenguaje inventado de los indios del libro sea tan fabricado como el de los cuentos de *La venganza del cóndor* de Ventura García Calderón o la novela *Tungsteno* de César Vallejo, no nos da, como en estos libros, la impresión de ser hechizo sino veraz? Por la mejor destreza literaria de Arguedas para 'desordenar' artísticamente el español, desde luego. Pero, también, porque en *Yawar fiesta* una forma expresiva pintoresca, que se ofrece al lector como espectáculo, no desentona en absoluto, más bien coincide con la intencionalidad profunda de un relato que, antes que denunciar los horrores sociales en las alturas andinas, se proponía reinvindicar el derecho a la existencia de una cultura quechua, a través de una de sus más controvertidas creaciones, precisamente un espectáculo: esa 'fiesta sangrienta' que, como para que no haya equívoco al respecto, ostenta el libro desde su título.

La cultura invicta

Ahora bien: *Yawar fiesta* no es, como muchas novelas costumbristas, una superficial apología de una fiesta local. En verdad, la anima un propósito desmesurado: congelar el tiempo, detener la historia. La novela es un alegato contra la modernización del pueblo andino, una defensa sutil y disimulada, pero vigorosa, de lo que hoy se llama multiculturalismo, la evolución separada y autónoma de las culturas y el rechazo de una integración a la que se percibe como un proceso de absorción destructivo de la cultura indígena por la cultura occidental. Esta problemática aparece bellamente simbolizada en una anécdota de fuerza y color: los conflictos e incidentes que provoca en el pueblecito serrano de Puquio la decisión del gobierno central de prohibir la corrida de toros indianizada – el *yawarpunchay*, con capeadores espontáneos, dinamita, borrachera y enjalmas – que tradicionalmente celebran los ayllus en las Fiestas Patrias, el 28 de julio, día de la independencia nacional, y de reemplazarla por una corrida española ortodoxa, lidiada en un coso cerrado y por un torero profesional.

La historia está presentada por el narrador con la habilidad necesaria para que, al final, al lector no le quepa la menor duda sobre la conclusión que aquél quiere hacerle compartir: que quienes se empeñan en suprimir el *yawarpunchay* no entienden ni respetan la cultura – las costumbres, las creencias y los ritos – de los indios y, en verdad, quieren despojar a éstos de algo precioso: su identidad. En esta pretensión anti-india coinciden todos los personajes 'extranjerizantes' de la novela, sean los principales obsecuentes al Subprefecto, los serranos 'alimeñados', los costeños prejuiciosos contra todo lo andino y los mestizos e indios aculturados, los 'chalos', a quienes el irse a vivir a Lima y ciertas doctrinas foráneas han confundido y culturalmente descastado.

Defender la 'fiesta sangrienta' no es defender la barbarie, pese a que esta corrida consista en una exhibición de salvajismo, sino una identidad cultural que, pese a la explotación secular, la ignorancia y el aislamiento en que se encuentran los indígenas de los Andes, sobrevive e incluso se renueva, pero en sus propios términos, es decir, aclimatando lo ajeno – como lo ha hecho con la fiesta española de la lidia del toro – a su propia tradición andina, mágica, colectivista y animista, una tradición nítidamente diferenciada de la invasora (española, costeña, cristiana, blanca, y occidental).

Hasta el capítulo quinto, el narrador de *Yawar fiesta* es una presencia discreta y relativamente imparcial, pero en las páginas en las que se declara el conflicto – la prohibición de la corrida sin diestros – abandona su apariencia de neutralidad y, aunque sin demasiado exhibicionismo, toma partido con quienes defienden el *toropukllay*. Lo hace ridiculizando a los principales que apoyan al Subprefecto y se distancian del comerciante don Pancho Jiménez, e insinuando que actúan así no por convicción sino por servilismo, para congraciarse con la autoridad. Más tarde, en ese mismo capítulo, los muestra en la sesión del Concejo convocada para discutir el tema haciendo gala de racismo, pues todos ellos parecen creer, con 'El señor vecino notable Cáceres' que todos los indios son 'de retrasado cerebro'.[7]

¿Por qué se banderiza el narrador con quienes defienden la corrida india? No porque ignore la violencia y la crueldad que anidan en ella y de las que son víctimas los pobres capeadores campesinos, como el Wallpa, a quien el Misitu despanzurra, sino porque ella representa una creación cultural y un símbolo de la soberanía del pueblo quechua, porque el *yawarpunchay* que, en un principio, fue una imposición colonial, ha sido arrebatado a la cultura extranjera, transformado y asimilado al acervo propio. Para el narrador, 'extranjero' es un concepto negativo, algo que implica peligro, amenaza, traición a la cultura de la que se forma parte. Por eso el narrador ridiculiza a esos 'mistis' del jirón Bolívar dispuestos a vender su alma, que se atreven a proclamar: 'Necesitamos de autoridades que vengan a enseñarnos y que estén resueltas a imponer la cultura del extranjero' (102).

Ideología, aculturalismo y traición

Estas críticas no apuntan sólo a los principales de Puquio, 'alimeñados' y racistas; también a los 'chalos' bienintencionados que están a favor de suprimir la corrida india para traer el progreso a Puquio, un progreso que para los lucaninos emigrados a Lima y admiradores de Mariátegui, promotor del socialismo y del marxismo, tiene una clara orientación política e ideológica. El narrador amonesta sin eufemismos a los 'cholos leídos' por tomar partido contra la cultura del pueblo del que salieron y por aliarse –

---

7. ARGUEDAS, *Obras completas*, II, 107.

cegados por una visión abstracta del progreso – con los 'mistis' y la autoridad corrupta. Es verdad que sus motivos son altruistas: traer la modernidad a Puquio, impedir que continúe una fiesta bárbara en que muchos indios son destripados para diversión de los espectadores blancos. Para el narrador ésta es una manera errónea de encarar el problema, una suerte de petición de principio, pues delata un supuesto occidentalizado, 'blanco', anti-indio, de la idea de progreso, en la que todo lo que diverge o contrasta con ciertos patrones pre-establecidos por el colono o conquistador es rechazado como expresión de atraso y barbarie. Si aceptara esta concepción, al campesino quechua no le quedaría otra alternativa, para alcanzar 'el progreso', que la asimilación al mundo de los blancos: renunciar a su lengua, a sus creencias, a sus usos y tradiciones. Y para el narrador – portavoz evidente en esto del José María Arguedas que escribió *Yawar fiesta* – desindianizar a los indios ('salvar a los indios de las supersticiones', como dice Guzmán, uno de los 'cholos leídos') es un crimen todavía peor que explotarlos, discriminarlos y maltratarlos (170).

Entre la magia y la ideología, el narrador de *Yawar fiesta* no vacila: elige la primera. Por eso nos induce a compartir la secreta simpatía y el respeto que siente por el mestizo don Pancho Jiménez y por el terrateniente don Julián Aranguena, quienes, frente a la problemática de la identidad cultural, muestran una lucidez mayor que la de los 'cholos leídos', tomando partido a favor de la preservación del *toropukllay*. Aunque el primero sea un negociante sin muchos escrúpulos y el segundo un abusivo explotador de los campesinos, ambos tienen, por lo menos, un acendrado sentido del terruño y de las costumbres propias, no se avergüenzan de ser lo que son, no renuncian a su idiosincracia de provincianos y serranos, no aspiran a convertirse en 'extranjeros', a 'alimeñarse', y, aunque sea a su modo rudo e instintivo, defienden como suya una fiesta india.

Un mundo de machos

Ambos tienen, además, otro mérito sobresaliente en este mundo visceralmente machista de *Yawar fiesta*: son valientes. El machismo es un tótem que todos reverencian en la realidad ficticia: blancos, mestizos e indios. Las oposiciones y antagonismos entre razas, culturas y regiones desaparecen en lo que concierne a la relación del hombre y la mujer, pues, no importa cuál sea su educación, su procedencia o su patrimonio, todos los hombres son machistas. Y de manera tan obstinada y excluyente que las mujeres casi no figuran en la sociedad que describe la novela, o, mejor dicho, cuando asoman, siempre en apariciones furtivas, no parecen estar dotadas del mismo grado de humanidad que los varones sino, más bien, pertenecer a una especie inferior, a medio camino entre el ser humano y el animal o los objetos.

Todos son machistas: 'mistis', 'chalos' e indios, los principales desprecia-bles como don Demetrio o los rescatables como don Julián, el generoso don Pancho o la ruindad humana que es el Subprefecto. Todos rinden culto a la fuerza física y creen que el coraje – el desplante, el desprecio a la vida propia y ajena, la temeridad e incluso el sadismo – representan un valor. Todos des-precian por igual a las mujeres, presencias que están allí para ser golpeadas sin motivo, a fin de que de este modo el macho afirme su superioridad ante sí mismo, o para que desfogue en ellas su rabia y sus contrariedades. Todos usan la palabra 'amujerado' como un empobrecimiento de la condición mas-culina, algo que roza la ignominia. El propio narrador participa de este pre-juicio, a juzgar por la naturalidad con que presenta las actitudes abusivas y despóticas de hombres contra mujeres en la realidad ficticia (en tanto que adopta siempre una distancia crítica cuando se trata de los atropellos y exac-ciones que padecen los indígenas) y él mismo se vale de expresiones como 'hasta el más amujerao' (de los comuneros) en un sentido despectivo (161).

Pero, la condición de extrema inferioridad de la mujer en este mundo – víctima entre las víctimas – se hace sobre todo manifiesta en que ella no es nunca convocada por el narrador como protagonista ni actora de sucesos: sólo comparece esporádicamente y siempre como horizonte, sombra o bulto. Se mueve en colectividad, es un paisaje, y, se diría, su única razón de estar allí es llorar o rezar por las proezas o tragedias de los hombres, y prestarse a ser empujada, insultada o maltratada cuando éstos necesitan volcar en alguien sus accesos de rabia. Así le ocurre a la mujer del 'misti' don Jesús, por ejemplo, quien, furioso por haber sido víctima de un timo por parte del corrupto Sub-prefecto, arroja a aquélla un plato de mote en la cara ('porque su rabia contra el Subprefecto no se había calmado todavía', 147). Y en otro momento los in-dios k'ayaus la emprenden a puntapiés contra sus mujeres por la razón más baladí: para que saquen a los niños de la plaza del barrio (154). Cuando, rabiosos por haber sido privados de su fiesta tradicional, los campesinos de los ayllus de Puquio insultan al torerillo español Ibarito II, ¿qué le gritan?: '¡Mujerao!' (191).

La rabia

Estas formas de conducta son expresiones de un fenómeno más general, característico del mundo de José María Arguedas, y que François Bourricaud, en uno de los buenos estudios sobre el machismo en esta novela, llama 'el desplazamiento de la agresividad'.[8] Para desahogar los accesos de furor que los acometen, y que resultan de los abusos que sufren o de la frustración de sus expectativas y que, muchas veces, no tienen razón aparente, los hombres ejercitan la violencia física contra algo o alguien más débil que ellos o incapaz de defenderse: las mujeres, muy a menudo, pero, también, los subordinados – siervos, empleados, niños – o los animales, las plantas o los meros objetos. Interpretar esta 'rabia' en términos socio-psicológicos, como rebeldía empozada ante un estado de cosas intolerable que se exterioriza en explosiones individuales anárquicas e irracionales de los explotados, no da cuenta cabal de la manera como este fenómeno funciona en la realidad ficticia. Por lo pronto, estos arrebatos emocionales se apoderan de los personajes – de manera transitoria pero periódica – con prescindencia de su raza y su posición social: tanto a explotadores como a explotados, a costeños y serranos, los ciegan e impulsan irresistiblemente a destruir, hacer daño, torturar o asesinar. En la realidad ficticia esta 'rabia' de la que de pronto es presa un individuo o un grupo al que enajena y convierte en una bestia maligna es más una plaga mágica o una misteriosa fatalidad inherente a la condición humana que una 'transferencia' freudiana de los rencores y sentimientos de desquite que inspiran en los débiles las exacciones y brutalidades de los fuertes.

Los ejemplos en *Yawar fiesta* de los exabruptos de 'la rabia' en los ánimos varoniles son abundantes, además de los citados de mujeres humilladas y golpeadas. Luego de una reunión con don Pancho Jiménez, que parece terminar en buenos términos, el Subprefecto, al ver alejarse al comerciante por la plaza en sombras de Puquio, ordena de pronto al Sargento, de modo totalmente arbitrario e inexplicable, que coja su rifle y lo mate por la espalda: '¡Tírele! Y quedará tumbado como un perro' (117–18). Y, si el Sargento no hubiera desobedecido, allí habría terminado la existencia del emotivo negociante. Don Julián Arangüena, luego de una tentativa frustrada de capturar al Misitu, dispara a ciegas contra sus propios concertados, que han huido, espantados ante el impetuoso animal, y, luego, al cielo, en una curiosa mezcla de

---

8. François BOURRICAUD, 'El tema de la violencia en *Yawar fiesta*', en *Recopilación de textos sobre José María Arguedas*, ed. Juan Larco, Serie Valoración Múltiple (La Habana: Centro de Investigaciones Literarias, Casa de las Américas, 1976), 209–25.

exultación y exasperación por su propio fracaso y por el admirable poderío de su toro, estado de ánimo que el narrador describe de manera inmejorable: 'Iba a matarlo, pero siguió disparando al cielo, de rabia, como de alegría' (136). Esta rabia que se confunde con la alegría lo lleva sin embargo a matar instantes después al pobre caballo de su mayordomo, el 'chalo' Fermín, para descargarse así de los restos de furor que todavía lo solivantan.

Las hazañas colectivas

La contrapartida a la rabia son esos arrebatos emotivos de generosidad que se dan a veces en individuos como don Julián Arangüena cuando regala a los comuneros k'ayaus el Misitu, el toro que es la niña de sus ojos, o de arrojo, como los que mueven a los capeadores el Honrao, el K'encho, el Raura y el Wallpa a enfrentarse temerariamente a los astados en el *yawarpunchay*. Pero es sobre todo entre los indios y de manera colectiva, cuando el individuo se halla disuelto en el grupo, cuando la persona desaparece en lo social, que esos arrebatos de entrega y sacrificio alcanzan su grado máximo de generosidad y altruismo. Así nacen las hazañas colectivas: la construcción de la plaza del mercado, en un par de meses, por los puquios en competencia con los parinacochas, o la construcción que los ayllus llevan a cabo de la carretera Puquio-Nazca – 300 kilómetros en 28 días – que el narrador describe como proezas épicas en las que se expresa lo más positivo de la idiosincracia quechua, su nobleza e idealismo. A veces, estas hazañas colectivas son beneficiosas para la comunidad en términos prácticos – es el caso, sin duda, del mercado y de la carretera – pero su utilidad no es lo que determina siempre su grandeza moral y cultural. Por ejemplo, sería difícil establecer qué provecho trae al pueblo de Puquio toda la energía y temeridad que los k'ayaus gastan en capturar al Misitu, otra realización colectiva que en la novela aparece como modélica. No, estas hazañas valen por sí mismas, por el simple hecho de realizarse, por la falta de cálculo egoísta con que se emprenden, porque muestran el poderío potencial de los comuneros, su capacidad de trabajo y sacrificio, la solidaridad y la voluntad de 'mover montañas' que las hace posibles. La noción de 'progreso', de 'modernización', en cierta forma, está reñida con el espíritu que preside esas hazañas colectivas. Así lo hace patente el narrador al describir lo que ocurre cuando, a partir del ejemplo que dan los puquios con la carretera a Nazca construida por acción comunal, se desata en la sierra central una fiebre constructora para abrir caminos hacia la costa; los gamonales quieren que esas rutas pasen por sus haciendas y, entonces, construir carreteras se vuelve un 'negocio', algo despreciable que desnaturaliza un esfuerzo colectivo que en un principio había sido desinteresado, 'puro'.

El comercio degradante

De una manera todavía tímida, se manifiesta así algo que en posteriores novelas de Arguedas adquirirá una forma más precisa: el rechazo a la civilización urbana, al mercado, al mundo industrial. El cálculo mercantil, el afán de lucro, son una manifestación de egoísmo y de individualismo, algo que ensucia y degrada la vida, un fenómeno de ciudad. Lo humano sólo conserva su limpieza ética – aunque sea en la miseria y en lo que desde aquella perspectiva urbana representa el atraso – en el mundo rural: allí el hombre está en estrecho contacto con la Naturaleza, lo colectivo prevalece sobre lo individual, el sentimiento sobre el cálculo, y la razón no ha derrotado aún a lo espiritual, lo religioso y lo mágico.

Estos supuestos aparecen en *Yawar fiesta* de manera mucho más elaborada que en la primera versión de la novela, el cuento *Yawar (Fiesta)* de 1936. Al cotejar ambos textos se advierte lo mucho que ha mejorado la técnica narrativa de Arguedas y cómo se ha ido refinando y complicando su mundo literario en los cuatro años intermedios. El cuento es un relato de filiación costumbrista y folklórica, en el que el habla de los indios carece de re-elaboración literaria y suena caricatural. Las tomas de posición del narrador sobre lo que narra son constantes y explícitas, su sentimentalismo y truculencia devalúan su testimonio e irrealizan la historia ('¿Pero a quién le importaba esa sangre? ¿Quién sentía pena por ese cholo rajado de arriba abajo por las astas del toro?', 135). La violencia que en el cuento muestran los 'mistis' – principales o policías – roza lo inverosímil: ambos se solazan con la sangre y el sufrimiento indio de una manera que se diría demoníaca, en tanto que los comuneros, aunque capaces de 'hazañas colectivas', como la construcción del mercado de Puquio, no personifican, como en la novela, bajo su primitivismo, una rica y antigua cultura; son una masa embrutecida por el cañazo, 'el veneno de la costa', que los insensibiliza; los capeadores se lanzan, enloquecidos y codiciosos, contra los toros y se hacen cornear por las libras (monedas) que las señoritas de Puquio han prendido en las enjalmas con ese propósito corruptor. La maldad de los blancos tiene que ver con su individualismo y con la práctica del comercio; por eso 'sus almas eran casi siempre enemigas unas de otras, porque estaban dominadas por el espíritu del negocio, por la ambición; los indios, no.'

Lo que más diferencia a ambas versiones es que, en la de 1940, ha aparecido un nuevo sector social, una cuña entre los indios y los 'mistis' que en la de 1936 no existía, los mestizos o 'chalos', y con ellos una nueva dimensión de la realidad: la ideológica, la de las ideas progresistas empeñadas en transformar la sociedad para establecer la justicia. Esto representan esos humildes lucaninos emigrados a Lima, el estudiante Escobar, el chofer Martínez, el conductor de ómnibus Rodríguez, el sastre Gutiérrez, a los que el viaje a la capital y los oficios y actividades que allí realizan han ido desindianizando y comenzando a 'aculturar', algo que, como vimos, el narrador reprueba, pues lleva a estos ingenuos muchachos, en su afán de trabajar por la modernización de Puquio, a hacer causa común con el Subprefecto y los 'mistis' – los explotadores de los indios – en un crimen mayor: la prohibición – o, peor, su 'extranjerización' – de una creación cultural del pueblo quechua.

Lo que nubla el recto juicio de los 'chalos' y los induce a ser cómplices de la autoridad política y los gamonales es, al transplantarse al mundo de la costa y de Lima, haber empezado a perder sus raíces étnicas y culturales. Pero, afortunadamente, éstas no han desaparecido del todo, como se advierte cuando los vemos, contagiados por el espectáculo de los comuneros llevando al pueblo al Misitu que acaban de capturar, pedir al *varayok* (alcalde indio) que les permita arrastrarlo a ellos también. Es decir, actuar, por un momento al menos, no en función de su razón sino de emociones y pulsiones atávicas, como lo hacen los indios.

La derrota de la razón

Lo que la razón dicta a los 'chalos' es acabar con la fiesta india, que para ellos es manifestación de atraso, un atroz espectáculo en el que los comuneros son corneados para diversión de sus verdugos ('¡Nunca más morirán indios en la plaza de Pich'kachuri para placer de esos chanchos!,' dice Escobar, 130). Estas ideas les vienen a los lucaninos de José Carlos Mariátegui (1894–1930), fundador del Partido Comunista y escritor y periodista divulgador de las ideas marxistas en el Perú, cuyo retrato preside en la novela las sesiones del Centro Unión Lucanas y a quien los 'chalos' invocan con respeto, llamándolo 'werak'ocha' y 'taita' (padre y señor) (131). Aunque Arguedas no estuvo nunca inscrito en el Partido Comunista, en muchas ocasiones declaró que la lectura de los ensayos de Mariátegui y la revista que éste dirigía, *Amauta*, había tenido influencia decisiva en su formación. Por otra parte, en los años en que escribía *Yawar fiesta* estuvo bastante cerca de los comunistas y su correspondencia con Manuel Moreno Jimeno lo muestra enviando artículos al periódico del Partido 'Democracia y Trabajo' y vendiendo bonos para su financiación, pruebas evidentes de que, sin ser un militante, aprobaba por lo menos en buena parte las tesis ideológicas racionalistas, modernizadoras y occidentalizantes del marxismo frente al problema indio.[9]

Pero al ponerse a escribir la novela, siguiendo su inclinación natural, los dictados espontáneos de su espíritu, sus 'demonios', fueron más fuertes que sus simpatías ideológicas y terminaron por introducir en *Yawar fiesta* una paradoja a la que esa historia debe en gran parte su tensión dramática. Pues, aunque el narrador se esfuerce por subrayar todas las buenas intenciones que guían a los 'ideólogos' mestizos en sus propósitos modernizadores, la historia que cuenta los hace aparecer como obnubilados y ciegos frente al problema del pueblo andino, víctimas de una mistificación intelectual que les impide abordar este asunto de manera cabal, no sólo como una lucha contra los despojos económicos y los abusos políticos que padecen los indios, sino, a la vez, como una lucha por la preservación y defensa del ser andino, de sus ritos, creencias y costumbres que, precisamente por ser antiguos y apegados a la tradición, garantizan la identidad y perennidad de 'lo indio'. Al elegir el socialismo contra la 'magia', los 'chalos' han dejado de formar parte de su pueblo y comenzado a ser aliados de sus enemigos.

El narrador, en cambio, enfrentado a ese dilema, opta abiertamente por el *yawarpunchay* y todo lo que él simboliza: la originalidad y la fuerza de una cultura con profundas raíces en el pasado y en la recia geografía de esos Andes de enhiestas montañas, cielos inmarcesibles y abismos escalofriantes cuya secreta vida de mitos y prodigios y de intensa espiritualidad sólo ella conoce.

La victoria simbólica

Aunque ella se insinúa a lo largo de toda la novela, esta cultura mágica y ceremonial, arcaica y andina, quechua y rural, irrumpe con todo su colorido y fuerza atávica a partir del capítulo VII, 'El Misitu', en el que el narrador nos pone al tanto de las creencias míticas y las prácticas mágicas de los indios de la puna, los k'oñanis, quienes se resisten a que los comuneros k'ayaus se lleven para torearlo en la fiesta del 28 de julio al toro de don Julián. Para ellos, este animal es una figura legendaria y semidivina: lo creen salido de las aguas de una laguna (Torkok'ocha) en una noche de tormenta y dotado de

---

9. ARGUEDAS, *La letra inmortal*, 100.

atributos mitológicos.[10] En ese mismo capítulo vemos al narrador confundirse con el brujo Kokchi cuando éste hace una ofrenda a la montaña tutelar de los k'oñanis (el taita Ak'chi) para que proteja al Misitu y luego lo vemos, desde la perspectiva de los k'ayaus, compartiendo con éstos la ceremonia mágico-religiosa en que los comuneros van a su vez a pedir la protección de otro espíritu de las montañas (el auki Karwarasu) para capturar al toro.

Así aparece, en todo su relieve, un mundo indio ancestral, animista, irracional y mágico que coexiste, semi-soterrado, con el más moderno y occidentalizado de Puquio, y que, aunque, como éste, tiene divisiones y fracturas – k'oñanis y k'ayaus discrepan sobre el Misitu – denota, pese a su primitivismo, un carácter genuino, una autenticidad de la que adolece aquél, que, además de degradado por el servilismo y la crueldad, luce un semblante de total bastardía, de mala imitación, de ramificación mostrenca, algún modelo remoto y alérgico a ese lugar de los Andes y a sus gentes. En cambio, el de los indios surge como un trasunto natural de aquel paisaje bravío y de la idiosincracia del pueblo quechua, una cultura que emana de la experiencia vivida y que, aunque discriminada y explotada por los forasteros blancos, no ha sido aún corrompida, pues en ella no tiene vigencia el interés egoísta, el 'negocio' no destruye el vínculo social comunitario y colectivista – todo se hace en función de la comunidad, instancia moral superior a la del individuo – y lo espiritual, lo religioso – el diálogo con lo trascendente – sigue presidiendo las actividades humanas.

Ese diálogo con el trasmundo se lleva a cabo de manera continua y a través de la ceremonia, la música y la danza, mediante las cuales se produce una integración de lo humano con lo divino y del individuo con el mundo natural, un mundo que, a diferencia de lo que ocurre en la otra cultura, para los comuneros es sagrado y vivo, pues lo habitan los dioses tutelares de cuya benevolencia u hostilidad dependen el éxito o el fracaso de las empresas humanas. Por eso, la captura del Misitu por los comuneros, descrita en el capítulo X, que significativamente lleva como título el nombre de 'El Auqui' (dios supremo de la montaña), no es una proeza deportiva sino una fiesta

---

10. Para Gladys C. MARIN, *La experiencia americana de José María Arguedas*, Colección Estudios Latinoamericanos (Buenos Aires: Editorial Fernando García Cambeiro, 1973), 66, la realidad mágica aparece desde el primer capítulo de la novela, cuando el narrador, al describir Puquio, compara el jirón Bolívar, la calle de los 'mistis', con una culebra, el Amaru, animal que en el mundo mitológico indio representa el mal, la destrucción y la muerte. De este modo, el narrador estaría sutilmente calificando de entrada a los principales blancos del lugar como los malvados de la historia que va a referir.

religiosa, con desfiles, ofrendas, la inmolación del *lay'ka* (brujo) y la música de esas trompetas de cuerno, las *wakawakras*, cuyos lúgubres y vibrantes sonidos, multiplicados por los ecos de los cerros, ejercen una función encantatoria, llenando de misterio, de pavor, de inquietud y, también, de exultación, a los vecinos de Puquio cuando llega la hora de la fiesta. Es este contexto el que da todo su sentido a la presencia de esos *dansak*, los bailarines Tunkayllu y Tayta Untu (que reaparecen en muchas ficciones de Arguedas, y, sobre todo, en su bello relato *La agonía del Rasu-ñiti*) a quienes vemos recorrer las calles del lugar desde la víspera de la fiesta, trazando su misterioso laberinto de pasos y golpes de tijeras, como emisarios de un más allá, de un panteón de dioses y espíritus del que la música sería manifestación privilegiada.

Es este contexto el que explica y justifica el *yawarpunchay*, la bárbara fiesta con que, en el último capítulo, culminan estos preparativos rituales. Ella termina por imponer sus propias leyes, su incontenible fuerza mágico-religiosa portadora de la fe y la solidaridad del pueblo indio, sobre las deleznables intrigas y prohibiciones de la autoridad costeña y su corte de 'mistis' serviles y de 'chalos' aculturados que pretendían reemplazar 'el yawar punchay verdadero' por ese simulacro foráneo, la corrida española con el torerillo traído de Lima, Ibarito II, a quien los extraños y revueltas del Misitu expulsan del coso. Cuando, convocados por los gritos de la multitud, incluidos los de los 'mistis', salen los capeadores de los ayllus a enfrentarse al Misitu, y estallan los cartuchos de dinamita y, pese a toda la conjura de los 'mistis', se restaura la corrida en su sesgo indio tradicional, hay como un discreto suspiro de alivio en el narrador quien decide suspender allí, en ese momento de apogeo del espectáculo, la narración. Ese final no es gratuito: la muerte del Misitu con el pecho destrozado por los explosivos de los comuneros es la victoria – fugaz, simbólica – de una cultura que, aunque derrotada muchas veces y denigrada por sus enemigos, renace en espectáculos como éste y muestra en ellos su capacidad de supervivencia, su indoblegable voluntad de no desaparecer ni ser asimilada.

¿Cabe imaginar una ficción que, a pesar de sus denuncias y su indignación frente a las iniquidades que infligen los 'mistis' a los indios, sea más *conservadora* que *Yawar fiesta*?

MARIO VARGAS LLOSA

IN WHICH NERUDA,
APPROACHING HIS SEVENTIETH BIRTHDAY,
STRAYS INTO POST-MODERNISM

IN A DISCUSSION of Neruda's *Odas elementales* (1954), Robert Pring-Mill, 'medio bromeando', has coined the term *güimsicalidad* to describe a new quality in the writing of the then nearly fifty-year old poet. 'Esta *güimsicalidad* consiste en una sumamente delicada aleación del humorismo irónico . . . caracterizada por cierta agudeza (a veces casi quevedesca) . . . y por un si-es-no-es de caprichoso', and it sustains 'múltiples cambios de tono'.[1] Just as José Miguel Ibáñez-Langlois is able to see Nicanor Parra's *Versos de salón* (1953–1962: that is to say, the same period, more or less, as from Neruda's *Odas* to his *Plenos poderes*) as representing 'una decompresión de la angustia' in burlesque, playful, and parodic mode in the wake of the existentially fraught *Poemas y antipoemas,* so too does the Nerudan *güimsicalidad* become the catalyst for a process of (partial) self-demystification, a sequence of deliberately contradictory *tomas de posición*.[2] In *Estravagario* (1958) this same quality comes bubbling up, with an admixture of more robust, knock-about humour and a further opening up to the astringencies of popular wit (in structure and in turn of phrase). It is central to what Federico Schopf has called the 'curioso juego de ocultación y mostramiento' surrounding the poet's coming to terms with the pressures and *desengaños* of the era of de-Stalinization and vital to the new 'liberated attitude', an attitude of *desacato*.[3] It also al-

1. Robert PRING-MILL, 'El Neruda de las *Odas elementales*', in *Coloquio Internacional sobre Pablo Neruda (La obra posterior al «Canto general»)*, ed. Alain Sicard (Poitiers: Centre de Recherches Latino-Américaines de l'Université de Poitiers, 1979), 261–300 (262–63).

2. José Miguel IBÁÑEZ-LANGLOIS, 'La poesía de Nicanor Parra', in Nicanor Parra, *Anti-poemas: Antología (1944–1969)*, ed. Ibáñez-Langlois (Barcelona: Seix Barral, 1972), 9–66 (44).

3. Federico SCHOPF, 'Recepción y contexto de la poesía de Pablo Neruda', in *Pedro Lastra, o la erudición compartida: Estudios de literatura dedicados a Pedro Lastra*, ed. Mario A. Rojas & Roberto Hozven, La red de Jonás (Mexico City: Premià Editora, 1988), 332–72 (364). See also René DE COSTA, *The Poetry of Pablo Neruda* (Cambridge, Mass.: Harvard University

lows diversity, a continuation of the tonal variations identified by Robert
Pring-Mill, the emergence of 'el movimiento perpetuo | de un hombre claro y
confundido, | de un hombre lluvioso y alegre'.[4]

The playful Neruda has not been given much room on the pages of academic critical writings. Even as recently as November 1993 at the 'Simposio
Internacional sobre Pablo Neruda' a number of conversations and more formal interventions made reference to this lack of attention.[5] Robert Pring-Mill
himself suggested one evening during this event that non-Chilean critics did
well to be wary of the topic, given that the jokes so often drew on specifically
Chilean forms of humour, on localized topics, and on the shared experiences
of small groups of friends. During the *sesiones de investigación* of the Simposio, Hernán Loyola was able to remind his audience of another curious critical
blindness, one which I want to suggest here, in the barest of terms, is related
to that other absence: if we all knew, or thought we knew, the Neruda of
Modernity, where might we locate the entry of his texts into Post-Modernity;
and is there not a wide range of possible post-modern readings of Neruda?

High humour and high theory might not immediately reveal their relationship to one another, but from *Estravagario* onwards, in an intermittent way,
Neruda can be seen slyly deconstructing himself. A post-modern individual
emerges who has many of the characteristics of such a subject as summarised
by Pauline Marie Roseman: often a poem will construct a subject who is
'aware of [his] own fictionality' and who 'misbehave[s] in a comic fashion'.
There is certainly a subject here who is 'relaxed and flexible, oriented towards
feelings and emotions, interiorization, and holding a "be-yourself" attitude'
and who in doing so 'looks to humour and fantasy'. Moreover, if post-modern
individuals are 'characteristically free of totalizing global projects such as
those of socialism' though ready 'from time to time [to] affirm struggles
against the state and the system', then moments of political and per-
sonal/political scepticism from *Estravagario* onwards, make the textualized
Neruda, at least, post-modern.[6] Even more so when, as de Costa suggests,

---

Press, 1979), 198–99, and Jacqueline TAUZIN, 'Sobre *Estravagario*: el desacato', in *Coloquio
Internacional*, ed. Sicard, 337–59.

   4. Pablo NERUDA, *Obras completas*, 4th edn, 3 vols (Buenos Aires: Losada, 1973), II, 707.

   5. The Simposio was held at Oxford and Warwick from 12 to 16 November 1993 and was organized by Robert and by John King.

   6. Pauline Marie ROSEMAN, *Post-Modernism and the Social Sciences: Insights, Inroads, and
Intrusions* (Princeton: Princeton University Press, 1992), 52–54; the ideas being summarised
here are those of Gilles Lipovetsky.

Neruda is engaged in a project of liberation from selves constructed in past writing.[7] Most apparent of all the possible post-modern characteristics in Neruda's later texts is the questioning of the status of the self and the construction of an extremely equivocal relationship to previous writings and the wider traditions they drew upon. There is a strong sense, especially in the wry poems of the posthumous collections, of a failure of confidence in what Fredric Jameson suggests was the predicate of the modernist aesthetic, 'the invention of a personal, private style' linked to 'the conception of a unique self and private identity, a unique personality and individuality, which can be expected to generate its own unique vision of the world'.[8] Old styles, words themselves, are looked at askance and often in a spirit of black comedy: 'Repertorio', the opening poem of the posthumously published *Defectos escogidos* (1974), ends with the words 'yo que hablo por hablar hablo de menos: | de cuanto he visto, de cuanto veré | me voy quedando ciego' and the status of poetic vision is left only half-playfully in perplexing shadow.[9] Even that close cousin of such a dismissive attitude, the constant adoption of robustly anti-intellectual positions which can so entrance and infuriate the reader of the poems of the post-1935 Neruda, is a transparently evasive strategy which for all its occasional leadenness is never far from the *güimsicalidad* that allows plurality of self-representation and offers us a new Neruda.[10]

Much has already been written on the question of changes and fragmentations of the poet's identity in Neruda's poems and on the related processes of *reconciliación, unificación,* or *superación.* For Alain Sicard, Neruda's discovery in *Estravagario* of the plural self is 'una experiencia de la fragmentación' and, as such, means that 'la introspección autobiográfica es un reconocimiento

---

7. DE COSTA, *The Poetry*, 198–99.

8. Fredric JAMESON, 'Postmodernism and Consumer Culture', in *Postmodern Culture*, ed. Hal Foster (London: Pluto Press, 1983), 111–125. There are many elaborations and critiques of this particular approach of Jameson's: see, for example, Margaret A. ROSE, *The Post-Modern and the Post-Industrial: A Critical Analysis* (Cambridge: Cambridge University Press, 1991), 65–85 and 94–97.

9. Pablo NERUDA, *Defectos escogidos* (Buenos Aires: Losada, 1974), 9–11.

10. See Sylvia MOLLOY, *At Face Value: Autobiography in Spanish America* (Cambridge: Cambridge University Press, 1991) on Neruda's 'crusade against the book that his writing, and even his habits as a rare book collector, consistently question' (21), and Enrico Mario SANTÍ, *Pablo Neruda: The Poetics of Prophecy* (Ithaca, NY: Cornell University Press, 1982), which proposes (17) a reading which 'challenges . . . the anti-intellectual image that Neruda himself fostered and that continues to prevail among many of his admirers, if not among many critics'.

de sus límites por parte del individuo'.[11] This 'recognition' means for the poet that 'su propia existencia halla su unidad en una continua superación de las vidas fragmentarias' and autobiography becomes 'un modo ... de acceder a ... lo "general" ' precisely because 'al advertir la fragmentación del yo individual, el poeta advierte su radical insuficiencia y la profunda dependencia de la colectividad histórica en que se encuentra'.[12] Although not concerned with the same dialectical processes, Jaime Alazraki coincides with Sicard's view that the recognition of the fact of one's fragmentary nature leads on to the discovery of the unity of the self. The poetry of the period 1951–1969 is 'una travesía hacia adentro' and 'una reconciliación': 'los hombres y las cosas se reconocen en una misma dimensión, en una sola substancia, en una unidad cósmica donde la vida y la muerte se confunden como la luz y la sombra se confunden en la penumbra'.[13] The poems of the sort I am concentrating on here also appear to find radically insufficient both *la colectividad histórica* in its traditional, Old Left forms and the shadow-world of inner reconciliation.

As I have been able to argue elsewhere – thanks largely to Robert Pring-Mill's encouragement – a number of poems in *La rosa separada* (1973), *Jardín de invierno* (1974), and *El mar y las campanas* (1973) look to materials from the poet's past and transmute them, creating out of them new cores of significance for themselves.[14] Equally though, there are poems, notably in *Defectos escogidos* (1974), *El corazón amarillo* (1974), and *Libro de las preguntas* (1974), which disruptively take the earlier *güimsicalidad* to extremes. Here are poems that borrow with such ease from earlier attitudes that they put ironic inverted commas around the whole otherwise deadly serious project of remembrance.[15] There are poems which seem to have no intention of setting up any dialogue with the past, and poems which set out to do this but fail. The lack of overall unifying structures and a fragmentation of lines or poems reveal not only that the process of the conquest of 'la discontinuidad' suffers major setbacks to the very end but perhaps also that these texts are participating in a post-modern

---

11. Alain SICARD, *El pensamiento poético de Pablo Neruda*, tr. Pilar Ruiz Va (Madrid: Editorial Gredos, 1981), 339.

12. SICARD, *El pensamiento*, 338–41.

13. Jaime ALAZRAKI, 'Poética de la penumbra en la poesía más reciente de P. Neruda', *Revista Iberoamericana*, 39, nr 82/83 (1973), 262–91 (289).

14. Christopher PERRIAM, *The Late Poetry of Pablo Neruda* (Oxford: The Dolphin Book Co. Ltd, 1989).

15. NERUDA, *El corazón amarillo* (Buenos Aires: Losada, 1974), and NERUDA, *Libro de las preguntas* (Buenos Aires: Losada, 1974).

scepticism about grand schemes, including those of redemption: the meta-narratives convoked and rewritten in the poems of commitment and convic-tion of the poet's thirties and forties are now questioned, sometimes whimsi-cally, sometimes bleakly. This erring from the realm of the monolithic Neruda of literary myth has caused some interesting critical differences. Some readings of these late poems find in them a gravity consistent with the grimmer texts of *El mar y las campanas* or *Jardín de invierno*, whereas others have expressed concern at a lack of unity and a failure to be 'great poetry'.[16]

Reading some of these apparently perplexing later poems of Neruda from the perspectives of *posmodernidad* as well as *güimsicalidad* can liberate us from the phantom need to find either grave coherence or a safe, separate cat-egory of flippancy which might explain away the worrying absence of connec-tion with any serious writing. In 'Repertorio' it is announced that

> Hay de todo en la cesta: sólo son
> cascabeles aquí, ruidos de mesa,
> de tiros, de cucharas, de bigotes:
> no sé qué me pasó ni qué pasaba
> conmigo mismo ni con ellos,
> lo cierto es que los vi,
> los toqué y como anda la vida
> sin detener sus ruedas
> yo los viví cuando ellos me vivieron,
> amigos o enemigos o paredes,
> o inaceptables santos que sufrían,
> o caballeros de sombrero triste,
> o villanos que el viento se comió,
> o todo más: el grano del granero
> las culpas mías sin cesar desnudas
> que al entrar en el baño cada día
> salieron más manchadas a la luz.

> *(Defectos, 10)*

16. SICARD, *Pensamiento*, esp. 416–25, 445–55, 463, 467, 471; Giuseppe BELLINI, 'Con-tinuidad y novedad en la poesía póstuma de Pablo Neruda', *Quaderni di letterature americane*, 1 (1976 [a special issue on Neruda]), 25–49; Carmen DÍAZ CASTAÑÓN, 'La poesía póstuma de Pablo Neruda', *Archivum* (Oviedo), 29/30 (1980), 191–252; Guillermo ARAYA, 'La poesía póstuma de Pablo Neruda', *Revista de Crítica Literaria*, 5 (1979), 61–86 (62); Manuel DURÁN & Margery SAFIR, *Earth Tones: The Poetry of Pablo Neruda* (Bloomington: Indiana University Press, 1981), 173–75.

The title 'Repertorio' itself had been used before in *Estravagario* (*Obras*, II, 611–12) and its re-use here suggests that the poet's repertoire of titles itself is limited (in *El corazón amarillo*, 7–19, the opening poems are simply called 'Uno', 'Otro', and 'Otro más', in an even more blatant acknowledgment of this exhaustion). The earlier 'Repertorio' had declared (612) 'Yo soy el que fabrica sueños . . . | y hago crecer seres sin rumbo | que aún no podían nacer', revealing, half-jokingly, a nostalgia for the status of the poet as 'un pequeño dios'. In the later poem, though, other selves are all too much in evidence and threaten the individual's integrity ('yo los viví cuando ellos me vivieron') as much as they threaten to become the random objects ('cascabeles' and so on) with which they share the pronoun 'ellos' or to dissolve back into the gastronomic, literary, and popular cultures of 'villanos', 'caballeros de sombrero triste', 'ruidos de mesa', 'tiros', and 'cucharas'. Now our post-modern poet is as much a 'ser sin rumbo' as those earlier creations. When the poem ends with 'yo que hablo por hablar hablo de menos: | de cuanto he visto, de cuanto veré | me voy quedando ciego', not only is it referring back to the quirky contradictions of *Estravagario* but it is signalling even here, in a garrulous and loosely structured piece, the poet's awareness of one of the fundamental principles of the late poetry at its most serious, that 'no hay nada más que descifrar, | ni nada más que hablar: eso era todo'.[17]

Were this only a striving after the music of silence it would represent unproblematically a Modernist poetics after the manner of Juan Ramón Jiménez or Wallace Stevens: but the gesture is more equivocal than that. Things in this rattle-bag are simply there, in a chaotic amalgam, and unconcerned with notions of pure expression, origins, coherence, wholeness, or even decorum. In 'Piedrafina' (*El corazón amarillo*, 45–48) a highly self-conscious comedic subject who may or may not be autobiographical refers to a flirtation and insists on 'desmesura' (47): 'mis inaceptables instintos | y la insaciable vanidad | que me lleva a tantos errores'. 'Repertorio' takes up the quirky position of 'el archivista [. . .] de los defectos | de un solo día de mi colección' (*Defectos*, 10) and here the fault is turned into a post-modern and comic virtue in that the wider schemes of history, personal and public, are eschewed: days are so many specimens, isolated in the collector's basket. Similarly 'ya nadie llora, se pasó de moda | la bella lágrima como una azucena, | y hasta el remordimiento falleció' (10–11). Along with moral seriousness, the claims of

---

17. 'Animal de luz', *Jardín de invierno* (Buenos Aires: Losada, 1974), 83–85 (84).

high culture are lightly questioned: the dream-factory is not in the ownership of the individual (even if he is capitalizing on his own fame and output) but is part of the external commerce of stories, songs, jokes, pictures, words and noise.

Both disconnection and indiscriminate inclusion inform the *Libro de las preguntas*, a book which does not even pretend to be concerned with sequences of thoughts. Being a miscellaneous collection of elaborations on themes and procedures first thought of by Neruda in 'Por boca cerrada entran las moscas' (*Estravagario*) and by Nicanor Parra before that, it reworks old ground for all the seeming freshness of its questions, and is in fact the culmination of a period of hoarding which dates at least as far back as 1958.[18] Unlike the serious questions of *Estravagario*, which are comfortably and meaningfully contained in a framework of fond ambiguity and paradox, the questions with a sting in the tail in *Preguntas* are effective precisely because they strike the reader as being out of context. They abound in *aperçus* about the wonder and colourfulness of a world seen in such close-up that the wider scheme is often quite forgotten. Nearly all is pastiche and surface, as would befit a postmodern text and every now and again an effort is made to pull things together; the effect is only to tease the reader into looking for depth and coherence.[19] There are fragments of familiar Nerudian territory in this book, but the highly charged images which used to serve as reference points in complex areas of thought now speed past, vivid and recognizable as what they elsewhere are, but unconnected and denatured. In similar fragmentary mode, the 'Triste canción para aburrir a cualquiera' (*Defectos*, 61–64) looks at a lifetime's experience and fails to see any sense in it. Its structure is evidently an illustration of how a life – 'toda la vida' – can end up in fragments which do not cohere although they are at least jumbled into a common negative category, linked by the word 'no' which is repeated obsessively throughout (as, for example, 62: 'Toda la vida me pasé la luz | sacando cuentas,| pero no de libros, | pero no de perros, | pero no de cifras, | no'). It concludes:

> Toda la vida me pasé la muerte
> sacando cuentas

18. SCHOPF, 'Recepción', 365. Writing to Volodia Teitelboim on 17 January 1958, Neruda says, 'Tengo un librito en el que escribo mis pensamientos como ser: a qué hora comemos? Lo que es un perro!': Volodia TEITELBOIM, *Neruda*, 5th edn (Santiago de Chile: Ediciones BAT, 1992), 386.

19. See JAMESON, 'Postmodernism'.

> y si salí perdiendo
> o si salí ganando
> yo no lo sé, la tierra
> no lo sabe.
>
> Etcétera.

(63–64)

Given the enormous importance elsewhere of things telluric, such a throw-away conclusion is as self-consciously scandalous as it is obliquely grim.

 Similarly, in 'Otro' (*El corazón amarillo*), the solemn land becomes an eccentric's hideaway, a refuge from a carnivalesque, grotesque world whose values still infiltrate the poet's refuge. Even a weary heart is here able to avoid the loss, if liveliness and colour and exasperation can wear a smile:

> De tanto andar una región
> que no figuraba en los libros
> me acostumbré a las tierras tercas
> en que nadie me preguntaba
> si me gustaban las lechugas
> o si prefería la menta
> que devoran los elefantes.
> Y de tanto no responder
> tengo el corazón amarillo.

(13–14)

Many of the poems allow the serious region of *lo deshabitado* to echo back to the reader a wry sense of oneness with the world in a spirited and frivolous manner. Concentration on anecdote, verbal show, and banter even allows retirement into solitude, which elsewhere is such a serious and symbolic activity, to be talked of enigmatically, comically, and with a kind of mischievous worldly wisdom. 'Canción del amor' (*El corazón amarillo*) – another poem, as Robert Pring-Mill has observed, 'whose humour is closely akin to that of Chilean *poesía popular*' – stands worlds away from the metaphorical winter landscape of the poetry of solitude of the late years.[20] It takes love as something immediate – a kind of isolated, bright, and constantly present fact of life, to be celebrated with a naive directness and no reference to past or future cares or to prior texts. Its lightness of tone carries over into the structure: it is

---

 20. Robert PRING-MILL, 'Introduction', in Pablo Neruda, *A Basic Anthology*, ed. Pring-Mill (Oxford: Dolphin Book Co., 1975), xv–lxxxi (lxxv).

the only poem of the period to have full end rhyme, and that in a jokily irregular pattern. The poet, with charming self-consciousness, declares his own in-
competence (52) – 'y no tengo tono ni tino | para cantarte mi canción, | . . .
en mi violín que desentona' – making light of what elsewhere is a grim topic,
artistic failure. In 'Uno' (*El corazón amarillo*) comic self-denigration is the
key note:

> No hallo explicación halagüeña
> a mi destino intermitente,
> mi vanidad me conducía
> hacia inauditos heroísmos:
> pescar debajo de la arena,
> hacer agujeros en el aire,
> comerme todas las campanas.
> Y sin embargo hice poco
> o no hice nada sin embargo,
> sino entrar por una guitarra
> y salir cantando con ella.

(10)

These lines, racing on ahead of logic and making 'agujeros en el aire', are
characteristic of the tendency to put on a performance with insubstantial materials. Of the 'inauditos heroísmos', the absurd activity of eating the bells is
the most significant. For a moment it radically adjusts a whole world-view
built up in the late poetry by its irreverence towards the deadly serious meditations on the sea and the bells. In shifting perceptions so sharply it has the
true epigrammatical force which so many of the *preguntas* seek after and –
deliberately or not – fail to attain. As if conscious of having got nowhere in
particular in this poem, and as if content to celebrate precisely its vagabond
quality, Neruda ends it in a way which diverges from earlier modes of *güimsicalidad*. The semi-chiastic 'sin embargo . . . sin embargo' is pure *Estravagario*,
but whereas an *Estravagario* poem says it is disorganized and naive but is not,
only pretending to be uninterested in the seriousness that is the reverse side of
its humour, 'Uno' succeeds in dodging seriousness altogether.

In this strange world, 'el que fabrica sueños' half playfully and half seriously
skips in and out of the realm of fact, breaking a life story into fragments and
mixing what has been with what has not. The new repertoire wants to refuse
to make distinctions between poetry, the raw clutter of the material world,
and the impossibly proliferating world of images and words which is post-

modern culture. 'Es necesario para mí | este pan | de los cuentos, | de los cantos,' says the untitled poem which begins 'No hay mucho que contar'.[21] Rather than striving to live on in an integral inner world, here the speaking subject feels impelled to tip out the contents of that world – the 'cesta' of 'Repertorio' (*Defectos*) – for all to see and touch. Although this involves displaying failings, and risks disorder at a period when concentrated expression and the refinement of experience is at a premium, the impulse becomes a part of the *deber del poeta* itself, now seen not so much as an all-inclusive, self-sufficient programme but rather as an opening up to diversity:

> Yo con mis manos debo
> llamar: Venga cualquiera.
>
> Aquí está lo que tengo, lo que debo,
> oigan la cuenta, el cuento y el sonido.
>
> Así cada mañana de mi vida
> traigo del sueño otro sueño.

> (*El mar*, 52)

This uncertain vision – where the self is constructed of a sequence of dreams, and poetry slips into joke or list or tale or plurivalent sound – makes the old politics of duty newly personal and reveals yet another *ser sin rumbo* in these texts: or the erring, possibly post-modern Neruda.

CHRIS PERRIAM

University of Durham

---

21. *El mar y las campanas* (Buenos Aires: Losada, 1973), 51–52.

INDEX

Dates are AD unless otherwise indicated. Historical figures are given in full, followed in parentheses by brief identifying details and dates, where known. Modern scholars are listed by surname and initials alone. The following abbreviations are used:

auth.	author of	fl.	flourished
b.	born (in)	k.	king of
(a)bp	(arch)bishop of	bro.	brother
ca	circa	mo.	mother
r.	reigned	d.	died (in)

Abelard, Peter (Paris theologian and philosopher, 1079–1142) 126
acting : see Plays and playhouses
Ad Herennium 20
aesthetics and art theory 117–128; see also Literary theories, fashions, and criticism
al-Abbas, 'Ali ibn (commentator on Galen, fl. 10th c.) 27
Alain de Lille (French humanist and poet, 1115/18–1202/3) 19
Alazraki, J. 210
Alberti, Leon Battista (architect and humanist, 1404–72) 122
Alberti, Rafael (writer and politician, b. 1902) 168, 175, 177–178
Albertus Magnus, St (German philosopher and theologian, ca. 1200–1280) 27
Alcover, A. 32
Alfonso V of Aragon (r. 1416–58) 14
allegory : see Literary theories, fashions, and criticism
Allen, J. 78
Alonso, A. 75–76
Álvarez Quintero, Joaquín (dramatist, 1873–1944) 151
Álvarez Quintero, Serafín (dramatist, 1871–1938) 151
Amadei-Pulice, M. 116
Amor y Vázquez, J. 111
analogy and analogical argument 37, 47–52, 55–56, 58, 61, 63, 76, 95, 126–27, 151, 154, 164, 176
Anderson, A. 149–64
Anglo-Catalan Society iii, xi
Aquinas, St Thomas OP (Doctor angelicus, scholastic theologian and philosopher,

1225–74) 3, 8, 27–28, 32, 122
Ara, J. 79, 105
Araya, G. 211
Archer, R. 3–15, 20, 26
Argensola, Bartolomé Leonardo de (chaplain to María de Austria, historian and poet, 1562–1631) 157
Arguedas, José María (Peruvian novelist and ethnologer, 1911–69) 189–206
Argüelles, Agustín (statesman and principal author of the 1812 Cadiz Constitution, 1776–1844) 179
Argüelles : see Madrid
Aristotle 3, 8, 9–10, 20, 27–28, 37, 49–50, 54–56
Armas, F. de 78, 81, 92, 114
Arniches, Carlos (dramatist and librettist, 1866–1943) 151
Asturias, Miguel Ángel (Guatemalan novelist and essayist, 1899–1974) x
Aubert, L. 163
Auclair, M. 152
Augustine, St (bp Hippo, Father of the Church, 354–430) 10, 23, 29, 51, 122–23, 125–27
Ausonius, Decimus Magnus (Latin poet, d. ca 395) 154–55, 162
Avancini, Nikolaus SJ (poet and dramatist, 1611–86) 115
Avicenna *recte* Abû 'Alî al'Husayn ibn Sînâ (Persian physician and philosopher, 980–1047) 27–28, 49
Aznar Soler, M. 168, 178
Azorín (pseud. of José Martínez Ruiz, novelist, 1873–1967) 151

TABULA GRATULATORIA

Justo Alarcón
Andrew A. Anderson
David G. Anderson
The Anglo-Catalan Society
Robert Archer
Pamela Bacarisse
Lola Badia
Paul A. Ballard
Geoffrey R. Barrow
Bernard P. E. Bentley
Anthony Bonner
Stephen Boyd
The Library, University of Bristol
Bulletin of Hispanic Studies
Rosalba Campra
Fernando Cervantes
Marie-Thérèse Church (née Grealy)
Silvia Coll-Vinent
Jaime Concha
Graeme Creffield
David Davies
G. A. & C. G. Davies
Charles Davis
Alan Deyermond
Victor Dixon
Sheila Downie-Jorge
Instituto Cervantes, Dublin
Martin J. Duffell
Peter N. Dunn
Peter Dymond
Hans Flasche

Biblioteca Catalana, Deutsch-
    Katalanische Gesellschaft,
    Frankfurt-am-Main
Margit Frenk
Derek Gagen
Ángel M. García
Joan & Elizabeth Gili
Martin & Kate Gili
Nigel Glendinning
John Gornall
Clive Griffin
Nigel Griffin
James M. Grist
J. B. Hall
Anne Hamelin (née Montague)
J. N. Hillgarth
Richard Hitchcock
Fred Hodcroft
Anne Hogg
David Hook
James Iffland
Ron Keightley
John King (Eton College)
Jeremy Lawrance
Warburg Institute, University of
    London
Juan López-Morillas
Ian R. Macdonald
Bernard McGuirk
Melveena McKendrick
John Rylands University Library of
    Manchester

David Mee
Ian Michael
Dominic Milroy, OSB
Enrique Montero
R. J. Oakley
Margaret O'Leary
Christ Church, Oxford
Exeter College, Oxford
Interfaculty Committee for Latin-
    American Studies, Oxford
New College, Oxford
St Catherine's College, Oxford
St Peter's College, Oxford
Taylor Institution, Oxford
Trinity College, Oxford
Arseni Pacheco
Christopher Pagett
David Pattison
John Pelham
Ralph Penny
Chris Perriam
Frank Pierce
Dario Puccini
Margaret A. Rees
Geoffrey Ribbans
Jeremy Rigden
Stephen Roberts
Jeremy Robbins
Xon de Ros
Peter Russell
John Rutherford
Geraldine M. Scanlon

Karl-Ludwig Selig
The University of Sheffield
Joan Shenton
Alison Sinclair
Hilary Dansey Smith
R. N. Smith
Verity Smith
Amadeu Solé-Lerís
Rosalie & Alan Soons
The University of Southampton
The Library, Southern Illinois
    University at Carbondale
Eric Southworth
Alan Swan
Rosalind A. M. Temple
Lore Terracini
Arthur Terry
Colin Thompson
Douglas Town
Ronald Truman
Ángel Julián Valbuena-Briones
J. E. Varey
Mario Vargas Llosa
John & Laura Wainwright
Ana & Daniel Waissbein
Bruce & Nancy Wardropper
Eileen Whelton
David Williams
Margaret Wilson
Hensley C. Woodbridge
Alan Yates